PRAISE FOR CATHY GLASS

'Poignant and revealing ... real-life stories such as these have helped to move and inspire a generation'   *Sunday Mirror*

'A true tale of hope'   *OK!* Magazine

'Heartbreaking'   *Mirror*

'A life-affirming read ... that proves sometimes a little hope is all you need'   *Heat* Magazine

'A hugely touching and emotional true tale'   *Star* Magazine

'Foster carers rarely get the praise they deserve, but Cathy Glass's book should change all that'   *First* Magazine

'Cannot fail to move those who read it'   Adoption-net

'Once again, Cathy Glass has blown me away with a poignant story'   The Writing Garnet, book blogger

'Brilliant book. I'd expect nothing less from Cathy ... I cried, of course'   Goodreads review

'... gripping page-turner from start to finish ... emotive and heart-wrenching ...'   Kate Hall, book blogger

Unwanted

ALSO BY CATHY GLASS

THE MILLION COPY BESTSELLING AUTHOR

CATHY GLASS

Unwanted

**The care system failed Lara.
Will she fail her own child?**

Certain details in this story, including names, places and dates, have been changed to protect the family's privacy.

HarperElement
An imprint of HarperCollins*Publishers*
1 London Bridge Street
London SE1 9GF

www.harpercollins.co.uk

HarperCollins*Publishers*
Macken House, 39/40 Mayor Street Upper
Dublin 1, D01 C9W8, Ireland

First published by HarperElement 2023

3 5 7 9 10 8 6 4

A catalogue record of this book is
available from the British Library

ISBN 978-0-00-858442-9

Printed and bound in the UK using 100%
renewable electricity at CPI Group (UK) Ltd

ACKNOWLEDGEMENTS

A big thank-you to my family; my editors, Ajda and Holly; my literary agent, Andrew; my UK publisher HarperCollins, and my overseas publishers, who are now too numerous to list by name. Last, but definitely not least, a big thank-you to my readers for your unfailing support and kind words. They are much appreciated.

IN THE BEGINNING

When I first started writing my fostering memoirs it broke new ground. No one before had written about the hidden, sometimes secretive world of fostering and the social services. Over the years I've received thousands of emails and messages from around the world, many from care-leavers. While some said their time in care was a positive one, many did not, which saddens me greatly. Some felt they were not cared for or loved, and far too many had multiple placements. Some had to move upwards of thirty, fifty or more times. How could this be allowed to happen?

This is the story of Frazer and Lara. Their lives began very similarly. Frazer's mother managed a drug fix just before she went into labour and Lara's just after she'd given birth. She was found injecting herself in the hospital toilet.

CHAPTER ONE

NON-ACCIDENTAL INJURIES

It was the end of October. My previous foster children had just left and I was anticipating a few days, maybe even a week, child-free, when I hoped to be able to wind down after a rather traumatic year fostering during the pandemic. I could catch up with friends and my family.

My adult son, Adrian, was married to the lovely Kirsty. My daughter Lucy was living happily with her partner, Darren, and had blessed me with my first grandchild, Emma, now two and a half, and a treasure who made us all smile. My other daughter Paula was still living with me, so there was just the two of us and our rescue cat, Sammy, at home. I'd been divorced for many years. Paula had recently returned to work after being furloughed during the peak of the pandemic, so it felt as if life was gradually returning to normal. Of concern was that the R number – used to calculate the spread of the coronavirus – was rising, particularly in some areas. We were regularly reminded on television and billboards to stay safe by sanitizing our hands, wearing a face mask in enclosed public spaces and social distancing. This had become known as the 'hands, face, space' rule.

It was Thursday morning when Joy Philips, my supervising social worker (SSW), telephoned. All foster carers in the UK have a supervising social worker whose job it is to support, monitor, advise and guide the carer and their family in all aspects of fostering. They also advise the carer on their training requirements and generally make sure the children in their care are well looked after.

'How are you?' Joy asked. It wasn't simply a polite question. The pandemic was still ongoing so she needed to know.

'Well,' I confirmed.

'No one in your household is having to self-isolate or is awaiting a Covid test result?' She asked this most times she phoned.

'No.'

'Good. So you're ready to take your next child?' Referrals usually come through the carer's SSW.

'Yes, although I was hoping to take a few days off.'

Sometimes it felt like a never-ending stream of children coming through my door who for various reasons couldn't live at home. Yet despite fostering over 150 children since I began all those years ago, I always gave each child the love and care they needed and deserved. My daughter Lucy arrived as a foster child and became my adopted daughter. Other children have returned home or gone to forever families.

'You will be able to take some time off as this placement isn't needed until Monday,' Joy said.

'All right. Good.'

'It's for a little boy, Arthur, he's just one year old. He went to an emergency carer yesterday, but she can only keep him for the weekend so he will need to be moved on Monday.'

'OK. Why is he in care?'

'Suspected non-accidental injuries,' Joy said, and my heart went out to him. 'His mother has been struggling for a while. She went to the doctor about herself, but the doctor noticed bruises on the child's face. He examined the child and found more bruises on his legs and body. His mother is denying harming him and says he is accident-prone.'

'I can take him on Monday,' I confirmed.

'Thank you. I'll let his social worker know and she'll be in touch.'

We said goodbye.

The poor child, I thought. I'd fostered children before who'd arrived with suspected non-accidental injuries, including cigarette burns, scalds, cuts and bruises, and it didn't get any easier. But I put my concerns for him aside for now – I'd do enough worrying once he arrived – and continued with my day as planned. I spent the afternoon with Lucy and Emma and on my way home dropped in at Adrian's. He was still working from home but was pleased to have a break. Kirsty, a teacher, was in school. My family lived locally so we were able to see each other regularly. Sadly, my dear parents, who'd been so supportive of my fostering, had now passed.

Once home, I prepared dinner for when Paula arrived back from work. Later, as we ate, I told her what I knew of little Arthur and that he would be with us on Monday. I share information with my family on a need-to-know basis. Paula was part of my household so needed to know almost as much as I did, and certainly anything that would affect her. If, for example, a child arrived who'd been sexually abused, then we put in place extra measures, especially around bath- and bedtime, and when we had visitors, so that everyone felt safe. Thankfully that wasn't the case with Arthur (as far as I knew), although, like me, Paula was upset that he was thought to have non-accidental injuries. No child should ever suffer.

After we'd eaten, Paula went to her room to relax and I watched the evening news. I learnt that cases of Covid were rising around the world and in England they were rising 'significantly faster' than predicted. Secondary school children had the highest rate of transmission, and there was talk of another lockdown.

Arthur's social worker, Claudette Brimstone, phoned me the following afternoon and our conversation didn't get off to a good start.

'Thank you for agreeing to take Lara and Arthur,' she said. 'We were really struggling to find a mother-and-child placement.'

'I didn't,' I blurted. 'Sorry. There seems to have been some confusion. I thought I was just having Arthur.'

'Oh. That was the original plan, but the judge didn't accept our recommendations. She wants Arthur kept with his mother while we carry out a parenting assessment. It seems your supervising social worker wasn't updated.'

'Indeed. That rather changes things.'

'Does it? You're approved to foster all age groups and you have experience of mother-and-baby placements.' She would have seen this on my file.

'Yes, but I was expecting just Arthur …' I paused. 'He's a year old?' I checked, in case this was wrong too.

'Yes. His mother, Lara, is twenty, a single parent, and has faced her own challenges. She was in and out of care herself and has no real family to support her. She lacks parenting skills.'

'Joy said Arthur had suffered suspected non-accidental injuries.'

'Yes, that was the concern of her doctor. But in court Lara's lawyer pointed out that we'd had no previous concerns about her abusing her child, that the boy was thought to be very accident-prone, and the cuts and bruises could have easily been sustained as a result of rough play, tripping and falling. It's impossible to know. The judge ruled that Lara and Arthur were to be found a mother-and-child placement while they were being assessed. Your reports will form part of the assessment.' I knew this was standard practice. 'Assuming you can take them, of course. If you really can't, we will have to try to find somewhere else, but it's not going to be easy.'

'So you want to move them on Monday, not today?' I checked.

'That's correct. Arthur can have his cot in with you if you don't have a spare bedroom. We don't want them in the same room, to begin with at least.'

'They can have their own rooms, that's not an issue. How long is the placement likely to be?'

'Four months, although it could be extended.'

'All right. I'll take them.'

'Thank you. I'm anticipating collecting Lara and Arthur on Monday morning and then coming straight to you.'

'Where is Lara now?' I asked.

'With her boyfriend, but she won't be seeing him again once she's with you. He's not the child's father and has a history of violence. Lara will sign an undertaking not to divulge your address to him.'

'I'm pleased to hear that. Is it possible he harmed the child?'

'It was suggested, but Lara is adamant that Arthur's bruises were a result of him falling. The emergency foster carer took him to the hospital for a scan and there are no signs of previous or new fractures.'

Which was a relief, although, of course, a child can be beaten without sustaining fractures.

'Well, if there is nothing else, I'll see you Monday,' Claudette said, winding up. 'I'll email you the placement forms.'

'Thank you.'

Having said goodbye, I spent the rest of the afternoon hoping I'd done the right thing in agreeing to look after Lara and her son, and getting their bedrooms ready. Now Adrian and Lucy had left home I had the space; the larger bedroom would be Lara's and the cot would go in the smaller room next door. I assumed the social worker wanted them separated because of the suspected non-accidental injuries. If they were sharing a room it would be more difficult to monitor what was happening at night. Lara would be expected to do all the caring for her child, so if, for example, he woke at night she would tend to him, although I would be on hand. Part of the foster carer's role in a mother-and-child placement is observation and record keeping, as well as giving support where necessary.

As I worked, the enormity of what I'd committed to hit me. It was a huge responsibility. When I'd had a mother-and-baby placement before it was purely to support and guide the mother in her parenting; there'd been no suggestion of her harming her child. Now I would need to watch Lara and Arthur very carefully every minute of the day and if he woke at night. I'd never forgive myself if he sustained another injury while in my care. It crossed my mind that it would have been so much easier to just look after Arthur, but the judge had decided to give Lara another chance, and I needed to as well.

CHAPTER TWO

LARA AND ARTHUR

I told Paula when she came home from work that evening that we'd be looking after Lara as well as Arthur. She had mixed feelings too. She was also concerned at the possibility of another lockdown, and the effect it would have on her job. She had an administrative position in the offices of a local manufacturing firm. At the start of the first lockdown she'd worked from home for a short while until the number of new orders coming in had fallen and there hadn't been enough work, so she'd been furloughed. She had returned to the office a month ago, but workers had been warned that if order numbers were still low and didn't pick up soon, some of them would be made redundant. Many businesses were struggling because of the pandemic, despite a good furlough scheme. I reassured her as best I could and said the situation we were in was unprecedented. Until now, pandemics had only been the subject of films for us.

Claudette Brimstone, Lara and Arthur's social worker, emailed me the placement information forms and I read them after dinner. As well as containing basic details like Lara's and Arthur's full names, dates of birth, ethnicity (white British; language spoken: English), religion (none) and the care plan, the forms gave a potted history of what had been going on. Lara was twenty and the only child of a single mother who had died from a drug overdose when Lara had been seven years old. With no relatives to look after her, she'd been taken into care where she'd remained until eighteen. She didn't appear to be in contact with any of her foster carers, which I thought was a pity. The box on the form that asked whether the young person was known to smoke or abuse alcohol or drugs said: *No known drug abuse but Lara smokes and drinks alcohol. This could be an issue around Arthur.*

Arthur's date of birth was 5 October so he was just one year old. Details of his father: *Unknown*. His mother was Lara Lewisham. The social services had become involved when Arthur was six months old after a neighbour had overheard an abusive argument in the flat where Lara and Arthur were living with her boyfriend. It didn't give the boyfriend's name, but he was ten years older than Lara and had a history of violence. The social services had been monitoring the situation, although due to Covid restrictions many of their visits had been virtual – online. I read that Arthur was up to date with his vaccinations and was walking, but didn't have any language yet, which wasn't surprising at his age. Neither of them had any allergies or special needs, but Arthur was still receiving most of his nutrition from formula milk. There was the comment: *The foster carer will need to teach Lara how to wean her son.* There were details of their doctor and the health clinic they attended. Then followed the type of placement, the reason for it and its duration, which I already knew. During the assessment there would be weekly meetings between Lara, the social worker and me to see how things were going. Coming to the end, I closed the file and felt the responsibility even more. What I observed and wrote in my reports would ultimately contribute to whether Lara kept her son. I hate sitting in judgement on others, but sometimes in fostering it's necessary in the best interest of the child.

On Saturday morning I did the weekly shop and stocked up on groceries and other household items, as my family was about to double in size. Once home, I unpacked, then took out the toy boxes that contained early-years toys. Having been fostering for over twenty-five years, I've built up a large collection of toys, puzzles and games for all ages of children, as most carers do. I also had spare clothes to fit most ages and sizes of children for those who arrived as an emergency with only what they were wearing.

That afternoon I spent some time tidying the garden. We were in the throes of autumn and there was always something to do. I raked up fallen leaves and also began giving the hedge its annual trim. At six o'clock I drove to a friend's house for her birthday dinner. Paula was out with a friend. Once Lara and Arthur were with us, we wouldn't both be out at the same time as Lara wasn't to be left alone with her son to begin with. Paula was one of my nominated sitters, but I wouldn't give her the responsibility of looking after Lara and Arthur until I knew Lara could be trusted with Arthur. This would be my last night out for some time.

As it turned out I wasn't the only one who wouldn't be going out socializing for some time. While driving home after a lovely evening I heard on the car radio that Boris

Johnson, our prime minister, had announced a second lockdown, starting on Thursday and lasting for four weeks, although unlike the first lockdown schools and colleges would remain open. The restrictions were necessary 'in order to save lives and prevent a medical and moral disaster'. After which England would revert to the tier system and the furlough scheme would be extended.

The news bulletin continued by reminding us what lockdown meant. That from 5 November people in England should stay at home and only go out for education, work (if they couldn't work from home), exercise, a medical reason, escaping injury or harm, shopping for food and essentials, and providing care for vulnerable people. Non-essential shops, leisure and entertainment venues would close. Pubs, bars and restaurants would only be allowed to operate takeaway and delivery services.

It wasn't good news but like most people I felt that if this was what was needed to prevent deaths and stop the virus spreading then we had to accept it and cooperate.

Paula arrived home shortly after me, also having heard the news.

'Just as well I went out tonight,' she said glumly. 'I suppose I go to work on Monday and see what happens.'

'Yes. That's all you can do, unless your work contacts you before and tells you not to go in.'

We were also told not to panic-buy as had happened during the first lockdown earlier in the year, but that didn't stop some people trying to stockpile food, especially non-perishables like tinned goods, toilet paper and flour. I'd just done my weekly shop so had no need to buy more, but by Sunday afternoon supermarkets were again having to ration the number of similar items each customer bought to prevent shortages. I phoned Adrian and Kirsty that afternoon and we discussed the latest news. He was an accountant and had access to all the files he needed from home so would continue working remotely as he had been doing since the first lockdown. The government advice had been to work from home if possible. Kirsty was relieved the schools would be remaining open; like many teachers, she worried about the effect closing them had on children, not only on their education, but on their social skills and mental health too.

Paula and I watched a film together on Sunday evening. She hadn't heard from her work so the following morning she went in as usual while I waited for Lara and Arthur to arrive. Just after eleven o'clock Joy, my supervising social worker, telephoned, having just heard that the placement was for Lara as well as her son. Sometimes SSWs are kept well informed, other times not so much.

'Sorry about the mix-up,' she said. 'Do you have everything you need?'

'Yes, I think so.'

'And you're well?'

'Yes.'

'Will Lara have had a Covid test before she arrives?' Joy asked.

'I don't know. It hasn't been mentioned.'

'Some of our young people are being tested. What time are they expected?'

'I'm not sure exactly. Claudette said she'd collect them this morning and then come straight to me.'

'I'll try to contact Claudette and then get back to you.'

'Thank you.'

Accepting a new child – in this case a mother and her child – during the pandemic ran the risk of bringing the virus into the home, and for this reason some foster carers, especially those with underlying health concerns, had stopped fostering for the time being. Once Lara and Arthur were living with me I could protect us all, following the government guidelines, but I had no idea if they were already infected. It would help put my mind at rest if Lara arrived having had a negative test.

I'm often nervous when awaiting the arrival of a new child. Once they're with me I'm so busy there isn't time to be anxious as I concentrate on their needs. I couldn't settle to anything that morning and kept checking my phone. Paula had promised to text me when she heard about her job and Joy was going to phone me. Then just before midday Claudette phoned to say they were on their way, and ten minutes later the doorbell rang. My heart rate stepped up a few paces as I went down the hall to answer it. Before I opened the door I unhooked a face mask from where I kept them on the coat stand in the hall. Lara – tall, blonde, slender and wearing a padded jacket – was holding Arthur. Beside her was a woman I took to be her social worker. Shorter than Lara, Claudette looked to be in her early forties. She wasn't wearing a coat, despite the cold. Both women were wearing masks but Arthur kept pulling Lara's mask down.

'Hello, I'm Cathy,' I said. 'Lovely to meet you. Come in.' I stood aside to let them pass.

'Shall I take off my shoes?' Lara asked, seeing some of our outdoor shoes paired in the hall.

'Yes, please, we usually do.' I smiled, although she couldn't see it under my mask.

Lara slipped off her jacket and hung it on the hall stand, then kicked off her shoes. She pulled off Arthur's blue canvas toddler shoes and dropped them on top of hers. I could see a faint bruise on his left cheek.

'Which room are we in?' Claudette asked, already halfway down the hall.

'The living room – it's straight ahead of you,' I replied.

'You need to take off your shoes first,' Lara called after her.

Claudette stopped and then returned to leave her shoes with ours. Well done, Lara, I thought. I didn't ever make an issue about visitors not taking off their shoes, but my family and our friends always took ours off. I think it's unhygienic to wear outdoor shoes indoors, especially when there are infants in the house. They may be crawling or playing on the floor and are therefore susceptible to dirt and germs that might have been walked in.

'How are you?' I asked Lara as we went into the living room.

'All right, I guess. Thanks for having me and Arthur.'

'You're welcome, love.'

Arthur was struggling to be put down and, once in the living room, she set him on the floor where he rushed over to explore the toy boxes.

'Can I take off my mask now?' Lara asked.

'Yes, of course,' I said.

'Can you wait until after I've gone?' Claudette said.

'No, it's making me hot,' Lara replied. 'I'll keep away from you. You can sit over there and I'll sit here.'

Claudette sat in the chair Lara pointed to while she sat on the sofa, which was on the other side of the room. I too sat away from Claudette, although I kept my mask on.

Social workers' visits were still being kept to a minimum to reduce their chances of catching or spreading coronavirus. The rest of the meetings were online, but placing a child or young person required the social worker to be present.

My first impression of Lara was that she was feisty and spoke her mind, which should help me when looking after her. Some children or young people who arrived were so withdrawn and introverted that it made gauging their needs very difficult. From what I'd seen so far I felt sure Lara wouldn't hesitate to tell me what she needed.

Claudette had taken her laptop from her bag and was concentrating on the screen. Arthur, having spent a few moments tipping out the contents of the toy boxes, now headed for the living-room door. Lara went after him.

'Can I close this door?' she asked me. 'Or he's going to be everywhere.'

'Yes, sure.'

She pushed it shut and returned to the sofa with Arthur, where he immediately wriggled from her lap. He was a sturdy little chap and clearly very active. He had fine blond hair, a bit lighter than his mother's. He was like a hurricane as he zipped around the room and I knew we would need to keep a close eye on him. At his age children have no fear of danger.

'Did you receive the placement information forms?' Claudette asked, glancing up from her open laptop.

'Yes, thank you,' I replied.

'Do you have any questions?'

'Joy, my supervising social worker, phoned, and wondered if Lara had had a Covid test.'

'Have you?' Claudette asked Lara.

'Yes, I had a sore throat and a temperature.'

'When was that?' Claudette asked.

'About a month ago. But the test said I didn't have Covid.'

'So not recent?'

'No.'

'Do you want Lara to have a test?' Claudette now asked me and then answered her own question. 'There doesn't seem much point now she's here.'

'There's no point,' I agreed. 'If anyone shows symptoms, I'll arrange a test.'

'Who else lives here?' Claudette asked, although it would have been on my file.

'Just my daughter Paula.'

'And how old is she?'

'Twenty-seven. You'll meet her later,' I told Lara.

'Do you have everything you need to look after Arthur and Lara?' Claudette asked me.

'Yes, I think so. I've put his cot in the room next to Lara's.'

'I'll have a look in a minute,' Claudette said.

'I've got his bottles and formula in the car,' Lara said.

I nodded, although we needed to start weaning Arthur soon. Our cat, Sammy, appeared on the patio and I was about to show Arthur when he spotted him through the glass. Before I could stop him he ran straight into the patio window with a bang. I jumped up and rushed to him.

'Are you all right?' I asked, very concerned. He looked a bit startled but otherwise appeared to be unharmed. 'You must be careful or you'll hurt yourself.' It was something I would be telling him a lot over the coming weeks.

'I assume it's toughened glass,' Claudette remarked as she typed.

'Yes.' It was one of the many safety requirements in foster carers' homes.

'Come on, let's play with some toys,' I said to Arthur, and led him back to the toy boxes. But, unsure of me, he wanted his mother and ran to her and clambered onto her lap, which was nice to see.

'Do you have a stroller for him?' Claudette asked me.

'Yes.'

'Mine's broken,' Lara said. 'The rest of my things are in her car.'

'We'll bring them in shortly,' Claudette told her as she typed.

'How have you been managing without a stroller?' I asked Lara.

'I carry him everywhere, but he's heavy. When I go into shops it's a nightmare. He pulled over a whole rail of dresses in one shop. We had to leave.'

I could imagine the scene. 'Don't worry. I've got a stroller and most other things you'll need.'

Claudette quickly completed her online placement form with a few more questions, then closed her laptop and returned it to her bag.

'You can show me around now,' she said, standing. 'Lara, if you're coming, please put on your mask.'

'I'll stay here,' she said.

Claudette looped her bag over her shoulder and headed out of the living room. I showed her our kitchen-diner. She nodded and went down the hall, then in and out of the front room. I opened the child-safety gate to let her go upstairs. She went briefly into Lara's and Arthur's rooms, nodded, and quickly looked into the other rooms.

'You'll need to supervise his bathing,' she said as we returned downstairs.

'Yes, I will.'

Arthur appeared at the safety gate but there was no sign of Lara. Claudette, in front of me, opened it and then called, 'Lara, you need to come and get him so I can unload the car.'

Lara came into the hall, picked up Arthur and carried him into the living room. I helped Claudette unload her car, stacking the bags and boxes that contained Lara's and Arthur's belongings in the hall. As we worked Arthur suddenly appeared at the open front door. I took him by the hand and led him back into the living room where Lara was sitting on the sofa checking her phone, oblivious.

'Can you keep him in here while the front door is open?' I said. 'He could run into the road.'

'Yes, sure,' she said amicably. But it was concerning she hadn't spotted the danger. I closed the living-room door so he couldn't get out, and helped Claudette.

Once we'd finished unloading her car, Claudette went into the living room and said a quick goodbye to Lara. I saw her out and took off my mask.

As soon as she'd gone Lara came into the hall, followed by Arthur.

'I need a ciggy,' she said with a sigh. She took a packet of cigarettes and a lighter from her jacket pocket and went out the front door, assuming I would look after Arthur.

I knew then I was going to have to put in place some ground rules pretty quickly and speak to Lara as directly as she did to others. If I didn't do it now, it would be more difficult later.

CHAPTER THREE

SETTLING IN

Arthur wasn't happy suddenly being left alone with a stranger. He looked close to tears, despite my efforts to try to interest him in the toys I'd set out.

'Mummy won't be long,' I told him. We were in the living room while Lara had her cigarette in the front garden.

He began sucking his fingers so I thought he might be hungry. It was mid-afternoon and I wondered when he'd last had anything to eat and drink. Despite his diet only being formula milk, he was well built and seemed healthy. I gave Lara a few minutes to finish her cigarette, then, holding Arthur's hands, I took him down the hall. I picked him up before I opened the front door; he was so quick I knew he would be outside in a flash. Lara had finished her cigarette but had stayed in the front garden to talk on her phone. She stopped as soon as she saw us.

'I won't be long,' she said.

'When was the last time Arthur had something to eat or drink?' I asked.

'This morning. Before Claudette collected me.'

'I think he's hungry and his nappy needs changing.' It felt very full through his clothes.

'Can you do it?' she asked. 'His stuff is in one of the bags in the hall.'

'I think it would be better if you did. He's not familiar with me yet.' Arthur was struggling to be put down to get to his mother. Also, there was the matter of Lara being responsible for Arthur's care – one of the stipulations of the placement agreement.

'I've got to go,' Lara said to whoever she was talking to. 'I'll phone you later.'

'I can help you,' I said as she came indoors. 'But you need to see to Arthur's care.'

'I know.'

Once the front door was closed I put Arthur down and he went straight to his mother. She found a bottle of formula in one of the bags and carried him into the living room where she sat on the sofa and fed him as one would a much younger baby. He was clearly very hungry and sucked ravenously, his little hands clutching the bottle. He finished and threw the bottle onto the floor.

'Cheeky bugger,' Lara laughed, and picked it up. 'Shall I get him some more milk?'

'Did Claudette talk to you about weaning him?' I asked.

'Yes, I've got one of those pouches in the bags. She said you'd tell me what to do.'

'I will. Has he had any solid food?'

'Diesel used to give him a chip to suck to keep him quiet, but that's all. Sometimes it had ketchup on it.'

'Diesel was your boyfriend?' I asked.

'Yes, but not any longer. He was bad news. I'll be better off without him. So once Arthur starts eating proper food he'll sleep at night, right?' she asked.

'Starting him on solids should help,' I said. 'Has he been waking up much?'

'Every three to four hours. I'm knackered.'

'I can imagine, but don't worry.' I smiled. 'We'll get him into a better routine. Now, I suggest you change his nappy and then, instead of giving him another bottle, we try him with some solid food. It can take a while to wean a baby so the sooner we get started the better.'

'OK. Cool. You've got a nice house,' she said pleasantly.

'Thank you, love. It's your home too for now.'

'I've heard that before!' Lara laughed but then wouldn't tell me what she meant.

'Let's see to his nappy and get him more comfortable,' I said.

We went to the bags in the hall. Arthur ran into the front room and began to explore.

'His nappy stuff is in that one,' Lara said, pointing. 'But I'm out of cream and nappy bags.'

'We'll put those on a list and go shopping tomorrow,' I said. 'If you take Arthur upstairs, I'll bring up the bag.'

Lara retrieved Arthur from the front room, lifted him over the safety gate and then stepped over herself.

'It opens like this,' I said, showing her the latch.

'Oh. We didn't have those in the flat.'

There was a stairgate at the top too and she opened that.

'This is your room,' I said as we went round the landing. 'And Arthur's is right next to yours.'

'Fantastic! Look! We've got our own rooms,' she said, clearly delighted. My heart went out to her. She was so child-like in her enthusiasm.

'Did Arthur share your room before?' I asked as we went into his room.

'You must be joking! Diesel wouldn't have allowed that. Arthur's cot was in the living room with all his stuff. Diesel hated having him there. He said I could stay but the kid had to go.'

'Charming. Did he ever lose his temper with Arthur and hit him?' I asked. Lara appeared to like a direct approach.

'I've already been asked that,' she replied. 'Not as far as I know. He was rough with me, but I don't think he ever hurt Arthur.'

'How long were you there for?' I asked as Arthur explored his bedroom.

'About four months.'

'And before then?'

'The council put me in a bed and breakfast.'

It wasn't the best way to start parenthood, but during my fostering career I'd heard of worse. I got out the changing mat and laid it ready on the bed. 'Do you have baby wipes?' I asked, looking in the bag.

'No. I ran out of those too. Everything is so expensive.'

True, if you were on a low income, but then smoking was very expensive and bad for Lara's health. However, I decided to leave that conversation for another time.

'Claudette said I had to notify the benefit office now I'm here,' Lara said.

'Yes, that's correct. Have you got any money?'

'A little.' Lara would be expected to manage her income and buy what she and Arthur needed, although I would buy household items that we all used.

Lara laid Arthur on the changing mat and took off his trouser bottoms. I saw small bruises on his knees and shins.

'Are those the marks your doctor was worried about?' I asked.

'And he's got some more on his bottom and back, as well as that one on his face. They asked me how he got them, but I don't know. He's always running into things and falling over. I think that social worker has got it in for me because I was brought up in care. Like mother, like daughter.' She threw me a humourless smile.

'I don't think so, love,' I said. 'You are your own person. You won't make the same mistakes. My daughter Lucy hasn't.'

I then told her a little bit about Lucy as she continued to change Arthur's nappy. (I tell Lucy's story in my book *Will You Love Me?*) Lara was interested and asked questions.

'Pity you didn't adopt me,' she said as I finished. 'Things might have turned out differently.'

'They still can,' I said. 'You're only young. You have your whole life ahead of you. You can make of it what you like.'

'Maybe,' she replied, without much conviction.

'I know you can,' I said positively. I had to believe that there was a good chance Lara could make the necessary changes to be able to keep her son, otherwise there was no point in her being with me, and Arthur would go into long-term care or be adopted.

* * *

That first day was all about settling Lara and Arthur in, so they felt at ease in what would be their home for the next four months, possibly longer. I suggested I showed them around.

'Yes, sure, why not?' Lara replied easily.

Arthur had given up trying to pull open the drawers of the wardrobe and was now trying to climb into his cot.

'Does he usually have an afternoon nap?' I asked. Most infants his age do.

'Sometimes he falls asleep in the day. It's good when he does. It gives me a break,' she said.

'Roughly what time?'

'Whenever he wants.'

'We could try to get him into a routine. Once I've shown you around the house and he's had some food we could put him in the cot for a sleep. He might nod off if you stay with him. It will also get him used to his room ready for tonight.'

'Sure,' Lara replied amicably, checking her phone.

I began the tour in Arthur's room by opening the wardrobe door, and then showing her the storage compartment beneath the single bed for his belongings. We continued next door to Lara's bedroom where Arthur immediately began exploring.

'I haven't had such a nice room since I left foster care,' Lara said regretfully. 'But I ran away from there. I didn't know what was good for me back then.'

'When was that?' I asked.

'When I was about fifteen, but I was always running away,' she admitted.

'Why?'

'Lots of different reasons. Sometimes I didn't fit in. Other times I just didn't want to play happy families when I couldn't have a family of my own. The children's home was a bit better. We were all the same there. But I had to leave when I was eighteen.'

'Then where did you live?' I asked, keeping an eye on Arthur.

'All over the place, sofa-surfing, before I had him.'

'Where's his father? If you don't mind me asking.'

She shrugged and changed the subject. 'Nice garden,' she said, glancing out of the window.

'Thank you.'

Arthur was now on the bed and about to start jumping. I instinctively reached out to steady him as Lara continued to look around the room.

'If we can get him off for a little sleep, I can help you unpack,' I said to Lara. For it was clear we weren't going to be able to do much while Arthur was awake.

'Yes, sure.'

I lifted him off the bed and then showed them the rest of the upstairs. 'I sleep in here,' I said, opening my bedroom door. 'And that's Paula's bedroom,' I told them as we passed. 'She should be home around six o'clock.'

I showed them the bathroom, where Arthur tried to pitch himself head-first over the edge of the bath.

'Do you want to stand in it?' I asked him, and lifted him in. He was naturally curious, as most toddlers are, so it was better he explored carefully with us there.

His socked feet slipped on the dry bottom of the bath, which he thought was great fun. But I saw the danger of him falling and banging his head on the hard porcelain so

I held him carefully. 'You can have a bath tonight,' I said, and lifted him out.

He went to his mother. She was checking her phone. 'If you take his hand, we can go downstairs,' I told her.

At the top of the stairs I unfastened the stairgate and let them down first, then after going through I shut it behind me. Downstairs I gave Lara the password for the Wi-Fi router so she could access the internet on her phone and any other electronic devices she had with her, then I took her and Arthur into the kitchen-diner, the only room they hadn't been in.

'You're well organized,' Lara said, referring to the highchair, which I'd put ready at the table.

'Hopefully,' I smiled. 'I find it helps with children.'

I showed her the spaces I'd made in the cupboard and fridge for her and Arthur's food. While she was with me Lara would be living semi-independently, taking care of Arthur and herself with my help and support where necessary. This included shopping and cooking, although I would sometimes offer her our meals as well. Arthur was now trying to pull open the freezer door, which was child-locked, as were all the other cupboards at floor level.

'Shall we try him with the food you've brought?' I suggested.

'Yes, sure. But I haven't got a spoon or bowl, just bottles.'

'Don't worry, I've got what we need.'

Arthur ran after his mother as she went to the bags in the hall. I took the opportunity to check my phone. There was a text from Paula: *Going to be furloughed again!* with a raised-eyes emoji face depicting exasperation. *See you later. x*

Yes. See you later, I replied. *Try not to worry. At least you are being furloughed and still have a job. xx*

For now, she texted back. So I assumed there was still the possibility she might be made redundant.

There was also a message from Lucy: *Firework display on Thursday cancelled due to lockdown*. It was Bonfire Night on 5 November and traditionally it was marked with fireworks events. We'd been planning to go to a local display, but like all other group events it wouldn't go ahead now.

I texted back with an emoji of a disappointed face and the message: *I'll phone later. Lara and Arthur have just arrived. xxx*

Lara returned with a pouch of baby food. She was also checking her phone again so didn't see Arthur go to the cat's water bowl and dip in his hand.

'No, yucky,' I said, pulling a face, and drew him away. 'That's for Sammy, our cat. Not little boys.' I wiped his hand. 'Do you want a drink of water?'

'He can't answer you,' Lara said, without looking up.

'No, but children learn language by hearing words repeated over and over again. He will understand more than he can say.'

'Oh shit!' she said, still looking at her phone. 'I've got to attend a parenting class.'

'Really? We're going into lockdown again on Thursday. You'd better check it's still on.'

As Lara texted her social worker, I looked at the pouch of ready-prepared food, a blended mixture of vegetables including sweet potatoes, which could be served at room temperature. I took a bib, food bowl, plastic spoon and sippy cup from the cupboard, filled the cup with water, and set them on the table, ready.

Once Lara had finished on her phone I suggested she put Arthur into the highchair to feed him.

'Fasten the belt to stop him falling out,' I added.

She did, but Arthur didn't like having his movements suddenly curtailed and began to protest, squirming and kicking his legs.

'Look, food!' I said, showing him the packet to distract him.

'He's never been in one of those chairs before,' Lara said.

'He'll soon get used to it; if not, feed him sitting on your lap for today. Mummy's going to feed you,' I told him with a big smile.

'Am I?' Lara asked uncertainly.

'I'll help. He's likely to spit it out to begin with.' I fastened the bib around his neck and he stopped fidgeting and tugged it quizzically.

'Can he suck this straight from the packet,' Lara asked, looking at the instructions.

'He could but it's better to put some in the bowl to get him used to having his food on a spoon. It's very different to sucking.'

I joined Lara at the table as she squirted some of the blended mixture into the bowl, then looked at me. 'You have a go first,' she said, unsure, and slid the bowl and spoon towards me.

'Mmm, yummy,' I said, showing him.

I scooped a little of the food onto the spoon and put it to his lips. He looked startled and Lara burst out laughing. Arthur then grabbed the food end of the spoon, squelching the gooey mixture between his fingers. Lara laughed even more.

I tried again with some more food with the same result – puréed vegetables everywhere except in his mouth. Arthur thought it was fun and was laughing too. On the third attempt some went past his lips and his face was a picture of surprise, intrigue and disgust. Putting his fingers into his mouth, he fished out some of the food and examined it. Lara was laughing so much she was bent double, clutching her sides.

'It's all new to him,' I said, smiling. 'Not just the taste but the texture too.' I popped some more into his mouth.

He spat some out but then swallowed the rest.

'Good boy,' I said. 'Yummy. Well done.'

I clapped and he grinned. I gave him another two spoonfuls and then said to Lara, 'Your turn. I'll get a cloth to wipe him down.'

'A hose more like it!'

As she fed him I went into the kitchen, found a clean muslin cloth and ran it under the tap to dampen it. Returning to Arthur, I began wiping away the food that was spread over the tray of the highchair, his hair and, of course, his face and hands. Lara continued to give him small amounts on the spoon, which he was swallowing. I praised her and suggested she pause and give him some water from the sippy cup. He grabbed it from her hand and threw it to the floor. She laughed. I picked it up and wiped it and she tried again – this time with more success. Feeding Arthur was a new experience for her, as it was for him. They were learning together, and feeding a child (as well as giving them nutrition) helps bond mother and child, just as it did when she bottle-fed him.

After about ten minutes it was clear Arthur had run out of patience. I praised them both and we cleaned him up.

'Shall we try him in his cot?' I suggested after a while, when his food had had time to digest.

'Oh yes, please,' Lara said, with a heartfelt sigh.

She lifted him out of the highchair and we went upstairs, where she was going to put him in his cot fully dressed.

'Best to take off his tracksuit so he sleeps in his vest and nappy,' I said. 'The house is warm and you don't want him to overheat. Also, he'll come to associate undressing and his cot with having a sleep.'

'You're going in your cot, mate,' Lara said, and took off his top and bottoms. She lifted him into the cot and gently laid him down. Arthur immediately stood and wanted to be out.

'Keep resetting him,' I said. 'Raise the sides of the cot and stroke his forehead through the slats.'

'I used to put him in the cot at Diesel's place to keep him out of the way,' Lara admitted.

'It may take a few days before he starts associating his cot with sleep, but we'll get there. Just keep resetting him.'

'Shall I get him his dummy?' she asked.

'If he uses one, yes.'

Lara returned with the dummy, laid Arthur down again and put it into his mouth. Arthur stood up.

'Go to sleep, good boy,' she said gently.

He was grinning at me so I moved out of his line of vision and stood outside the bedroom door, from where I could still see them as Lara continued to resettle him.

'It's just us now,' I heard her tell Arthur. 'We're in our new home. This is your bedroom. I've got one too.'

Eventually Arthur stopped trying to stand and I heard Lara say, 'Good boy. There's no sofa for me to lie on so I'm going to lie on that bed where you can see me.'

I waited on the landing, thinking that if Arthur went to sleep it would give Lara and me the chance to unpack. After a few minutes it went quiet so I looked in. They were both sound asleep, Arthur on his side in his cot facing his mother, and Lara on the single bed facing her son. I really hoped this was going to work out for them, for I'd already noticed the bond between Lara and her son – something you don't always see when a child comes into care.

CHAPTER FOUR

I'D NEVER HURT HIM

While Lara and Arthur slept I put the time to good use. I took their bags upstairs and stacked them on the landing ready to unpack later. I checked my emails and also began the daily record I had to keep for the social services, which would ultimately contribute to Lara's parenting assessment. Foster carers are given extra training in order to take a mother-and-child assessment placement. The parenting doesn't have to be perfect but 'good enough', which is a recognized term and covers four key areas:

The parent's ability to meet the child's health and developmental needs.

How well they put the child's needs first.

How they provide routine and consistent care.

And if they can acknowledge problems and engage with support when necessary.

In practical terms this means assessing how well they feed and change their child, keep them safe, show love and affection, stimulate them, put boundaries in place and offer stability. It's what most parents do automatically, often having learnt it from their own parents or care-giver. Problems can arise if a new parent hasn't had a good role model, but parenting assessments take this into account as well as other factors that may have affected the family, such as housing, employment and income. No parenting is perfect, but it has to be adequate to meet the child's needs and keep them safe.

Lara had only just arrived so my observations were very limited, and of course I wouldn't be drawing any conclusions for some time. I did, however, make reference to the bond I'd already noticed between them, and that Lara had been happy to accept my suggestions on weaning and settling Arthur into a better routine. I'd also had to note that she'd gone outside to smoke. But as she'd only had one cigarette since arriving I was hoping she would be able to give up in time.

Lara and Arthur slept for an hour. I heard Arthur wake first and I went upstairs. He was standing in his cot, rattling the side, ready for off. Lara was still asleep. I was tempted to leave her to sleep and take Arthur downstairs, but if she was allowed to keep Arthur then at some point she'd have sole care of him so would need to be awake when he was.

'Lara,' I said gently. 'Arthur is awake.'

She came to with a start.

'Where am I?' she gasped, sitting bolt upright on the bed.

'You're with me, Cathy.'

'Oh, yes. You gave me a shock.'

'Sorry, love. You both had a little sleep. It's nearly four o'clock and Arthur is awake.'

'OK,' she said, rubbing her eyes. 'I'll leave him in his cot while I have a ciggy.'

'I think he'd like to be up now.'

She stood, lifted Arthur out of the cot, checked his nappy didn't need changing and went downstairs. She put Arthur in the hall, took her cigarettes and lighter out of her jacket pocket and disappeared out the front door, putting the lock on the latch so she could get back in. I'd give her a front door key later.

I took Arthur into the living room and played with him until Lara returned. She asked if she could make herself a cup of tea, so I showed her where everything was in the kitchen.

'He usually has another bottle now,' she said. 'Does he need it with that food?'

'Yes. He didn't have much. We'll reduce his milk as we increase the amount of solid food he is having.'

'I'll get his stuff,' she said.

'All your bags are on the landing,' I called after her.

Arthur followed her out and I went too, to check he couldn't get upstairs. The lower stairgate was closed. The fact that Lara had said he usually had a bottle about now suggested a routine of sorts, which was good. Often in parent-and-child placements the parent is very young, the baby only a few weeks or months old, and there is no routine at all. Arthur was a year old so clearly Lara had been managing to some degree at least. From what I'd seen so far she seemed to be doing quite well.

She came down with empty feeding bottles and the formula milk, and we went into the kitchen-diner.

I'd put another safety gate between the kitchen and the dining area as I was expected to, and I stayed with Arthur on the dining side while Lara went into the kitchen. She boiled the kettle for tea and to make up another bottle.

'I stopped sterilizing his bottles when he was a year old,' Lara told me as she worked. 'That's what it says online.'

'Yes, that's fine. Just make sure they are kept clean by washing them in hot water. And if you make up any food in advance, it should be stored in the fridge. You don't mind me telling you all this?'

'No. You go ahead.'

As I kept Arthur amused Lara offered to make me a cup of tea, which I accepted. I also told her where the biscuit tin was. She was careful as she carried the mugs of tea into the living room, keeping them right away from Arthur. Once seated, she placed her mug out of his reach and then dunked her biscuit into her tea and gave him some.

'Is that allowed?' she asked me, slightly worried.

'Yes, of course. If you want to give him a bit of biscuit, that's OK. Do you brush his teeth?'

'No. He's only got a few baby teeth,' she said, amazed.

'It's a good idea to start brushing them as soon as they come through. We'll put a baby toothbrush and tooth-paste on the shopping list for tomorrow.'

Lara said she'd start a list on her phone and propped Arthur with his bottle on the sofa, which left her hands free. He was good at holding his bottle. She saw me watching him.

'Is that all right?' she asked.

'Yes, love, don't worry. Although I wouldn't leave him alone with a bottle at night.'

'Because?'

'He could choke. Not likely at his age, but better to be safe than sorry.'

It seemed I was giving Lara a lot of advice, but she didn't mind, and in my experience it's better to begin as you mean to continue. As we drank our tea she asked about the many photos I had on the living-room walls. They were of my family and the children I'd looked after.

'I've got a photo of my mum,' she said. 'I'll show you later.'

'Thanks. I'd like to see it.'

'I loved my mum,' Lara said, which really moved me. 'I know we lived in chaos, but she did love me.' Lara had been seven when her mother died so would have memories of her. 'We were always on the move, going from one bed-and-breakfast lodging house to another, but her favourite place was London. All the hustle and bustle of the city. She said we fitted in. That's where I got my name from – Lewisham. I was born in the hospital there.'

'Very good.' I smiled.

'The Lara comes from Lara Croft in *Tomb Raider* – you know, the video game. Mum loved that game.' I nodded. 'She used to play it all the time.'

'It's nice you have happy memories of her,' I said, pleased that Lara felt relaxed enough to share them with me.

'They weren't all happy, not by a long way,' Lara said. 'I remember going hungry because Mum didn't have the money to buy us food. She used to send me to ask neighbours for food and sometimes we'd steal it. There were a lot of weirdos hanging around where we stayed, which was frightening. Other junkies, I guess. I remember hiding from the social worker. The rooms where we stayed were always in a mess. Mum didn't like cleaning. She said there was no point as it got messy again. We used to keep empty packets and tins of food in the cupboards to trick the social workers. They always checked the cupboards to see if we had food.' Lara smiled at the memory. 'But Mum meant well. She loved me, which is more than can be said for some of the foster carers. She just couldn't cope with a child. She struggled to look after herself. I guess it was because of the drugs. I'd never do drugs. I've seen what they can do.'

'I'm pleased to hear it. Although you know cigarettes and alcohol are types of drugs. They're very addictive.'

'Did that social worker tell you I drink?'

I nodded. 'It was included in the information I was sent.'

'There! I knew she had it in for me. I only used to drink because Diesel did. I told her that. We drank too much, then we'd argue. The neighbours heard and called the police. It wasn't my fault.'

'They would be worried that you or Arthur could be hurt,' I said.

'He was in his cot, he didn't get hurt,' she said, a little defensively. 'Anyway, I won't drink here. I can't.'

'And what about smoking?' I asked.

'Give me a break!' She laughed good-humouredly. 'It keeps me sane. I only smoke a few a day, and not near Arthur.'

'I understand. I used to smoke,' I said. 'Like you, it wasn't many, and I always went outside, but I'm pleased I gave up. Apart from it being bad for our health, cigarettes are so expensive.'

'I hear you,' she said.

I smiled. 'Good. I'm going to have to get some dinner going soon, for later. I was planning on making a cheese, pasta and broccoli bake. Would you like some?'

'Yes, please.'

'While I see to it, you could take Arthur into the garden for a while. Let him run off some energy.' Since we'd been in the living room talking he hadn't stayed in one place for longer than two seconds.

'Isn't it cold out there?'

'Wrap up warm and he'll be fine. Just for ten minutes or so. It will help him sleep tonight.'

The prospect of more sleep did it for Lara and she put on their coats and shoes and took Arthur into the back garden. I could see them through the kitchen window as I worked. Lara was on her phone as Arthur ran around, tumbled, picked himself up and continued running. Round and round the lawn and all over the garden. Many infants his age are very active, wanting to explore the world. As a parent or carer, we daren't take our eyes off them. Then I saw Arthur trying to clamber up the climbing frame, which was in the children's play area at the very end of the garden. I tapped on the window to get Lara's attention and I pointed to him. She went to the frame, lifted him off and continued her phone conversation. Arthur went straight to the climbing frame again and Lara removed him a second time. Then a third. The climbing apparatus was designed for older children, but a toddler could manage it with help. As soon as Lara put Arthur down he ran straight to it again. It was a game for him but not for Lara. Eventually she picked him up and, none too pleased, headed back up the garden. I busied myself preparing dinner.

'He's been a right pain,' she said, coming in the back door. 'Can we watch television?'

'Yes, sure, although children of his age are active. It's a good sign. They've recently learnt to walk so now they want to explore.'

She sighed and, taking off their shoes and coats, went into the living room. Presently I heard a children's programme on the television, but Arthur wasn't ready to sit still yet. Lara kept telling him, 'Come here.' 'Sit down.' 'You are a pain.' And so on. Then I heard him run down the hall and go into the front room. I left what I was doing and went to find him; I didn't want him in there unattended. The children's toys were either in the living room, the cupboards in the kitchen-diner or in the child's bedroom, so there was little to interest him in there.

'Come on, let's find Mummy,' I told him.

He grinned in his cheeky way, ran twice around the room, narrowly missing the corner of a bookshelf, then he was off down the hall and into the living room. I closed the front-room door and went into the living room where Lara was engrossed in the children's programme.

'Can you keep an eye on him?' I said. 'He can run up and down the hall, but I don't want him in the front room. It's not child-proofed and the computer is in there and important documents.'

'OK,' she said easily. 'What age do children sit and watch television?'

'Not for some while yet, love. He may like you to play with his toys with him.'

I returned to the kitchen and listened to Arthur running up and down the hall and banging on the front door. Then he began appearing at the safety gate that separated the kitchen from the dining area, peering at me and running off. 'Boo!' I said, each time he appeared. He chuckled, ran off and came back again. This game kept him amused for another fifteen minutes while Lara watched television.

Once I'd put dinner in the oven I suggested to Lara that she could give Arthur some more solid food. 'Then once we've had dinner we can unpack his belongings and start his bath and bedtime routine.

'Yes, bedtime sounds good,' she said.

As Lara gave Arthur some more of the blended vege-table mixture I sat with them at the table and talked to her about weaning in general: how we would gradually introduce new tastes and textures into Arthur's diet so eventually he was eating our food, mashed or chopped, and no longer needed formula milk. As with the previous meal he began taking some of the puréed vegetable out of his mouth, squelching it between his fingers and examin-ing it, which Lara found disgusting.

'I know it's messy,' I said. 'But he's interested in what the food looks like. It's perfectly normal. When we eat we'll give him some of our food to play with.'

'Yucky,' she said, as he smeared more around his face. Some went in his mouth, though.

Once Arthur had finished Lara cleaned him with a damp cloth and then gave him a bottle. He soiled his nappy so I went with them upstairs while she changed him, putting the used nappy into a plastic bag. Downstairs, I showed her where the dustbin was for the dirty nappy. Arthur resumed running up and down the hall, banging on the front door as he landed against it. I tried to get him interested in some of the toys they'd brought with them, but he preferred the hall and front door. The hall runs the length of the house from front to back so must have seemed very long to him.

'He's training to be an athlete,' I joked to Lara, but she wasn't impressed.

Sammy chanced to appear so, taking Arthur's hand in mine, I showed him how to stroke his fur. 'Nice and gently,' I told him. 'Down from his neck, like this.'

Sammy allowed Arthur to stroke him for a little while and then, when he'd had enough, he trotted off down the hall, pursued by Arthur who wanted to stroke him some more. The front-room door was closed so with nowhere to go Sammy leapt over the stairgate and sat on the third stair looking coolly at Arthur. Arthur stretched his arm through the bars of the gate, but no matter how much he tried he couldn't reach Sammy. I'm sure our cat knew what he was doing as he sat there, tantalizingly out of reach with a self-satisfied grin, watching Arthur as he tried to reach him. It kept Arthur occupied for some time, and even when he gave up he kept returning to check if Sammy was still there. Over the weeks to come it became Sammy's favourite place when he wanted respite from Arthur, or possibly just because he could! I am sure cats are far more intelligent than we give them credit for.

Paula arrived home a little before six o'clock and I introduced her to Lara. I'd already explained to Lara that Paula had been furloughed.

'Sorry about your job,' Lara said as they said hello, which was kind of her.

'Thanks.'

'And this is Arthur,' I said. With the arrival of someone new, he'd hidden behind his mother.

'Hi,' Paula said, peeping around her, but I could tell she was preoccupied.

'Let's check on dinner,' I suggested, which would give us a chance to talk.

Leaving Lara and Arthur in the living room, we went into the kitchen where Paula said she'd been told not to go into work the next day. Although lockdown didn't start until Thursday, management had decided to furlough those employees who weren't needed immediately. Paula was concerned that her job might be in jeopardy and ultimately she might lose it completely, which was the worry of many. I reassured her as best I could. It was an unsettling time, especially for young people who were very vulnerable in the fluctuating job market, either having not been in a position for long or looking for work on leaving school or college.

'I could help with the fostering again,' Paula offered. She'd been a big help last time she'd been furloughed when we'd fostered two sisters. 'But I guess as Lara is looking after Arthur I won't really be needed.'

'I'm sure Lara will greatly appreciate your help,' I said. 'But remember, she needs to do most of the looking after as this is an assessment placement.'

'OK.'

Paula went upstairs to change out of her office clothes while I put the finishing touches to dinner. We ate at the table in our kitchen-diner with Arthur in his highchair. I checked it was all right with Lara and then gave him some of the bake we were having, putting it in a child's bowl, with an infant's spoon and fork. I didn't expect him to start using the cutlery straight away; it was to get him used to it. It's usual to introduce infants of his age to first-stage cutlery and have them sit at the table. Needless to say, Arthur used his fingers to explore the contents of the bowl, squashing the food in his hand, wiping it over his face and the tray of the highchair, then putting some into his mouth. I was watching him as Lara ate.

'Well done,' I told Arthur as he sucked the food and then swallowed it. 'Good boy.'

I explained to Lara what he'd done and why I was pleased. Children of his age, given the opportunity, will normally use their hands to put food into their mouths and it's the start of feeding themselves.

As we ate, Lara talked to Paula. I think she appreciated the company of someone closer to her age, having been with me all day. She asked Paula about her job and what qualifications she had.

'I wish I'd done better at school,' Lara admitted. 'I failed most of my GCSEs.'

'You could always retake them,' Paula said.

'What, with him?' Lara exclaimed, as if it would be impossible.

'You could attend college part-time when they reopen,' I suggested. 'Some colleges have nurseries. Or you could learn remotely online.'

'Maybe,' Lara said with a shrug and changed the subject.

She talked to Paula about a local nightclub and some other venues she went to and asked if Paula had ever been to them, which she had. From what Lara said, and the phone calls she'd had during the day, it seemed she had two close friends and they often went out together in a group of three.

'Who used to babysit Arthur?' I asked nonchalantly, as he squashed some more food into his mouth.

'Diesel,' Lara replied. 'His mates used to come round with beers while I went out.'

'And you were happy that Diesel could take care of Arthur?' I asked.

'I guess so.' But she didn't seem sure. 'They put his cot in the bedroom and I left some bottles for him. Sometimes when I came back the place smelt of weed. Diesel and I argued, and he said he wouldn't smoke in the flat again, but he did.'

I didn't comment, but from what I knew of Diesel so far he'd be the last person I'd trust with any child of mine.

'I mean, there was no one else to ask to babysit and I had to get out,' Lara added. 'It was only once a week.'

'What would you do in the future if Arthur was living with you and you wanted to go out?' I asked.

'Not go, I guess,' she replied. 'Or ask you to babysit.'

I smiled. 'I could. It is important to find someone trustworthy. I've been a single parent for a long time and know how difficult it can be to have a social life. When my children were young I hardly went out at all.'

I thought Lara should know the responsibility and limitations that came with being a single parent.

After dinner Paula went to her room and I looked after Arthur so that Lara could unpack his belongings. She added to her list of what we needed to buy for him tomorrow. Once she'd unpacked his bags I suggested we ran his bath. Lara said she'd just been washing him whenever she had time, so I explained that having a bath-and bedtime routine helped prepare the child for bed, and the warm water relaxed them and helped them sleep.

I gave her what she needed, towels and so forth, and then stood to one side in the bathroom and let her get on with it. As she undressed Arthur I saw the other bruises she'd mentioned – on his back and bottom. Three small marks that had faded now but must have been more vivid when the doctor saw them.

'You know you never leave a child unattended in the bath,' I checked. 'Not even for a second.'

'Yes, I know,' she replied. 'Like I told the doctor and social worker, he got the bruises from falling over. I'd never hurt him. I know he can be a pain at times, but I'd never harm him.'

'Good.'

I wanted to believe her, but I'd heard other parents of children in care swear blind they'd never hurt their child and then it was shown that they had. I dearly hoped this wouldn't be true for Lara.

CHAPTER FIVE

HOMELESS

Once Arthur was asleep in his cot I suggested to Lara that she unpack her belongings so she felt more at home.

'It won't take me long,' she said. 'I'm good at packing and unpacking with all the moves I've had.'

She didn't have an awful lot. Most of the bags and boxes contained Arthur's belongings, so I wondered if she'd left some of her possessions at her ex-boyfriend's, but she said she hadn't and this was it. It appeared she'd spent what little money she had on Arthur. I was touched by this and thought it sad that at the age of twenty all her worldly possessions could be fitted into three small hold-alls, when you think what the average young person has. Lara's most precious possession was her smartphone, which was a recent model. She didn't have a laptop or any other electronic devices, and I told her she could use the computer and printer in the front room if she needed to. I then said I'd be downstairs in the living room if she wanted me, and left her to finish off unpacking.

Twenty minutes later Lara came into the living room carrying one of the holdalls full of clothes. 'This is our washing,' she said. 'I haven't done it for a while.'

'We'd better get a load in now then,' I said, and left what I was doing.

We went into the kitchen where I showed her how to use the washer-dryer. She didn't have any food items with her apart from Arthur's powdered milk and she now put that into the cupboard I'd cleared for her. I asked her if she wanted a drink and she had a glass of juice. I told her to help herself if she wanted anything. She seemed a bit awkward, which was understandable, and of course Paula and I would have to get used to having another adult in the house.

'It's bound to feel a bit strange to begin with,' I said. 'But I hope you'll soon feel at home. I think Arthur already does.'

'I can live anywhere,' Lara replied stoically, leaning against a kitchen cabinet as we talked.

'You've had a lot of moves.'

'Yes, especially when I was in care. Twenty-five that I can remember.'

I would like to say I was shocked, but I'd heard similar from other care-leavers who'd had multiple moves.

'That should never happen,' I said. 'Do you know the reasons for the moves?'

'Some,' she said with a dismissive shrug. 'But not all. I was a pain when I was growing up so I think some of the carers couldn't cope or had enough and wanted me out. But I don't know why I got moved when I was little. You just get used to it in the end.'

'You shouldn't have to get used to it,' I said sadly. 'Every child deserves a stable, loving home.'

'I remember a social worker saying that as she moved

me in with what was supposed to be my permanent family when I was twelve.'

'And it wasn't?'

'No. It lasted a week.'

That did shock me.

'I am sorry,' I said.

'It's not your fault.'

Yet I felt a collective responsibility for Lara having been so badly let down.

At the time of writing there has been no in-depth study into the reasons why some children in care have multiple moves; I think this research needs to be done. Many children in care stay with one foster family who become their permanent family – as good as any birth family – but sadly too many children have to move, sometimes repeatedly. Not only is it unsettling for the child to leave what they thought was their home, but if the move is out of the area then they have to change schools, which can disrupt their education and result in them losing their friends. One of the reasons I write my fostering memoirs is to try to raise awareness for looked-after children and hopefully improve the system. The child-care system in the UK is one of the best in the world, but there is always room for improvement, and more support needs to be put in so that a child can remain with their birth parents or foster carer.

'I liked the children's home I was in,' Lara added.

'More so than being with a foster family?' I asked. We were still in the kitchen. Some of my best conversations took place there. I think its homely feel invites confidences.

'Yes. We were all in the same position in the children's home. I didn't feel different.'

Lara had said similar earlier and it was interesting because it's generally assumed that children who can't live with their parents or a family member are better off in a foster family rather than a children's home. Lara may have been in the minority feeling this way, but until more research is done we won't know.

'I'm sure if I'd had a family of my own with someone to call Mum and Dad then my life could have been different,' she said. 'I hope Paula and your other kids know how lucky they are.' Which touched me deeply. 'Anyway, I'll be in my room. Shout when the washing is done.'

'OK, love. Check on Arthur when you go up, please.'

'I will.'

I heard Lara go into Arthur's room, which was directly above the kitchen, and then into her room. It wasn't long before I heard the rise and fall of her voice as she spoke on the phone, although it wasn't loud enough to wake Arthur. I went into the living room, still thinking about what Lara had said. I hoped I could undo some of the harm that had been done to her by all the moves.

Presently, Lara came into the living room to find me, looking a bit sheepish.

'Can I ask you a favour?' she said.

'Yes.'

'You know lockdown starts on Thursday?'

'Yes.'

'If I go out tomorrow, can you or Paula babysit Arthur? Shell is asking. It's our last chance to go out for a month.'

'And Shell is one of your friends?'

'Yes. Her real name is Shelby, but everyone calls her Shell. It's her idea.'

I smiled. 'Yes, I can babysit. You go.'

'Thank you so much! I didn't think you'd agree. Don't tell Claudette.'

'I'll have to mention it to her, but you're not doing anything wrong. You're entitled to go out every so often as long as you make proper arrangements for Arthur.'

'Good on you!' she said. 'I'll tell Shell.' And she disappeared up to her room.

I heard her on the phone again, presumably planning their evening. Of course she could go out; I thought probably once a week was reasonable once lockdown was lifted.

When the washer-dryer finished I took Lara's laundry up to her room. She was still on the phone, but her tone was different so I guessed she was talking to someone else. I knocked, she called, 'Come in,' and immediately ended the call.

'Everything all right?' I asked.

'Yes.'

'Here's your washing.'

'Thank you. I'm getting into bed soon. I'm knackered. I'll have a shower in the morning.'

'All right, love. Have you got everything you need?' I'd already given her fresh towels.

'I think so.'

'I'll say goodnight then. I suggest you switch off your phone at night so you get some sleep. Hopefully Arthur won't wake too often.'

When I'm fostering a young person with a phone I explain one of our house rules is that phones are switched off at night or left downstairs, but it was more difficult with Lara as she was an adult. I could only suggest it, and then if it became an issue I'd talk to her again.

I'd just gone into Paula's room to have a chat with her when we heard Arthur wake. Lara went to him almost immediately and then it went quiet. I went to check everything was all right.

'His dummy fell out,' Lara said. 'I've put it back in.'

'OK, love.'

Paula and I chatted for a while in her room and then I went to bed at around 10.30. Lara's room was quiet too. But at 11 p.m. Arthur woke and from then on he was awake nearly every hour. Exhausted, Lara took longer and longer to answer his cries, and at one point both Paula and I were on the landing going to Arthur before she was. It crossed my mind that he might be ill, but he didn't have a temperature and hadn't been sick, so I thought he was more likely unsettled by the move.

At 3 a.m. Lara gave him a bottle to get him off to sleep, and he then slept until 7 a.m. Strictly speaking, toddlers of his age shouldn't need a bottle at night, but we'd only just started weaning him and he was used to his bottle and doubtless found it comforting. Guidance changes and much of parenting relies on common sense.

When Arthur woke in the morning I was still in bed. I heard Lara's bedroom door open and it went quiet. Slipping on my dressing gown, I went to check on them. Lara had taken Arthur into her bed and he seemed fine. They were both watching the portable television I'd put in there. It was a children's cartoon and the colourful, fast-moving pictures were keeping Arthur entertained, as they were Lara.

'Well done,' I said to her with a smile, and she gave me the thumbs-up sign.

I took the opportunity to shower and dress and by the time I'd finished Arthur was running around the landing, babbling loudly, dashing any hope Paula may have had of catching up on her sleep. By 8.30 we were all downstairs having our breakfast of cereal and toast. After Lara had given Arthur some formula milk I suggested she try him with some hot oat cereal, which she'd had. He thoroughly enjoyed it so that was another new taste and texture he'd accepted in his weaning programme.

Lara was looking forward to going out that evening with her friend Shell. She told us they were meeting at 7 p.m. at a pub a short bus ride away. I asked her how she was getting home and she said by bus.

'All right, keep safe. Call me if there's a problem,' I said, as I would any young person in my care. 'The buses aren't always that reliable.'

She looked a little bemused at my concern. 'Then what?'

'I'd come and collect you in the car if necessary.'

'Really?'

'Yes. Which reminds me, I'll give you a front door key.'

I fetched the spare front door key and Lara put it in her purse for safekeeping. I also checked she had my landline and mobile numbers in her phone in case she needed to contact me. I said I wanted to go shopping that morning as soon as we were ready and we'd walk to our local High Street where we should be able to get what we needed. While Lara got Arthur ready I took the stroller from the cupboard under the stairs and set it up in the hall. Paula wasn't coming with us as she had some things to do. It was 10 a.m. when we left with Arthur in a warm all-in-one coat in the stroller and Lara pushing it. She had her list of what she needed on her phone, and I had a written list of household items, plus plenty of bags. She took the opportunity to have a cigarette as we walked and talked.

Our local High Street is about a ten-minute walk away and consists of one main road with shops on either side. It includes a large pharmacy and supermarket, and a number of smaller shops – for example, shoe repairers/ locksmith, a greetings card shop, newsagent, dry cleaners, opticians, estate agent and so forth, much as you'd find on many high streets. Two of the small shops that had been struggling to stay in business before the pandemic had closed since the last lockdown. I tried to shop locally if I could, but items such as furniture or clothes required a trip into the town or retail park. Having lived in the same area for many years, I often saw people I knew on my way in and out of the High Street. If we stopped for a quick chat, I introduced them to the child or young person I was fostering as a matter of courtesy. Aware that it was chilly and Arthur wouldn't be content to stay in the stroller for long, I kept these interactions to a smile and a 'Hi, how are you?'

Now it was the beginning of November, some shops already had festive decorations in their windows. This next lockdown would be another hard blow for many of the smaller businesses as non-essential shops had to close again. As we passed one shop that had closed the previous month Lara suddenly grabbed my arm.

'Look at that guy!' she hissed under her breath.

I'd already seen him. Huddled in the doorway of the shop that had once sold arts and crafts goods was a rough sleeper. His hoodie shielded much of his face and a sleeping bag covered his legs, but from what I could see of him he was in his twenties. To find a homeless person on our High Street was very unusual. The last time I'd seen anyone sleeping rough there had been about five years ago, and that was only for a few days – a middle-aged man, who'd been found a hostel.

'Poor lad,' I said. 'I thought all the homeless had been given places indoors during the pandemic.'

'Well, clearly he hasn't,' Lara said. 'I'll give him some money.'

She stopped the stroller and, delving into her coat pocket, took out some loose change. I stayed with Arthur and watched as she went back and placed the money in the outstretched hand of the young man. He nodded appreciatively and said thank you.

'Aren't *you* going to give him something?' Lara asked me accusingly as she returned.

'I'll buy him a hot drink and a sandwich,' I said. 'Then I know the money hasn't gone on drugs or alcohol.'

'Oh, right, yes, I see what you mean.'

'Let's do our shopping first and then I'll get him something to eat and drink on the way back.'

It was then Lara realized she hadn't brought a face mask with her – they were mandatory in all shops – so I gave her a spare one of mine. We went to the pharmacy as most of the items Lara needed for Arthur could be bought there, including baby wipes, nappies, and ready-made weaning food and snacks. Lara chose and paid for these while I bought household items, including more antibacterial wipes and hand gel. On our way out we passed a display of products to help people stop smoking

– nicotine-replacement patches, chewing gum and lozenges.

'I bought some of those patches once,' she said. 'It was cheaper to smoke!'

'I think you can get some free on the NHS if you are going to give up smoking,' I said.

She nodded absently and was about to continue out of the shop.

'If you want to try to quit again, we'll get some now and I'll pay for them,' I offered. The NHS was under so much pressure looking after those seriously ill with Covid that non-essential appointments were being delayed by many months. If she did decide to stop smoking, it was better she got started straight away.

'What if I don't manage to give up?' she said, pulling a face. 'Will you want your money back?'

'No, of course not.'

'OK then. I'll give it a go,' she said. 'Perhaps I can do it this time without Diesel giving me grief.'

I enquired at the counter and we were told we had to see the pharmacist first. He explained to Lara the different products available, and they discussed the best option for her, based on how many she smoked a day, her medical history and if she'd tried to quit before. They decided on the nicotine gum. The pharmacist also gave her some literature, which included a telephone number that offered support, although he wasn't sure if it was operating at present during Covid.

'I'll try not to let you down,' Lara said to me after I'd paid and we'd come away.

As we'd been longer than we anticipated in the pharmacy, Arthur was now growing restless in the stroller.

Lara opened a packet of baby snack food she'd bought in the pharmacy – cheese puffs – and put one in his hand. This kept him amused for a while until he dropped it. She tried another and that did find its way into his mouth, as did the next. He seemed to be enjoying them – another new taste and texture.

We completed the shopping, then headed back along the High Street where I stopped off at the bakery. I bought our bread, the sausage roll Lara wanted, and soup and a sandwich for the homeless man. Outside we took off our masks and I told Lara to keep hers in her jacket pocket so she'd always have one with her. As we neared the shop doorway where the lad had previously been we could see it was empty, although his sleeping bag was still there. We looked around but he wasn't in sight.

'Hopefully he's found somewhere to stay,' I said. 'But I'll leave this here in case he's coming back.' I set the pot of soup and packet of sandwiches in the doorway, and we left.

On the way home Lara had another cigarette. 'I may as well finish the packet before I give up,' she said. 'Then I won't be tempted.'

I could see the logic, sort of. 'Or you could throw away the rest,' I suggested.

She looked horrified. 'That would be a waste! I'll smoke this one and hide the packet.'

Just after we arrived home Claudette phoned Lara to see how she was getting on. I heard Lara say fine, that she had given up smoking and Arthur had been weaned, both of which were actually works in progress. Claudette also emailed us with the details of the review meeting she'd set up for Friday. There would be a weekly meeting to see how things were going for Lara and to share our observations – at present online.

Paula joined us for lunch, when Arthur had some of the new food Lara had bought for him. Then she put him in his cot for a nap. She lay on the bed in his room as she had the day before and, like yesterday, she fell asleep. Arthur woke after about an hour and Lara woke too. She gave him a drink and then Paula and I looked after him while she washed, dried and straightened her hair ready to go out later. She said she'd have to leave the house at 6.30 p.m. to meet her friend at 7 p.m. so I made an early dinner, some of which Arthur had. Then Lara asked if I could give Arthur his bath and put him to bed, which I'd sort of assumed I would be doing.

'Just give him his dummy if he cries,' she said, rushing out the front door.

'Have a nice time!' I called after her.

'Thanks. I will!'

Arthur was with Paula and me in the living room and, suddenly realizing his mother had gone, he ran down the hall looking for her. I picked him up and Paula and I distracted him with toys until it was time for his bath and bed. He enjoyed his bath, but it took over an hour to get him off to sleep – not surprising as the room was still new to him, and now he'd been left with someone he hardly knew. Every time I laid him down he stood up, then he grew fretful, so I gave him the dummy as Lara had instructed. Ten minutes later he was asleep.

Paula and I watched the evening news, which included a terror attack in Vienna, the forthcoming US election and, of course, the latest on Covid. The UK was to pioneer mass Covid testing on a scale not attempted before, and the number of those expected to be furloughed during the forthcoming lockdown was predicted to double. The World Health Organization (WHO) had published its weekly epidemiological update and we learnt that in the past week over 3.3 million new cases of Covid had been reported globally, making a total of 46 million cases and 1.2 million deaths. Having heard enough doom and gloom, we switched off the television. Paula went to listen to music in her room while I wrote up my log notes.

That night I heard Lara come in at around 11.30, flush the toilet and then go straight to bed. She wasn't especially noisy but I'm a light sleeper from years of looking after children. Arthur woke at 2 a.m., which was a huge improvement on the night before, but Lara was in such a deep sleep she didn't hear him. I could have resettled him, but she should. I gently woke her and she staggered half asleep into his room where she collapsed onto the bed in there and went back to sleep. I was able to settle him. He was happier now he could see his mother. He found her presence reassuring, which was another positive sign. Children who have been abused can shy away from an abusing parent and be wary and fearful around them. There was no sign of this in Arthur.

CHAPTER SIX

DIESEL

'Did you have a nice evening?' I asked Lara the following morning as we sat at the dining table.

'Yes, although I've got a hangover.'

I'd rather guessed that. She looked rough. She was still in her pyjamas and had smudges of last night's mascara under her eyes. I'd woken her just after 7 a.m. when Arthur had been calling out, ready to get up. She was now seated at the table spoon-feeding him hot oat cereal but unable to face any food herself. She was just drinking orange juice.

'It's all right for Shell,' Lara grumbled. 'She doesn't have a child and can stay in bed and sleep it off.'

I nodded sympathetically. I'm a morning person anyway and was now showered and dressed and enjoying coffee and toast with lashings of butter and marmalade, which Lara was eyeing disdainfully.

'I got talking to that guy,' Lara said, shovelling more cereal into Arthur's mouth even though he hadn't swallowed the last mouthful yet. He spat it out.

'Yuck,' she said, grimacing, and wiped it away.

'Slow down. Give him a chance to swallow one mouthful before you give him the next,' I said. 'Also offer him a sip of water every so often. What guy?'

'You know, the one we saw yesterday.'

'No.'

'The guy sleeping rough.'

'Oh. You spoke to him?' I asked, surprised.

'Yes. He was there last night. I saw him from the bus on my way back. I got off at the top of the road and then walked back into the High Street to talk to him.'

I paused from eating. 'Really? You need to be careful at that time of night.'

'That's what he said. He's called Frazer. He's twenty-three. I told him it was us who left the soup and sandwich. He said thanks.'

'I see. Why's he rough sleeping?'

'He hasn't got anywhere else to go. He was living down South but came here a few weeks ago. I'm not sure why. He didn't say. I think it's personal. He was sleeping in someone's shed. That's where he got the sleeping bag from.'

'What do you mean, he was sleeping in a shed?'

'Some guy lets homeless people kip in his shed.'

'Are you sure he's not making this up?' I asked, shocked.

'I don't know. He seemed genuine. He told me he used to be in foster care.'

'Really?' I exclaimed.

'That's what he said. I told him I'd been in care most of my life and was again now, sort of.'

'He needs to be indoors, not sleeping rough,' I said, very concerned. 'It's winter soon and we're in the middle of a pandemic. Hasn't he got anyone he can stay with?'

'I don't think so,' Lara said, finally offering Arthur his sippy cup. 'He seemed nice, but I think he's depressed. I used my phone to find the number of a hostel, but they were full last night and said he should go there today and try. I gave him the details.'

'That was very sensible of you,' I said, impressed. 'Well done. I don't think there's much more you could have done.'

'I hope he goes.'

'Yes, so do I.'

Once Arthur had finished his breakfast I looked after him while Lara showered and dressed. By that time Paula was up, and after she'd eaten I suggested we all went for a walk. Like many during the last lockdown, Paula and I had got into the habit of going for a walk each day. I thought it would be a good idea to start doing it again as another lockdown approached. The fresh air would help clear Lara's head and it was good for Arthur to spend time outside each day. Lara suggested that I might like to take Arthur so she could go back to bed, but I reminded her nicely that she was responsible for Arthur and I'd babysat the night before.

'I'll bring his dummy in case he plays up,' she said, a bit disgruntled.

But once we were outside she got over her bad humour and talked to Paula, and then me. She pushed Arthur in the stroller as we walked up the road and through the park, then once in the open countryside beyond I suggested she take him out so he could run around.

Now, at the height of autumn, the trees were an amazing mixture of reds, golds and yellows. As the wind stirred, leaves floated to the ground like confetti, joining those already there. I pointed out a flock of birds to Arthur that were circling overhead.

'They could be flying to a hot country for winter,' I said. 'Lucky them.' For all holidays were now on hold again due to the pandemic.

But as we walked through the beautiful countryside we also had to make sure Arthur didn't tread in any dog mess dotted not far from the grassy path we were following. I think it's appalling that dog owners leave behind their pet's mess. It's completely irresponsible. I also think there is a good case for making owners keep their dogs on leads in public spaces, apart from some designated areas that everyone is aware of. Parks are primarily for people, not dogs, although I know some would disagree.

Moan over, we had a lovely walk, and talked about many topics as we went, including Frazer, the homeless young man in the High Street. Paula was saddened and appalled that he'd been sleeping rough and wondered, as I did, what had gone so badly wrong in his life that had made him homeless. Lara was keen to know if he'd found a hostel and on the way back suggested we go to the High Street to see if he was still there. It wasn't exactly on our route back, but I agreed to go. We'd been out walking for nearly two hours and Arthur was asleep in his stroller.

Lara gave a little whoop of joy when she saw the shop doorway was empty. The sleeping bag had gone too. Paula and I were pleased, although of course this didn't necessarily mean he'd gone to the hostel. He could have just moved on to a different doorway in another town.

'I could call and find out,' Lara said.

'You have Frazer's mobile number?' I asked, surprised.

'No, he hasn't got a mobile. It was stolen. I meant, I could phone the hostel and ask them if he's there.'

'They may tell you,' I said doubtfully.

I could see Lara was feeling much better now and her hangover had gone. By the time we arrived home she was ready for something to eat, and so was Arthur. Lara was supposed to be preparing their meals as she would if she was living independently. But from what I knew she had relied heavily on ready-made meals, so I suggested we made omelettes together for lunch.

'How do you do that?' she asked.

'I'll show you.'

So while Paula kept Arthur amused I showed Lara how to make an omelette (see page 46 of my book *Happy Mealtimes*). We added sliced tomatoes and grated cheese for the filling to one and baked beans to another. I explained to Lara that you could add almost anything, but meat and vegetables needed to be cooked first.

'An omelette is a cheap, quick and nutritious meal,' I added, sounding like a television commercial.

I arranged some green salad in a bowl and we ate at the table. Arthur had some omelette followed by mashed banana. I was keeping a note of what he was eating in case Claudette wanted to know; also, we'd need to check he was still gaining weight as we began reducing his formula milk.

After lunch Lara showed Paula and me the one photograph she had of her mother. It was just a head and shoulders, taken in a photo booth of the type that can be used for passport photos. I looked at the woman in her twenties with similar features and hair colouring to Lara.

She was thinner than Lara – I supposed from being addicted to drugs. She was smiling, although there seemed to be a sadness in her eyes. The photo was clearly very precious to Lara. She kept it in the wallet compartment of her purse and the edges were scuffed from being repeatedly looked at. It was the only photo she had from her past.

'Didn't any of your foster carers or social workers make a Life Story Book for you?' I asked as I returned the photo to her.

A Life Story Book is a record of the child's time with the carer and includes photographs and memorabilia – for example, school certificates – and is considered part of good fostering practice. It's an aide-mémoire, which the child takes with them to supplement their own memories so they can retain a sense of their past. Having to move around so much can blur recollections for foster children, as they don't have their birth parents to keep a treasure chest of memories alive.

'Yes, I had a Life Story Book, but I burnt it when I was angry,' Lara admitted. She carefully tucked the photo into her purse. 'I set fire to it in the foster carer's bath. Which got me moved again.'

Even so, it was sad that all she had of her past, apart from her memories, was this one small photo. Since she'd had her own phone at the age of sixteen she'd taken photos, but before then, nothing.

'It's possible some of your foster carers may still have photographs of you,' I said. 'I keep some of all the children I've looked after.'

'I doubt they would of me,' she said, pulling a face, suggesting they were pleased she'd gone.

'I am sure some have, no matter how naughty you were. You could ask your social worker. It would really be up to her to contact the carers. The social services should have a record of all the carers you stayed with.'

'I'll think about it,' Lara said, and changed the subject.

Mid-afternoon Lara ran out of patience with Arthur, who was being his usual active self and wouldn't sit still for longer than two minutes. She decided to put him in his cot for a sleep. She took him upstairs and then lay on the bed in his room, but Arthur wasn't ready for a sleep yet. I could hear him bouncing in his cot and having a great time; then after a while he'd had enough and wanted to be out. His cries of mischief and delight changed to those of frustration. I went up. His bedroom door was closed but I could hear Lara on her phone. I knocked and went in.

'I have to go,' she said, and ended the call. 'He won't sleep,' she said to me.

'I know, so bring him downstairs. Don't just leave him in his cot to get upset.' I was concerned she'd continued with her phone call despite Arthur's obvious distress.

'Sorry,' she said, and lifted him out of his cot.

'He had a long sleep on the way home from our walk,' I pointed out. 'He may not need another one, or you can try him again a bit later.'

'I need to change him first,' she said. 'He's done a poo.'

'OK.'

I didn't immediately leave but waited by the bedroom door, watching Lara as she changed his nappy. She was very quiet.

'Is everything all right?' I asked. 'You don't seem your normal happy self.'

'It's Diesel. He won't leave me alone,' she said, concentrating on Arthur. He was wriggling, making nappy-changing difficult.

'I didn't think you were supposed to be in touch with him,' I said.

'He keeps phoning and texting. I've told him not to, but he still does.'

'Was that him just now?'

'Yes.'

'So don't answer his calls. Block his number if necessary.'

'That would really piss him off!'

'Does it matter?'

She sighed. 'You don't know him,' she said, and her voice caught.

'Lara, what's going on?'

She shrugged.

'Have you told him where you're living?' I asked, concerned. It was a condition of the placement that she didn't tell him.

'No. I'm trying to make it work here and start again, but he keeps phoning and telling me I'm useless, no good, and I'll fail at this like I do everything. Perhaps he's right.' She began to cry.

'It's all right, love,' I said, going to her.

I passed her the box of tissues. She wiped her eyes and I finished changing Arthur's nappy. Once he was ready I set him on the floor and closed the bedroom door so he couldn't run off. I gave him a toy from his cot to play with so Lara and I could talk.

'What's the matter, love?' I asked, sitting beside her on the bed.

She shrugged and took a moment. 'I know I seem confident and outgoing,' she began, twisting the tissue in her hand. 'But I'm not really. Inside I doubt everything I do. I've made so many mistakes. I don't want to end up like my mum.'

'You won't,' I said. 'You're doing very well.'

'I hope so, but it's difficult being alone. Diesel seemed just what I needed, to begin with at least. He took control, and just having him beside me made me feel secure. He's a strong guy and trains and takes supplements. But he can be very demanding and possessive, and kept telling me what to do. I didn't mind at first, but after I moved in with him it got worse. Everything I did was wrong and his way was right. I couldn't have an opinion or say what I thought.' She paused to wipe her eyes.

'He started accusing me of looking at other guys. Even on television – he'd say, "You fancy him, don't you?" Then he'd get angry or not speak to me at all. I'm not sure which was worse. I was trying to look after Arthur and didn't know what to do for the best. Diesel let me go out once a week with my friends. He even gave me money as I didn't have much, and he would tell me to have a good time. But when I got home it was different. He wanted to know all the details of where I'd been, who I'd spoken to, what I'd had to drink and so on. He'd had a few cans of beer and a smoke if his mates had been round, and he'd make fun of me in front of them. He accused me of seeing someone else and when I denied it he said I was lying and I had to prove I loved him. It was all so confusing. I didn't know what to do to make him happy. He could be nice sometimes, although he never thought much of Arthur. I'm glad that neighbour reported us because it made me leave him. I don't think I would have had the guts to do it without that happening.'

'I understand, love,' I said gently.

'But he wants me back and keeps phoning and texting.'

'Do you want to go back?' I asked.

'No. I want a fresh start.'

I nodded. 'Are you scared of him?'

'I guess so, although it's difficult because sometimes he can be really charming.'

'So are a lot of abusers,' I said. 'Lara, you're not the only one to have experienced something like this. Have you ever heard of coercive control?'

She shook her head.

'It's a form of domestic violence. The abuser exerts power over their partner and acts in a way that makes them feel threatened, humiliated, intimidated and confused. Their confidence goes, and they come to believe they can never live without their abuser. There isn't necessarily actual physical violence, but the victim feels like there could be.'

'That sounds like him. He only hit me a few times, but I always felt it could happen again.'

'Exactly. But even one assault is one too many,' I said. 'Violence has no place in any relationship. If you are serious about keeping Arthur and protecting him and yourself then you can't have someone like Diesel in your life.'

'I know, that's what Claudette said. But how do I stop him phoning and texting me?'

'Block his number. Each time you answer his call or reply to a text he'll take it as a sign you are encouraging him. I suggest you send one last text telling him your relationship is over and he must not contact you again. If he does, we'll report him to the police.'

'Really?'

'Yes, if necessary. And we need to tell Claudette he's harassing you.' Lara was looking at me uncertainly.

'Lara, Diesel doesn't know this address, does he?' I asked again.

'No, honestly. I haven't told him.'

I believed her and thought her hesitancy was probably a result of the power Diesel still held over her.

'I've never been without a boyfriend,' Lara admitted. 'I'll be completely alone.' Which was both revealing and sad.

'Better not to have a boyfriend than to be in a bad relationship,' I said. 'You've got friends and you've got us. I'll do all I can to help you through this.'

She gave a weak smile. 'OK. I'll text him now before I lose my nerve. Can you look after Arthur downstairs while I do it?'

'Yes, of course.'

I scooped Arthur into my arms, blew a raspberry on his forehead, which made him chuckle, and left Lara to text Diesel. Downstairs, I got Arthur a drink and then kept him amused in the living room, where we played with some early-years toys.

It was fifteen minutes before Lara appeared.

'I've done it,' she said. 'I texted him and then blocked his number. That's it. No more Diesel.'

'Well done,' I said, and dearly hoped that was so. She

needed to keep her resolve, for no court would agree to Arthur living with his mother if she returned to Diesel, who had a history of violence. Through fostering I knew of other mothers who'd chosen an abusive partner over their children and spent the rest of their lives regretting it.

CHAPTER SEVEN

MEETING ARTHUR'S NEEDS

From what I knew of Lara so far, I would describe her as kind, caring, lacking in self-confidence and impetuous. She didn't appear to have a temper but wore her heart on her sleeve and tended to leap where others would proceed with caution. This was evident in what happened next.

The following afternoon, less than twenty-four hours after finally finishing with Diesel, Lara told us she had a new boyfriend. She'd been on the phone a lot, but I'd assumed it was with her friends Shell and Courtney.

'That was quick,' I said as she announced the new love of her life.

'He's not at all like Diesel,' she said, unable to contain her excitement.

'Good.'

'You know him. Well, you've seen him at least.'

'Have I?' I asked, surprised. We were in the living room where Paula and I had been looking after Arthur while Lara had been in her bedroom talking on the phone.

'Yes, it's Frazer, the homeless guy,' Lara qualified.

'Oh.' And I'm sorry to say I couldn't share her enthusiasm, as all my preconceived notions about a homeless person not making good boyfriend material surfaced.

'Lara, you've only seen him twice briefly in the High Street.'

'I know, but I've spoken to him loads since.'

'You phoned him at the hostel?'

'Yes, but he wasn't there. He's been given a room in a hotel to use during the pandemic.' Which was government policy at present. 'It's not far from here – Graverly Road.'

I knew where she meant. I'd driven past the hotel. It was about two miles away, with white walls and a sign outside saying 'Bed and Breakfast'.

'Frazer and me have done a lot of talking and we've got heaps in common, both being in care and all that,' Lara said.

'I thought he'd had his mobile phone stolen. Has he been able to buy another?' I asked.

'No, that's one of things I want to talk to you about. He's been borrowing phones from others but they're getting fed up. He needs one of his own. I was wondering if you could loan me the money so he can get a phone. I'll pay you back, honest. We're going into lockdown today so it will be four weeks before we can see each other. We need to be able to text and call.'

Lara was so sincere and passionate in her request that I could easily have said yes and given her the money. I glanced at Paula, who was expressionless.

'Lara, love, phones are expensive,' I said.

'I'll pay you back, honestly.'

'How is Frazer going to afford to run a phone?'

'He has benefit money and he wants to get a job. Everyone needs a mobile.' Which is probably true.

'How much do you want?'

'A hundred and twenty pounds.'

Which made my decision.

'No. I'm sorry, Lara. That's a lot of money and you can't be certain it will be spent on a phone or that he will repay you.'

'He will. I know. He's a nice guy.'

She didn't know Frazer at all and neither did I. This money could easily have gone on alcohol or drugs.

'I'm sorry, love, no,' I said. But then I had an idea. 'Lara, I understand Frazer needs a phone and I have a spare he can have. All it needs is a new SIM card.'

'Does it work?' she asked dubiously.

'Yes, it will once it has a SIM in it.'

'Can I see it?'

'Sure.'

I went into the front room and took the phone from my desk drawer. It was only a couple of years old and had stopped working. I couldn't be without a phone so I'd replaced it while it was being repaired and now kept it as a spare. I returned to the living room and gave it to Lara. She seemed relieved it wasn't from a bygone era.

'OK, thanks. I'll give it to him,' she said.

'And here's ten pounds to buy a SIM to get him started. Tell him it's an early Christmas present.' I took the money from my purse. 'How are you going to get it to him? We're in lockdown.'

'We can meet outside when I go out for my daily walk,' she replied. 'Don't worry, I'll be careful. I'll be quicker if you look after Arthur.'

In fact, I would have to look after Arthur or go with Lara, as she was still suspected of harming him so couldn't go out alone with him yet.

'Arthur can stay here,' I said. 'But, Lara, you need to be very careful when you meet Frazer. Treat him as if he's carrying the virus. That's what the government is saying – treat those outside your home as if they are contagious. No hugging or kissing him, stay apart and stay outside in the fresh air.'

'I will,' Lara said, clearly eager to be off. So it seemed it had been planned in advance.

She threw Arthur a kiss and headed down the hall.

'Don't forget your mask and the hand sanitizer I gave you,' I called after her.

'I won't. Bye! See you soon.' The front door closed behind her.

So far today Arthur had spent more time with Paula and me than he had with his mother. I could see that Lara meant well and wanted to help Frazer, but I had concerns that she didn't always put Arthur's needs first as successful parenting requires.

Paula and I continued to play with Arthur as we had been doing for most of the day. At five o'clock, when Lara had been gone four hours, we gave him his dinner, and I texted her: *Everything OK?*

She replied: *Yes. I'll be back soon.*

At 6.30, when it was dark outside and there was still no sign of Lara, I texted her again and she replied saying she was on her way home. I ran Arthur's bath in preparation for him going to bed. He loved playing in the water with the plastic bath toys, as most infants do. As he played and splashed I knelt by the bath and began sponge-washing him. I heard the front door open as Lara came in.

'I'm up here bathing Arthur,' I called. 'Wash your hands first please before you touch anything.' It was government advice.

'I will.'

I heard her go into the kitchen, then her footsteps on the stairs. Paula was in her bedroom.

'I've plated up your dinner, but get Arthur into bed first,' I said to Lara as she came into the bathroom. I then stood and handed his care over to her.

Lara was clearly in a very good mood, exuberant, and talked non-stop about Frazer as Arthur sat in his bath. She told me what a lovely person Frazer was, that he would never harm anyone, and how he had come to the area to see his mother, hoping to live with her, but it hadn't worked out. That was how he had ended up sleeping on the streets.

'He said thanks for the phone,' she continued. 'And the money. We had to go to the supermarket to buy the SIM.' Non-essential shops were closed. 'We got a take-away hot chocolate and then walked and talked. The streets are empty.'

'They would be, love, we're in lockdown,' I reminded her.

I could see Lara's spirits had been greatly lifted from spending time with Frazer. She was happy, elated, and kept kissing Arthur.

'You're going to have a new daddy soon,' she told him.

'Lara, slow down,' I warned her.

'Only joking!' she replied with a laugh. Although I doubted she was, not completely.

'Has Frazer ever had a job?' I asked.

'Yes, holiday season on a pier. But he wants to go to college and train to be a plumber or an electrician.'

'They're good trades,' I said. 'And you say his mother lives in the area?'

'On the other side of town. He sees her once a year. He moved away with the foster family when he was little. You might have known his carers as you've been fostering a long time.'

'It's possible,' I said. 'What were their names? Do you know?'

'No, but Frazer has an unusual surname – Labette.'

'Good grief!' I exclaimed. 'Yes, I remember his carers, Jenny and Shawn, and I remember Frazer. But I never met his mother. I think she was originally from France.'

'That's right. She's got a lot of issues.'

'I looked after Frazer on respite twice,' I said. 'He'd have been about five or six years old then.'

'Really? That's fantastic. I'll tell him,' Lara exclaimed, and was about to rush off to phone him.

'And you're going to leave Arthur unattended in the bath?' I asked.

'You're here.'

'But I won't always be and you are in charge of Arthur's care while you're here. Paula and I have looked after him for most of the day and babysat on Tuesday evening. See to Arthur first and then once he's settled in his cot you can talk to Frazer.'

Lara looked hurt but it needed to be said. I was still getting over the shock of the homeless young man being the little lad I fostered all those years ago.

'I didn't smoke while I was out,' Lara said as she lifted Arthur out of the bath.

'Well done.' I passed her his bath towel and waited while she dried him, and then dressed him in his sleep suit. 'Give his teeth a little brush,' I reminded her.

She cleaned his teeth, still in very good spirits. I was expected to observe her. She then chased Arthur around the landing to his room, thereby undoing the relaxing effects of his bath. Lara squealed as she caught up with him, then picked him up, laid him in his cot and put his dummy in. But of course Arthur wasn't ready for sleep now and he spat it out. Grabbing the slats of the cot, he began jumping up and down.

'It's going to be ages before he goes to sleep,' Lara said with a sigh. 'Is it all right if I sit on the bed in here and text Frazer?'

'That's your decision but resettle Arthur when he needs it. He is your priority.'

'I know.'

I waited on the landing for a while and then went to my bedroom where I remained, listening out. I had to give Lara some responsibility while ensuring Arthur's safety. I heard her talking to him in a low, comforting tone. 'Sshh, go to sleep … I need to make a phone call …'

After about twenty minutes it went quiet and Lara went to her own bedroom. I went round the landing to check on Arthur and he was fast asleep. I knocked lightly on Lara's door.

'Yes?'

'Don't forget to have your dinner, love.'

'I won't.'

An hour later Lara came downstairs.

'Everything all right?' I asked.

'Yes, fine.'

We pinged her dinner in the microwave, and she took the plate and a glass of water up to her room and continued talking on the phone. I could hear the hum of her voice, but it wasn't loud enough to wake Arthur or disturb Paula and me. Lara was still on the phone when I went up to bed. I knocked on her door.

'Night, love. I'm going to bed. Make sure you get some sleep.'

'Yes. I'll have my shower in the morning.'

Arthur woke in the night around 1 a.m. and I was impressed by how quickly Lara answered his cries. She was in his room in an instant. When I went to check all was well I found Lara still in her day clothes as she settled Arthur.

'Haven't you been to bed?' I asked her.

'I'll go to sleep now,' she said guiltily.

Needless to say, the following morning when Arthur woke at 6.30 wanting to be out of his cot and playing, Lara wasn't in the mood.

'Can't you look after him?' she groaned as I woke her. 'Just for a few hours so I can sleep.'

It would have been easy to say yes, but that wouldn't have done Lara any good. If Arthur lived with her I wouldn't be on hand to step in so she could catch up on her sleep. What would she do then? Leave him in his cot to cry?

'Sorry, you need to see to him,' I said, feeling like a wicked witch. 'If he has a nap later, you could have a sleep then.'

Not pleased with me, Lara dragged herself out of bed and went into Arthur's room, took him out of his cot and returned to her bed. I doubted he was going to go back to sleep as he'd only just woken. I went downstairs to make a coffee and feed Sammy before I showered and dressed. From the kitchen I could hear Arthur running around in Lara's room, then I heard a crash and Arthur crying. I shot upstairs straight into Lara's room. She was holding him and about to pick up the bedside lamp that was on the floor. Its ceramic base had cracked.

'I'm so sorry,' she said. 'He tripped and fell.'

'I'm not worried about the lamp. Is he hurt?' I asked, going to him.

'I don't think so,' she said.

I checked him over. He didn't appear hurt, and his crying was easing. I think it was more the shock of tripping and the lamp falling that had upset him.

'Lara, this room isn't child-proofed. As well as the lamp and that mirror, you've left your hairdryer plugged in and within his reach. There's your make-up on the dressing table and your dinner things from last night. Supposing he'd got hold of your knife or fork, or had fallen on those? Or jabbed himself in the eye? You'd never have forgiven yourself. With a child his age there is danger everywhere, but they don't see it. Take him into your bed if you wish but you need to keep him amused with a book or something. He can't just be left to run around.'

'But he won't stay in bed, and I need a shower,' Lara protested.

'I know it's difficult with an infant, but you need to be vigilant all the time Arthur is awake. And try to enjoy him. Babies grow so quickly. I'm here to help but he is your responsibility.' Which I'd said before.

'I know,' Lara said.

'I'll look after him now while you shower and dress, but in future make sure you go to sleep at a reasonable time so you are able to care for him when he wakes.'

'I will.'

'And remember, we've got an online meeting with Claudette at ten o'clock.'

'What are you going to tell her?' Lara asked, concerned.

'That you love and care for Arthur, and are generally doing well, but I think you find the continuous responsibility a bit of a challenge sometimes. Is that fair?'

'I guess.'

Lara went to have her shower while I took care of Arthur.

I knew it wasn't going to be easy having an online meeting with Arthur running around, but this was about him as much as Lara, and their social worker would expect to see him as if she had made her first visit in person. Paula was dressed and on hand to help out if needed. I decided to use my tablet so we could move around easily if necessary. Lara felt better after a shower and some breakfast. She'd given Arthur breakfast, and had washed and changed him, dressing him in a new navy tracksuit. He was looking very smart.

At 10 a.m. Lara, Arthur and I sat on the sofa in the living room, the tablet between us, and I logged in to the meeting. Just Claudette was there. This meeting wasn't as formal as the chaired looked-after child (LAC) reviews

I attended when I fostered a child, although it was no less important, and Claudette would be taking notes. Arthur was sitting on his mother's lap.

'Wave to your social worker,' Lara encouraged him as Claudette appeared, and flapped his arm up and down to simulate waving.

Intrigued by the image on screen, Arthur leant in and licked it. I wiped it clean with a tissue.

'So how is it going?' Claudette asked Lara, smiling at Arthur's antics. 'He seems bright enough.' He was babbling at her now.

'I've stopped smoking and Cathy says I'm doing well,' Lara replied.

'Good. And how do *you* think you're doing looking after Arthur?' Claudette asked.

'Fine. I've finished with Diesel and got a new boyfriend.'

I saw Claudette's expression imperceptibly change.

'I think talk about Arthur first,' I said quietly to Lara. 'He is your priority.'

'Oh, yes, sorry. I forgot.'

But that was the problem: Lara could forget Arthur and put her own needs first.

CHAPTER EIGHT

FRAZER

Lara and Arthur had only been with me a week, so Claudette wasn't expecting a lengthy, in-depth appraisal. These weekly meetings were to see how things were progressing (or not) in respect of Lara parenting her son. We began by talking about the routine Lara was establishing for Arthur, which included a typical day – mealtimes, bedtimes, playtimes, outings, etc. A routine is considered important for children of all ages. Arthur was now standing on the sofa, between Lara and me, grinning and jumping up and down. I was steadying the tablet between us as we continued by talking about his sleeping, which had improved, the food Lara was giving him and our daily exercise during lockdown. I was letting Lara do most of the talking, adding my observations as we went. It was important that she self-assessed so she could reflect on her parenting skills and identify areas that needed work.

I said I was showing Lara how to cook simple dishes for her and Arthur. 'And clear up after,' I added, with a smile. Lara laughed. She didn't mind the cooking and eating part but left the pans, utensils and dishes for me. Arthur scrambled off the sofa and began exploring one of the toy boxes.

'Has Arthur had any illness, injuries or accidents?' Claudette asked. It was a standard question.

'No,' Lara said, then looked at me.

'Arthur is a very active child,' I said. 'He's taken a number of bumps but without doing himself any harm. He's on the go all day. Like most children his age, he doesn't see danger and can run into things. He needs watching the whole time, which Lara is learning to do. The bruises he arrived with have gone now and there are no new ones.' Which I knew was a double-edged sword. For while this was good news, it begged the question as to why the injuries had stopped now they were in my care.

I paused as Claudette made some notes, then I continued by saying that I was encouraging Lara to play more with Arthur.

'Play is important,' Claudette said to Lara. 'It will help Arthur's development and nourish the bond between you.'

'I'll play with him more,' Lara said.

'Good. Anything else either of you want to discuss in relation to Arthur?' Claudette asked.

Lara shook her head.

'I don't think so,' I said, keeping one eye on Arthur as he was now trying to squeeze behind the armchair.

'This all sounds very positive,' Claudette said. 'Well done, Lara. Now, tell me about your new boyfriend.'

Having been rather guarded in what she'd said about Arthur, Lara now revved up and began animatedly extolling the virtues of Frazer. I stood, went over to Arthur and removed him from where he'd jammed himself between the chair and the wall. I sat with him on the floor and kept him amused as Lara continued to tell

Claudette how she'd met Frazer, all the things they had in common – i.e. a life in care – and how he was not at all like Diesel and would never hurt a fly.

'Frazer is so kind and gentle, I know Arthur will like him,' Lara said, pausing briefly for breath. 'It's difficult meeting because of lockdown so Frazer is going to see me and Arthur outside.' This was news to me.

'You'll have to stay outside,' Claudette warned. 'The rules are that two people from two households can meet in a public open space, but not indoors or even in a private garden. Arthur is exempt.'

'Yes, I know,' Lara said. 'We read it online, but unlike in the first lockdown we can go out as many times a day as we like.' Clearly she'd done her homework.

'To exercise,' Claudette said. 'How many times a day were you thinking of?'

Lara shrugged. 'I don't know yet.'

'Am I expected to go with Lara when she takes Arthur to meet Frazer?' I asked from where I was sitting on the floor.

'Yes, please,' Claudette replied.

'Why?' Lara demanded.

'Because part of the foster carer's role in a mother-and-baby placement is to supervise. We can review you taking Arthur out alone in the future,' Claudette added.

'It won't be worth me going if *she's* going to be with me the whole time,' Lara said, disgruntled.

'Why? What were you planning on doing?' Claudette asked.

Lara fell silent and then said, 'Just talk and walk.'

'Then I can't see a problem with Cathy being there, can you?'

'Or I could leave Arthur here with Cathy and Paula while I meet Frazer,' Lara returned quickly, without thinking.

Claudette went quiet. I couldn't see her face from where I was sitting on the floor with Arthur, but I knew Lara wasn't doing herself any favours in terms of putting Arthur first.

'I have offered to babysit once a week so Lara can go out,' I said. 'I think that's fair. If it were just her and Arthur, living alone, it's unlikely she'd be able to go out more often than once a week as a single parent.'

'I agree,' Claudette said.

I could tell from Lara's expression she wasn't happy. 'So I've got to take Cathy with me every time I go out?' she asked.

'If Arthur is with you, yes, for now. I'll leave it for you and Cathy to decide when. We can review the arrangements in the future.'

There was more silence, then Claudette said, 'So tell me about Diesel.'

'I've finished with him,' Lara said bluntly. 'I don't see him any more.'

'But he's been in contact?' Claudette queried.

'He's been phoning and texting, but I've blocked his number. I won't talk to him again.'

'All right. Make sure his number stays blocked. Anything else I should know?'

'No,' Lara said curtly.

I thought it was important to end on a positive note so, leaving Arthur with his toys, I returned to the sofa to talk to Claudette. Lara angled the tablet towards me.

'I wanted to say that from what I've seen so far I think Lara is going to do well. She clearly loves Arthur and they have a strong bond. She is willing to learn and open to suggestions about his care, so I'm very hopeful.'

'Good, noted,' Claudette said. 'Well, if that's everything, we'll meet again at the same time next week. If anything comes up in the interim that needs my attention then phone. Have a good weekend. I was supposed to be going to my mother's birthday party, but that's been cancelled due to lockdown.'

'Oh dear, I am sorry,' I said.

'So am I. Hopefully we'll have a vaccine soon.'

'Yes,' I agreed.

We said goodbye. The call ended, and I closed the app.

'Silly cow,' Lara said, which I ignored.

'I think Arthur needs his nappy changing,' I said.

Without speaking, and clearly in a mood, Lara picked up Arthur and carried him upstairs to change him. I followed, then waited on the landing. I watched as she laid him on the changing mat and took off his joggers, then his nappy. Although she was annoyed with her social worker, I'm pleased to say she didn't take it out on Arthur by rough-handling him as I'd seen another parent do with her child. I heard her muttering, 'Bloody social worker. Miserable cow,' and so forth, but that was all. Despite her frustration and disappointment, and Arthur making nappy-changing difficult by wriggling and kicking his legs, Lara was gentle with him.

'Well done, love,' I said as she came out of his bedroom.

'I'm pissed off with that social worker. She's treating me like a child.'

'I know it may feel that way, but we have to do as she says.' I opened the stairgate and we went downstairs with Lara carrying Arthur.

'Can I meet Frazer this afternoon?' she asked. 'He's expecting to see me and Arthur. We arranged it last night.'

'Where?'

'He's going to get a bus here and meet us in the park at two o'clock. Please.'

'All right, but in future can we discuss which afternoons you meet?' I said. 'It's cold now so Arthur shouldn't be outside for too long, and I have things to do as well.'

'OK.'

And that was how I ended up acting as chaperone for Lara and Frazer.

I was in Lara's good books for the rest of the morning and couldn't do anything wrong. She was very attentive to me and Arthur. She played with him and offered to vacuum the whole house and help me make lunch. I could see she was in the first flushes of a new relationship and her world had been brightened by the promise of seeing her beloved. I could remember that feeling, just, from my teens and twenties – a high of adrenalin where the whole world looked beautiful and full of promise.

It was touching to see, and I was pleased Lara was happy, but naturally I had concerns. While she was with me I was responsible for her as well as Arthur, and despite what she thought, she hardly knew Frazer. All those hours she'd spent on the phone talking to him was positive, but it was no substitute for spending time with him, when over many months, even years, they would gradually get to know each other and their true personalities would start to emerge. Frazer had clearly faced many challenges of his own, resulting in him being homeless, which must have left some scars.

I thought back to Frazer the boy who I'd briefly known when I'd looked after him for respite care all those years ago. I remembered how he'd been very interested in cars and could identify many makes and models. He would point them out to me as I took him to and from school. I could also remember his foster carers, Jenny and Shawn. They'd started fostering when their youngest child had left for university. Frazer had been their first fostering placement and was supposed to have stayed with them long term. A couple of years later they'd moved out of the area, but we hadn't been friendly enough to keep in touch. Frazer should have been with them until he was eighteen. There'd even been talk of them adopting him. So what had happened to bring him back here?

I explained to Paula that I had to accompany Lara and Arthur to the park so she could meet Frazer. Paula remembered Frazer staying with us for two short periods, and that he liked cars, but that was all. She had only been young. She now queried if the parks were open, as they'd been closed during the first lockdown, but I knew from the news and from Lara that most parks were opening during this lockdown.

We had lunch just before 1 p.m., which Lara gobbled down, then fled the table to finish getting ready. I was slightly baffled by how much preparation was needed for a walk in the park in winter. Surely a sturdy pair of shoes and a warm coat was all that was required? Plus, a mobile phone. Lara was upstairs getting ready until 1.45 – the time she'd said we needed to leave to make sure we were in the park when Frazer arrived at 2 p.m. She rushed down and quickly put Arthur into his zip-up all-in-one padded suit. Unfortunately, babies don't regulate their bodily functions to fit in with adult arrangements. As she sat him in the stroller, ready for off, his expression changed. He went quiet and concentrated hard as he filled his nappy.

'Oh no!' Lara cried. Then looked uncertain what to do next. 'We'll be late if I change him.'

'You'll have to change him,' I said. 'You can't leave him sitting in a soiled nappy. It'll make his bottom sore. I am sure Frazer will understand if we're a bit late.'

I went upstairs with Lara to help her change Arthur, distracting him with a toy so he would lie still while she cleaned him. I left her to dress him while I put the nappy in the bin outside, and a few minutes later we were ready to leave again.

We nearly ran to the park; Lara was pushing Arthur in the stroller while I trotted alongside. It was the most invigorating exercise I'd had in a long while. We slowed our pace as we went in through the park gates.

'There he is!' Lara cried, and began waving at a man.

I thought I must be looking at the wrong person for the tall young man coming towards us was clean-shaven and smartly dressed in a three-quarter-length grey winter coat. When I'd seen Frazer in the High Street he'd been hunched forward, huddled in a shop doorway with his hoodie covering most of his face. Only as he drew close did I realize it was him.

'You look smart,' Lara said, smiling, and then kissed him full on the lips.

'Thanks. The coat was donated. I wanted to make a good impression.' He turned to me. 'Hi, Cathy.'

'Hello, Frazer, lovely to see you again.' We bumped elbows, the standard greeting during the pandemic. 'You look so much better than the last time I saw you,' I said, still struggling to believe it was him.

'I can shower and wash my clothes and clean my teeth in the hotel,' he said. 'A guy there gave me a haircut. I hope this lockdown continues so I can stay there.'

Lara was holding his arm now and kissing his cheek. I thought Frazer was looking a bit awkward.

'So this is Arthur?' he said, releasing himself and squatting down to talk to him. 'Hi.'

Arthur grinned and babbled.

'Say hi,' I encouraged.

'Does he talk?' Frazer asked me.

'Not yet but we're working on it.'

'He's cute,' Frazer said.

'He's hard work,' Lara said.

'I think all kids are, aren't they?' Frazer asked, looking at me.

'Sometimes.'

'Shall we go for a walk?' Lara suggested to Frazer. 'Cathy can look after Arthur.'

'I don't mind,' Frazer said, uncertain.

'You can go for a walk,' I said. 'I'll take Arthur to the play area and we can meet there in fifteen minutes.' Which I didn't think was what Lara had in mind.

'See you soon,' Frazer said easily. Lara linked arms with him and drew him away.

I watched them head off towards the duck pond and they soon disappeared behind the shrubbery. I pushed

Arthur into the children's play area. Although it was a fine day, there were only two other families there. Some of the play equipment – on which it was impossible to socially distance – had been taped off, as had alternate swings. I lifted Arthur out of the stroller and he ran towards the row of baby swings. I cleaned the frame with an antibacterial wipe before lifting him in. He liked the swing, as many infants do – it's soothing – and was content to sit there and be pushed.

The baby swings have support bars on all four sides, making them safe for young children. It wasn't long before Arthur's body relaxed against the back and his eyes began to close. He hadn't had a nap yet today and the soporific motion of the swing gradually lulled him to sleep. I drew the swing to a halt and gently lifted him out and into his stroller. He remained asleep so I fastened his harness and pushed the stroller to a bench that was in the sun. I'd sat there many times over the years when I'd brought children to the park. It was sheltered from any wind and caught the sun, so even in winter it was a cosy place to sit. Although looking after Arthur while Lara and Frazer went off wasn't what we'd agreed, I could understand her wish to spend time alone with him. If she didn't appear within a reasonable time, I would phone her mobile. Five minutes later they came into view.

'Frazer remembers coming here with you,' Lara said excitedly as I made room for them on the bench.

I looked at Frazer. 'Do you really? That must have been, what, seventeen years ago?'

'Yes, I can remember some of it,' he said. 'I remember the pond and the children's play area, although some of the apparatus has changed. I think there was a very tall slide.'

'That's right. It was taken down a few years back – health and safety regulations.'

'I remember I had a nice week with you and your family, and I was feeling good. Jenny and Shawn were coming to collect me and I was looking forward to seeing them again. I was happy with them then. I was calling them Mum and Dad.'

'I know. I thought they were supposed to be your permanent family.'

'They were,' he said, and his face clouded over.

'He doesn't want to talk about it, do you?' Lara said defensively, taking his hand.

'I can tell Cathy,' Frazer said. 'It's not a secret. It wasn't my fault, although I got blamed.'

'Blamed for what?' I asked.

'Attacking their kids.'

And I could see from the look of shock on Lara's face that this was the first she'd heard of it.

CHAPTER NINE

GOING OUT

'You didn't tell me,' Lara said quietly to Frazer.

'No, well. A lot of stuff has happened since then,' he replied, with a shrug.

'Whose children did you attack?' I asked.

'Jenny and Shawn's.'

'I thought their children were adults when you went there, and you were the only child in the family.'

'I was for a long time. Seven years. Then everything changed.'

'How?' I asked, glancing at Arthur, who was still fast asleep in the stroller.

'They started fostering two other kids and didn't want me any more.'

'Surely not?' I said.

'That's what it felt like. I was twelve and as far as I was concerned they were my mum and dad. I thought everything would stay that way, the same. Then one day I got home from school to find two younger kids there, Davy and Micky, brothers. No one asked me if they could live with us. They just appeared, and all Jenny's and Shawn's time was spent with them. I even had to swap bedrooms as mine was bigger and they had to share. I felt so unwanted.'

'I see. I am sorry,' I said. 'Did you tell Jenny and Shawn how you felt?'

Lara was quiet, listening to what Frazer was saying. I wondered how much of this she knew.

'I told Jenny and my social worker,' Frazer replied, the memory still causing him pain. 'But no one listened or cared about how I felt. They tried to explain why they were doing it – to help by giving other kids a home – but what about me? If they'd only stayed a few weeks I think I would have coped, but it became permanent. They couldn't go home so they stayed. Jenny told me she still loved me, but it didn't feel like that. Davy and Micky were brighter than me and did better at school. I always needed extra help. Sometimes they'd laugh when I got things wrong. I hated them, I really did. I started getting into trouble at school and began hanging around with a group of older lads. I was kicking off at home too. Really losing it. I think Jenny was scared of me. I was bigger than her by then. And the brothers were scared of me when I lost it, which pleased me.'

I nodded sagely. Sadly, it made sense. 'How old were Davy and Micky?' I asked.

'Eight and nine. They used to gang up on me so I always got the blame, even when it wasn't my fault. I knew Jenny wasn't coping with three of us. Shawn had had enough too. I thought they'd get rid of Davy and Micky. That's what they should have done. I was there first. It was my home. But nothing happened and I got more and more angry. Then one day when I got home I found Davy and Micky in my bedroom going through my things. I really lost it then. I went for them and Jenny called the police. They contacted the social services and I was taken away. I never saw them again.'

'I am so sorry,' I said. 'But surely Jenny or Shawn tried to contact you after you'd left? You'd been with them a long time.'

'Jenny tried to phone me, and the social services said I should see them even if it was just to say a proper good-bye. But I didn't want to. I was gutted. I felt completely rejected and unwanted, and I was still angry.'

'I'm not surprised.'

I could see what had happened; I'd heard similar before. There is always a shortage of foster carers and Jenny and Shawn had had a spare bedroom. Frazer was settled and doing well so they were asked (or offered) to foster more children, which sparked all Frazer's insecurities, which he expressed through anger. Could it have been handled differently? It's difficult to say. I am sure at the time Jenny and Shawn thought they were doing the right thing in offering a home to the brothers. Possibly the social services, desperate to place the boys, didn't give enough consideration to the effect it could have on Frazer. It was possible it could have worked out; two parents with three children should have been manage-able, except the brothers would have come with their own set of needs and challenges. One mistake I think Jenny and Shawn did make was forcing Frazer to swap bedrooms. That was his space, his room for all those years, and of course it would have caused resentment even in the most placid of children.

'I wouldn't behave like that now,' Frazer added remorsefully. 'I've learnt to control my anger.'

'Good,' I said. 'I'm pleased to hear it. So you were twelve going on thirteen at that time. What happened then?' I thought Lara should know as much as possible if she was getting into a relationship with Frazer. Also, as a foster carer, I was interested, feeling there were probably lessons to be learnt here. However, at that moment a large raindrop fell, quickly followed by another and another.

'It's raining!' Lara exclaimed. 'What are we going to do?'

'Say goodbye or get sopping wet,' I said, standing. 'Frazer, I'm sorry I can't ask you back. Covid rules.'

'I know,' he said, also standing. 'It's been good talking to you. Perhaps we can meet here again?'

'Yes, of course, love. Have you got everything you need where you're staying?' I asked.

'Yes. And thanks for the phone.'

'You're welcome.'

I raised the rainproof cover over the stroller where Arthur was still sleeping and took a couple of steps away as Lara and Frazer said goodbye. Frazer had entered the park by a different gate, which would take him to the High Street and the bus he needed. The rain was coming down faster now and everyone else had gone. Although Frazer's coat was smart, it didn't have a hood as Lara's and mine did. Frazer seemed to be ready to go but Lara was still holding his arm and giving him one last hug. I took another step away and waited.

'I'll phone,' Frazer suddenly said. And breaking away from Lara, he jogged off through the park towards the exit he needed.

Lara watched him for a moment and then joined me. I

could tell she wasn't pleased, and I wondered if it was because of something Frazer had said.

'What's the matter?' I asked as we hurried head-down through the rain.

'He spent most of the time talking to you,' she replied, disgruntled. 'We only had a few minutes together.'

'Oh, Lara,' I said, glancing at her. 'I'm sorry if that upset you. Frazer didn't seem to mind, and it was nice talking to him after all these years. He's had a rough ride.'

'So have I!' Lara replied tartly.

'I know, love. It's not easy for either of you.'

If I thought Lara was being a little churlish in her resentment of Frazer talking to me, I didn't say. But when she took out her phone to call him I felt I needed to speak.

'Lara, you've only just said goodbye. He won't be on the bus yet.'

'So?' she replied.

'I think you should give him some space. Let him phone you when he's ready. That's my advice anyway. And while we're on the subject, you are not supposed to be hugging and kissing someone who is not in your household. You don't know if he has the virus.'

'He hasn't!' she snapped. 'He told me they test them every day in the hotel.'

'Even so, it's still against Covid rules. Just be careful, not only for your sake, but ours too.'

With a huff, she returned her phone to her pocket and we continued home in the rain.

Once indoors we took off our coats and shoes and I lifted Arthur out of the stroller. He was awake now. Lara went upstairs to use her phone and came down five minutes later still in a bad mood.

'Frazer's not answering,' she said. I was in the living room giving Arthur a drink.

'He's probably on the bus,' I suggested.

'So? He can answer his phone.'

'He can, but perhaps he prefers not to talk in a public place. Give him a chance to get back to the hotel and phone you. And, Lara—'

'What?'

'I wouldn't tell him off for talking to me.'

'I wasn't going to,' she said moodily.

'All right, love.'

I suggested she give Arthur a snack, which she did. Then we returned to the living room where Arthur stood at the patio doors, face pressed against the glass, watching the rain. Lara sat on a nearby chair, phone in her hand, anxiously waiting for Frazer to call. I could see she had thrown herself into the relationship and expected Frazer to do the same. But from what I'd seen Frazer was a very different character, more laid-back and chilled, whereas Lara could be very intense. Eventually her phone rang and, picking it up, she headed out of the living room. Arthur tried to follow her.

'You stay here with Cathy,' she said, and closed the door behind her.

'Come on, little man,' I said, going to him. 'Let's find something for you to play with.'

But again, I had a flash of concern. Lara's priority was Frazer, and Arthur had taken second place. I understood she wanted a relationship, and I appreciated that as a single parent it was a difficult balancing act, but Arthur needed to come first.

When Lara reappeared about fifteen minutes later she was in a much better mood.

'Frazer didn't answer because he was on the bus with his face mask on,' she said.

I nodded.

'I told him what you said about giving him space and he said it's fine for me to phone him whenever I like.'

'OK, love.'

'It's probably because you're older,' she said. 'Your generation did things differently back then.'

'True.' Although I'm not sure human nature has changed much.

To make sure there was no misunderstanding between Lara and me in respect of when I would be babysitting Arthur or accompanying her and Frazer when they met up, I thought it best to state what I had in mind. To be honest, I would rather she hadn't gone out at all with the virus on the increase, but that wasn't an option. Unless you were 'clinically vulnerable' you were entitled to go out to 'exercise' with someone from another household as many times a day as you liked. I'd already said I would babysit Arthur once a week so Lara could go out. I now said I would accompany her and Frazer when they met with Arthur twice a week, which seemed very reasonable to me given the lockdown situation.

'As long as Frazer wants to meet,' I added.

'He will,' Lara replied determinedly.

The following day, Saturday, Lara looked upon as her 'night out'. But instead of meeting one of her girlfriends,

Shell or Courtney, as she would have done in the past, she arranged to see Frazer. She spent a long time getting ready but wasn't out for long because nothing was open, and it was cold and raining.

'Maybe you could talk to Frazer and your friends online?' I suggested. 'That's what I've been doing with my friends and family.'

'But it's not the same,' Lara bemoaned.

I agreed. I missed seeing and hugging my family and friends during these lockdowns, especially my grand-daughter, Emma. But as in other countries, our government felt it was necessary to reduce the spread of coronavirus, so we had to follow the rules.

We spent Sunday mainly at home apart from a quick walk after lunch, when Paula joined us too. During the afternoon, when we were in the living room talking, Lara told us more about her time in care. She said she'd lost count of the number of foster carers she'd had, and generally didn't have a good word to say about any of them, although one family stuck in her mind as maybe looking after her.

'So what happened that meant you had to leave?' I asked, puzzled.

She shrugged. 'I can't remember exactly. But back then it didn't take much to make me angry and trash the place. Trashing their homes and stealing from them usually got me moved. I wanted my mum and nobody could make that happen so I didn't want anyone else.'

'Have you ever had counselling or therapy?' I asked.

'A bit.'

'Did it help?'

'Other than giving me an afternoon off school, no.'

'Perhaps it wasn't the right time in your life,' I suggested. 'Would you consider it now?'

'Why? Do you think I need it?' she exclaimed with a laugh.

'We all need it sometimes,' Paula said.

I nodded. 'Some people find therapy useful,' I said. 'But it has to be at the right time and with a therapist you feel you can connect with. It was just a thought,' I added.

'I'll be fine once I've got a place of my own,' Lara replied. 'I'm not going to start raking over the past. Frazer understands me. That's what I like about him, and he'll make a good dad.'

I didn't say what I was thinking – that she was investing far too much in her relationship with Frazer too soon.

On Monday morning, unbeknown to me, Lara telephoned her social worker, which she was entitled to do. The first I knew of it was when Lara came into the kitchen where I was preparing lunch. Arthur was being looked after by Paula in the living room.

'Claudette says I can go out more than once a week as long as you can babysit,' Lara said.

I stopped what I was doing to look at her. 'You are going out more than once a week. As well as your Saturday night out, I'm going with you and Arthur so you can meet Frazer twice a week.'

'Without Arthur, I mean. If you can't look after him then I'm sure Paula will.' Which sounded as though she was trying to play us off against each other.

'We'll look after him together,' I said.

'This afternoon?'

'I could. It's your decision.'

'Thanks,' she said, and disappeared to phone Frazer with the good news.

Subsequently that week, Lara also went out on Tuesday, Wednesday and Thursday afternoons. Supposedly it was to buy something she needed from the shops, but each time she was gone for two to three hours, leaving Paula and me to look after Arthur. When she returned she didn't have any shopping with her. I was disappointed with her behaviour. It was deceitful and also she was taking me for a fool. I wondered again if she lacked the commitment to parent Arthur full-time. When she was with him she was a loving mother, but then she dropped everything to run after Frazer. Yes, she knew I was here to help out, which may have guided her judgement, but part of her being with me was for her to prove herself.

On Friday morning we had the weekly review meeting with Claudette. It started well with Lara and I talking about the good progress Arthur was making in his weaning, sleeping and play. Claudette then asked Lara about Frazer and listened without comment as Lara talked non-stop, ending, 'When I leave here and you find me a flat will I be able to live with someone?'

'You mean a partner?' Claudette asked.

Lara nodded.

'In principle, yes, although I think it's far too early to be thinking of that yet, don't you? You agreed to stay at Cathy's for four months in a mother-and-baby placement, unless you've had second thoughts?'

'No, I was just wondering about the future,' Lara said.

'I think we should concentrate on the present,' Claudette sensibly said, making a note about something.

'From what I'm hearing, Cathy and her daughter are spending as much if not more time looking after Arthur than you are.'

'That's not fair!' Lara exploded. 'I'm here most of the time.'

'Lara, I've placed single mothers younger than you with foster carers and they don't have a social life at all,' Claudette said. 'They put their own lives on hold to concentrate on their babies. You've been given a chance here. Don't let me down, Lara, please. Where is Arthur now?'

'On the floor, playing,' Lara said with attitude. 'Look! See?' She turned the tablet round so Arthur came into view.

'Thank you. He seems happy,' Claudette said. She would have read my log notes online too.

Lara turned the tablet so it was facing us again.

'I'm due in another meeting soon,' Claudette said, winding up. 'Is there anything else we need to discuss?'

'No,' Lara said bluntly.

'OK, we'll finish then. I'll see you at the same time next week, unless anything comes up in the interim, in which case call me.'

Claudette and I said goodbye; Lara mumbled, 'Bye.' I closed the app.

'I'm not giving up on Frazer,' Lara said, still annoyed. 'She can't make me.'

'No one is suggesting you do,' I said. 'Just that you put Arthur's needs first all the time.'

'And what about *my* needs?' Lara said, standing. 'No one thinks about me.'

'I do.'

But, upset and angry, she left the room, leaving Arthur with me. He looked sad, and with a heavy heart I went over and took him onto my lap. I held him close.

'It's all right, love,' I said. 'Mummy will be back soon.'

He was still looking at the door when, to my delight, he said his first word: 'Ma-ma.'

CHAPTER TEN

ACCIDENTS HAPPEN

I shot upstairs with Arthur in my arms and knocked on Lara's bedroom door.

'What?' she asked grumpily.

'Can I come in? Arthur has just spoken his first word. It was "Mama".'

I went in and after a lot of encouragement, from me repeating 'Mummy, Mummy' over and over again, Arthur finally grinned and said 'Ma-ma' again. Lara was delighted and her previous ill-humour vanished. He said it a second and third time and Lara kissed him all over. I took the opportunity to praise her for all she was doing right. I also talked to her about areas she could improve on. I said Claudette clearly wanted this to work for her, just as I did. She seemed to listen, then as I finished she asked, 'Can I still go out this afternoon without Arthur?'

'You're an adult,' I said. 'You need to make that decision. I can look after Arthur if you think it's right for you to go out again. You've been out every afternoon this week, and you will probably want to go out tomorrow as it's Saturday.'

I left her to think about what I'd said and went downstairs. A few minutes later she appeared. 'I've spoken to

Frazer and he says Arthur should come with us when we meet this afternoon like he did before.'

'So I'll be coming too, then.'

'Yes, please.'

We met Frazer in the park at 2 p.m. It was a cold but bright day with the wintry sun low in the sky. Frazer and Lara didn't go off alone as they had done before, and instead the three of us went to the children's play area, which we had to ourselves. I wiped the handlebars of the play equipment with antibacterial wipes before Arthur went on them. Lara and Frazer pushed him in the swing, rocked him on the rocking horse, helped him down the small slide and chased after him when he just wanted to run around. As I looked on I thought they could be any young couple with their child if you didn't know their histories and the struggles they'd faced in the past. As with many children who'd been removed from their homes and brought up in care, some of what they'd been through would be character-forming and help them deal with life's challenges. But other experiences would haunt them, possibly impacting on their happiness unless they were dealt with. All I knew of Frazer was what he'd told me when we'd met last time and the things Lara had said. Clearly a lot more had happened to him, especially from the age of twelve when he'd been taken from his foster carers by the police to ending up homeless, some of which he was probably still processing and couldn't talk about yet.

We were in the park for about an hour when the sun disappeared from view and the temperature dropped.

'I think we need to be getting home soon,' I said, concerned about Arthur.

Neither Lara nor Frazer protested. They said goodbye with an elbow bump, which may have been for my benefit, then Frazer jogged off through the park to the exit he needed as Lara came with me, pushing Arthur in the stroller towards our exit.

'I did well, didn't I?' she said.

'Yes, love.'

'I didn't hug or kiss him.'

'No.'

'So can I go out with him alone tomorrow? It's Saturday.'

'Yes, if that's your decision.'

'Don't say it like that. You make me feel guilty.'

'That certainly wasn't my intention,' I replied. 'But you need to take responsibility for your decisions. Remember that we are working towards Arthur living with you permanently when you will have full responsibility for him all the time.'

'It'll be different then,' Lara said. 'Frazer will be living with us.'

'And he's said that?'

'Sort of.'

As it turned out Lara didn't go out on Saturday with Frazer. He phoned her in the afternoon to say that someone in the hotel where he was staying had tested positive for Covid, and they all had to quarantine for ten days even though his test was negative. Lara was disappointed to put it mildly, while I was very worried. Frazer could have been incubating the virus when we'd seen him the day before. We'd been outside in the fresh air, which should have reduced the chances of transmitting it, but he'd picked up Arthur when he'd lifted him on and off the play equipment and had stood close to Lara. Close enough to transmit a virus? I didn't know. Also, he'd seen Lara every afternoon that week when she had said she was shopping. I doubted they'd just elbow-bumped then.

I told Paula what had happened and then took all of our temperatures, which were normal. I emailed Claudette to update her. Lara said that as she wasn't seeing Frazer that night could she see Shell or Courtney instead.

I said, 'No. There is a chance you could be incubating the virus. You need to stay here until we know for certain. I've emailed Claudette.'

'I'll stay in then,' Lara said, more easily than I'd expected. 'Nowhere is open anyway.'

We went into the garden on Sunday for some fresh air and exercise rather than going out. I made us a roast dinner, showing Lara what to do, then after we'd eaten she and Paula played with Arthur while I cleared up. In the afternoon we all spent some time online talking to friends and family. Each time Lara took or made a call she went to her room for some privacy. Like a lot of others, since the start of the pandemic I'd felt as if my social life had become more virtual than real. I was looking forward to a time when all this was in the past and we could simply arrange to meet — at a café, pub, restaurant, or in someone's home.

On Monday morning Claudette replied to my email saying she thought we should get tested to be safe, although it wasn't a government requirement. I went online and booked the next available tests for Lara, Paula and me, entering the details that were needed for all of us. The tests were for the following morning at our nearest drive-through testing centre, which was a football stadium car park not being used at present. This was before our government began supplying us all with free lateral flow tests to use at home.

Lara phoned her friends to say we were going to be tested and seemed to find it a bit of a giggle, until we arrived! At 10 a.m. the next morning we joined a queue of cars going into the test centre, when Lara finally appreciated the gravity of the situation.

'It looks like something from a pandemic movie,' she gasped.

'Except this is for real,' Paula said. Paula was in the passenger seat next to me and Lara was in the back with Arthur.

It was the first time I'd been to a test centre and I felt my pulse step up a beat as I followed the queue of cars snaking its way into the grounds. The occupants of all these cars believed they might have Covid and similar scenes were being enacted at multiple testing centres around the world! Large arrows and cones showed us where to go, and signs told us to stay in our cars. Gazebos had been erected every so often along the route to give staff some protection from the weather. Even so they wore coats under their blue Tyvek suits. They also wore blue disposable gloves, masks and Perspex face shields, emphasizing just how contagious this virus was.

I wasn't sure quite what to do but gradually it became clear. At the first stop I was told to open my window a little and was asked for our names, dates of birth, contact details and time of appointment. We were then told to go to the next stop where I wound down my window a little again and was handed three testing kits.

'Pull over there to do the test,' the staff member said. 'Follow the instructions on the packet, and if you are not sure wait in your car and someone will come to you. Once you've done the test seal them in the packets provided and continue to the drop-off point.' This was different to how I'd seen it on the news on television, where the tester had actually done the test.

I parked the car where we'd been directed to and began doing my test as Paula and Lara cautiously watched me. Looking in the interior mirror, I opened my mouth wide as the instruction leaflet said and rubbed the swab over the back of my throat, avoiding my teeth, tongue or gums. I had to put the same swab up my nose until I met with resistance. It was unpleasant but not painful. I put the swab into the tube and screwed on the lid, then waited as Paula and Lara did their tests. Infants weren't being tested. Lara gagged as she put the swab down her throat. 'I'm not doing this again!' she exclaimed.

'Let's hope we don't have to,' I said.

Once Paula and Lara had done their tests and sealed the swabs in the tubes and then the bags, I started the car and followed the arrows and cones to the drop-off bay where I left the three packages. All we could do now was wait for the result, which could take three days. Arthur had grown restless so Lara gave him a snack and a drink as I drove us home.

We had a nail-biting wait but on Thursday afternoon our results came through and they were all negative.

Frazer was still testing negative too. However, I heard from a family I knew who fostered that they all had Covid. The father was very unwell. An hour later Lara received a text from her friend Courtney saying she had it.

'Thank goodness you didn't see her last weekend,' I said.

'I know. I'll be more careful in future.'

I'm sorry to say that on Thursday evening Arthur sustained his first injury since he'd been with me. Luckily for Lara, I was there to witness it. Although I'd seen nothing in the way Lara treated Arthur to suggest she was capable of intentionally harming him, I was still expected to observe her closely. If she got up in the night to tend to him I was there too. I was hoping that in time, with her social worker's agreement, I could trust her more and wouldn't need to be so vigilant. However, that evening, Arthur had just had his bath and was in his sleepsuit, when Lara began chasing him around the landing. It was a game they both enjoyed, but he ran straight into the edge of his bedroom door. Because he ran everywhere full tilt, he slammed into it hard rather than just knocking into it. I was immediately by his side, as was Lara. Paula heard his cries and came to see what had happened.

'It was an accident,' Lara said, worried, picking him up. 'He just ran into the door.'

'I know.'

I was trying to see his face to assess how badly he'd been hurt but he had it pressed to his mother as she comforted him. Eventually she was able to turn his head so I could see his face. The skin wasn't broken but there was a red mark on his forehead and a very small lump.

'We need to get a cold compress on that,' I said. 'Bring him downstairs.'

Concerned for Arthur, Paula came too. He wasn't one to make a fuss so this must have really hurt him as he was still crying loudly. In the kitchen I took a bag of peas from the freezer, wrapped it in a clean wet cloth and showed Lara how to apply the compress to Arthur's forehead.

'A cold compress helps ease the pain and reduce swelling,' I said.

Unlike most parents, as a foster carer I had the benefit of basic first-aid training. But I was wondering if we needed to take him to A&E as it was a head injury. When dealing with an injury or illness in a looked-after child the benchmark rule is: what would I do if they were my own child? Lara kept the cold compress on Arthur's forehead and presently he stopped crying. I checked the area, and the swelling was no worse. Now it had stopped hurting him, he wanted to be off his mother's lap and running around again.

'He seems OK,' I said. 'If he was drowsy or the swelling was getting worse I'd say take him to hospital to be checked. But I don't think that's necessary. We will just keep an eye on him.'

'It was an accident,' Lara said again, still very worried.

'I know, love. Accidents happen, but given how easily Arthur gets hyped up, especially at bedtime when he's tired, it's probably not a good idea to chase him and get him overexcited. It also makes it more difficult to get him off to sleep.'

'Will you tell Claudette it was an accident?' Lara asked.

'Yes, of course.'

I went with Lara as she took Arthur to his bedroom. Paula stayed downstairs. I waited out of sight on the landing as Lara settled him in his cot. He wanted to play so it was over half an hour before he was asleep. When Lara went to her bedroom I checked on Arthur. He was flat on his back and fast asleep. The swelling on his forehead was going. I came out and as I passed Lara's bedroom I could hear her on the phone telling someone about the accident. I would need to include it in my log notes as I was supposed to.

I checked on Arthur again during the evening and before I went to bed. Each time, Lara was on the phone. Arthur woke once in the night and Lara settled him, although I got up too. The following morning the swelling on his forehead had almost gone, leaving a red mark that was turning into a small bruise. Lara was still very worried about what Claudette would say. We had our weekly meeting that morning.

'Accidents happen,' I told her again as Lara gave Arthur breakfast. 'We just have to keep them to a minimum.'

'But supposing you hadn't been here and there was just me and Arthur. How could I prove it wasn't me who hurt him?'

I could appreciate her concern. Because his previous injuries were suspected to be non-accidental, any injury could raise the same concerns for some time to come.

'It might help if you kept a log,' I suggested. 'Like a diary. I keep a log for all the children I look after. You've seen me writing it online. It includes what they've done that day, any appointments, illnesses and accidents, even minor ones. It might be something you could do.'

'Is that what other parents do?' Lara asked.

'I don't think so. But it would help substantiate what you say. So for yesterday you'd write a few lines about what you did with Arthur and then say that at bedtime you were chasing him around the landing, playing, and he ran into his bedroom door. You'd include that you used a cold compress, but we decided it wasn't necessary to seek medical advice and just monitored him.'

'Did I?'

'We did. I checked on him during the evening and you did when he woke at night.'

'I guess I should have checked during the evening too.'

'It's best to err on the side of caution when it comes to little ones,' I said. 'And if in any doubt, seek medical help.'

'I will.' She looked at me thoughtfully. 'Do you think they were accidents when he got hurt when I left him with Diesel?' she asked. 'He always said they were.'

'I've no idea. What do you think?'

She shrugged.

'Did Arthur often get hurt when you left him with Diesel?'

'I guess so. I mean, Arthur used to have accidents when I was there as well, but when I was out it was more serious.'

'How?' I asked, very concerned.

'He had marks on him and he would be very upset and not let Diesel near him. He looked frightened of him. One time when I got back he had a burn on his hand that could have come from a cigarette. Look. He's still got a scar.'

Lara picked up Arthur's right hand and showed me a small round white patch of skin, which looked like a scar.

'Did you leave Arthur with Diesel again after that?' I asked, struggling to hide my disquiet. The scar was old, but Arthur had arrived in care with more recent injuries.

'I didn't have any proof it was him,' Lara replied. 'Diesel said Arthur must have run into a cigarette and burnt himself. He got angry if I doubted him. I know it sounds bad now but at the time I accepted what he said. I needed to get out once a week to see my friends. Diesel liked me to go out too so he could have his mates round. I always did what he said. I guess I was frightened of him.'

'If you were frightened of Diesel, imagine how little Arthur must have felt,' I said.

We both looked at Arthur sitting in his highchair, grinning mischievously, the remains of porridge around his mouth. So cute, adorable and vulnerable. My heart went out to him and what he had been through. At his age he was totally at the mercy of those who were supposed to be looking after him.

'As a parent our first priority has to always be our children,' I said to Lara. 'Always. Even if it means us not going out or doing the things we want to. Most parents have to make big sacrifices in many aspects of their lives when they have children. Life is never the same again.'

I didn't think Lara would intentionally harm her child, but that she could put him at risk by prioritizing her own needs. Those seemed to include having a boyfriend at all costs.

'Have you told Claudette of your suspicions about Diesel harming Arthur?' I asked.

'Sort of. A bit. I mean, I told her Arthur had accidents but not that I thought Diesel could intentionally hurt him. I can't prove anything.'

'Even so, I think she needs to be told.'

'All right. I hope Diesel doesn't find out,' Lara added. I knew then she was still scared of him.

'He's not been in touch with you again, has he?' I asked.

'No.'

But that was to change the following week.

CHAPTER ELEVEN

WIDER PROBLEMS

I usually like to start any review about a child or young person I am fostering by saying something positive, but at our online meeting that morning Lara leapt straight in.

'When you see Arthur you'll notice he's got a bruise on his forehead,' she told Claudette, in a rush to confess. 'He ran into his bedroom door last night. Cathy was there. She saw it was an accident. I made him better and he's all right now, but he's got a bruise where he banged himself.'

'Can you show me, please?' Claudette said.

Lara picked Arthur up from where he was playing on the living-room floor and sat him on her lap. I angled the tablet so Claudette could see his forehead.

'Yes, I see what you mean,' she said. 'How did it happen?'

As Lara told her, Arthur grabbed the tablet and kissed the screen where Claudette's face was.

'That's nice,' she said with a smile. 'He seems all right now.'

'Yes, he is,' Lara said, wiping the screen. Arthur wriggled from her lap and she finished what she had to say about the accident.

'We used a cold compress and he made a quick recovery,' I added. 'I've included the details in my log. But Lara also needs to tell you what she told me about previous injuries Arthur sustained.'

Lara now told Claudette more or less what she'd told me: that Arthur was accident-prone but suffered more injuries when she left him with Diesel, which she'd had to do sometimes or it all became too much for her. I hoped Claudette appreciated her honesty.

'Let me have a look at the scar,' Claudette said.

Lara took the tablet to Arthur, showed Claudette the mark on his hand and returned to the sofa.

'I'm assuming the paediatrician saw it when Arthur first came into care. Are there any other scars?' Claudette asked Lara.

'No.'

Claudette made a note and we continued with the other business of the meeting: Arthur's progress (including that he'd said his first word – 'Mama'), how Lara was meeting his needs by providing routine and consistency, and so forth.

'Lara is always willing to learn,' I said, which I knew would count in her favour.

Claudette asked to see the toys Arthur was playing with and Lara showed her. Then she wanted to see their bedrooms as she would have done if she'd visited in person. Lara took the tablet upstairs while I stayed with Arthur. It would give Lara a chance to talk to her social worker in private if she wanted to.

Lara wasn't gone long and was smiling when she returned, so I guessed Claudette had been pleased with what she'd seen and what Lara had told her. The meeting ended on a positive note with Claudette and me praising Lara for the progress she was making, although I knew that what Lara had disclosed about her life with Diesel wouldn't simply be forgotten. Lara would need to demonstrate that she had learnt from her mistakes, and I didn't think we were there yet.

The weekend was largely uneventful. Like many others, Paula, Lara, Arthur and I went out each day for a walk and then returned home to continue our socializing by phone and online. I also began my Christmas shopping using online stores more than I had in previous years. There was just over a month until Christmas and non-essential shops wouldn't be allowed to reopen for another week. I was planning a family Christmas at my house. It would be made even more special by having my grand-daughter and Arthur with us. I think children help make Christmas. Lara was looking forward to it too and was busy ordering presents online for Arthur.

Although we'd been warned by the government to expect a tier system of restrictions when lockdown ended on 2 December, I didn't envisage it impacting on our plans for Christmas. We weren't in a very high-risk area where the infection rate was rising sharply so I didn't foresee any problems.

Lara seemed happy over the weekend, although she said she was missing Frazer, who still had another two days to quarantine. But then on Monday she was quiet and withdrawn from the moment she got up. I asked her if anything was wrong and she said there wasn't. She spent a lot of time on her phone, usually going to her room to talk and leaving Arthur with me. I respected her privacy but asked her again if anything was wrong. She said there wasn't. However, that evening after Arthur was in bed Lara came to me in the living room.

'I'm in big trouble,' she announced, and burst into tears.

'Oh, love. What is it?' I asked, going to her. 'I knew something was wrong.'

'It's not my fault,' she wept, her face in her hands.

'What isn't?'

I passed her some tissues and drew her to the sofa where I sat next to her.

'Lara, what is the matter? I can help but I need to know what the problem is.'

'It's Diesel,' she said, and my heart sank.

'Are you in touch with him again?' I asked, keeping the censure from my voice.

'No. Not really. Sort of.'

I looked at her as she wiped her eyes.

'Can you explain?' I asked her gently.

'He knows I'm living here.' She sniffed. 'He's got this address. He's threatening to come here if I don't unblock his number and take his calls.'

'How has he found out?' I asked, aware of the seriousness of this.

'Shell told him.'

'Your friend told him? Why?'

'He asked her.'

'So Shell is in contact with Diesel?'

Lara nodded and wiped her eyes again. 'He found her on –' She named a dating website. 'They got talking and they're seeing each other now. You know, dating. She feels sorry for him. He told her he had an unhappy childhood and said bad things about me that aren't true. He said he had some of my belongings and wanted to return them to me, and she gave him this address. Oh, Cathy, he could turn up here any time and ruin everything.'

I knew, as Lara did, that this could jeopardize her staying with me. Claudette would have made it clear to her before she came that she must not divulge my address to her ex-partner as he was considered a risk.

'It's not your fault,' I reassured her, although I wasn't sure that made much difference to the outcome. Now we're so connected online it's easy to find someone through social media and it's a constant worry for those fleeing domestic violence.'

'Should I phone him and try to talk to him?' Lara asked.

'No. It didn't do any good before, did it?'

She shook her head.

'If Diesel does come here, don't answer the door. I'll deal with it. Are you on any social media websites?' I asked.

'I was – that's how I met Diesel – but I took my profiles down before I came here.'

'That was sensible.'

'Claudette suggested it.'

'All right, love. I'm glad you've told me. We'll phone Claudette first thing in the morning and see what she wants to do.'

'Shell didn't mean to make it difficult for me,' Lara said, making excuses for her friend. 'She won't believe how nasty Diesel can be. I've tried telling her, but he's been all nice to her. He's persuaded her that the problems we had were because of Arthur and he never wanted children. Shell's told him she doesn't want children either, but that's not true. She loves kids. She used to keep wanting to see Arthur. Diesel has brainwashed her. Shell can't see it, but then neither could I.'

I nodded sympathetically. 'You've warned Shell. I don't think there is much more you can do. We'll talk to Claudette tomorrow.'

'Will I have to leave here?' Lara asked dejectedly. 'That's why I didn't tell you straight away. I've been so worried.'

'It will be Claudette's decision. But don't encourage Diesel in any way by contacting him, will you?'

'I won't. I promise.'

'What does your other friend, Courtney, say about this?' I asked. 'The three of you are very close.'

'She says she wants to keep out of it and be friends with us both.'

'All right.'

So often in fostering we don't just look after the child; we get drawn into the wider problems involving friends and family. It's knowing when to stop. My protective instinct was to phone Shell and warn her of what she was getting into, but that would have been a step too far.

I had a restless night worrying about Lara and Arthur having to move. The following morning Lara said she too had lain awake for much of the night. We had breakfast – Lara didn't eat much – and then, with Paula looking after Arthur, Lara telephoned Claudette. She wanted me to be present so we went into the front room where she put her phone on speaker. Claudette guessed something was amiss – we were phoning her at the start of office hours. Lara told her that Diesel knew my address and how he obtained it. We heard Claudette sigh.

'Will I have to leave?' Lara asked anxiously.

There was a pause before Claudette asked, 'How long has Diesel known your address?'

'Shell told him last week, but I didn't find out until Sunday night.'

'And he hasn't shown up yet?' Claudette asked.

'No.'

'Not as far as we know,' I added.

'Cathy, I'm reluctant to move Lara. She and Arthur are settled with you, and it will be very difficult to find another mother-and-baby placement – impossible at short notice. I have concerns, but my feeling is that if Diesel was going to turn up and cause trouble he would have done it by now. What do you think?'

'Yes, I agree. I would like them to stay if possible. If he does start coming here and causing trouble then we'll have to rethink.'

'Let's go with that then,' Claudette said, to my relief. 'Lara, are you happy with that?'

'Yes, but I hope he doesn't come here.'

'It might be a good idea if you let it be known that if he does bother you, you'll call the police and apply to court for a non-molestation order. I don't think there are grounds to apply for one yet.'

A non-molestation order is granted by a court and prohibits an abuser from contacting the victim, even from coming within a certain distance of the person or their home. They can be immediately arrested if they do.

'I don't know what you mean about "let it be known",' Lara said, although I did.

'You talk regularly to Shell and Courtney, don't you?'

'Yes.'

'So let them know the police will be called if Diesel tries to contact you,' Claudette explained. 'I'm sure the message will get back to him.'

'Oh, I see what you mean,' Lara said. 'But what if he still comes here?'

'Do what we've said: call the police and tell me. I'll help you apply for a non-molestation order.'

Lara looked slightly less anxious now, while I was pleased with the decision Claudette had made.

After we'd said goodbye Lara decided she'd text rather than phone Shell and Courtney. The three of them messaged a lot through a WhatsApp group they'd set up so all of them could see the same message at the same time.

My social worker told me if Diesel comes here I will have to call the police and he will be arrested, Lara wrote.

It wasn't exactly what Claudette had said but it clearly made the point. Lara was expecting an immediate reply from Shell and Courtney, and when that didn't come she began to worry they were 'siding with Diesel' and wouldn't speak to her 'ever again'. She kept checking her phone and asked me if she should call them. I advised her against it and to give them more time. Shell was going out with Diesel so I guessed she might be weighing up what to do for the best. We had lunch and still neither of them had replied, which I agreed – from what I knew of them – was a little unusual. Then we went out for our walk. As we were returning a message finally arrived from Shell.

Diesel's dumped me! Seems you were right, Lara. He is a prick! Sorry I doubted you!

Lara immediately phoned Shell and they talked as we walked. There were plenty of expletives from Lara about Diesel's behaviour. Paula and I learnt, as did passers-by, that Diesel had only been dating Shell to 'get at' Lara. Incredibly, now having dumped her, he'd contacted Courtney through the same dating app and had tried to chat her up too. Lara was outraged and sympathized with what Shell had been through and then said she needed to speak to Courtney so she'd phone Shell again later.

And so the drama continued all the way home.

Once indoors Paula and I looked after Arthur as the phone calls and texts continued on and off for the rest of the afternoon. By dinnertime the three girls were best friends again and presenting a united front. Shell and Courtney had blocked Diesel's number on their phones as Lara had already done. They also removed him from their contacts lists on all their social media accounts so he shouldn't be able to contact any of them. Over dinner Lara told us Diesel was now trying to chat up a friend of Courtney's who Lara didn't know, poor girl. But it seemed he had moved on, so I was hoping that would be the last we heard of Diesel, although of course we couldn't be sure.

Frazer's quarantine ended and he was still testing negative so Lara asked me if I could babysit Arthur the following day so she could see him. I agreed. She'd had a worrying time and seeing Frazer lifted her spirits.

'Just be careful. Elbow bumps only for now,' I reminded her.

Having dealt with the drama of Diesel finding out my address, that evening I settled down with a mug of tea, hoping to unwind. I loved looking after Lara and Arthur and hoped I was helping her to be able to keep him, but it was hard work. I rarely had time to myself. Arthur was asleep in his cot and Paula and Lara were in their bedrooms. I sipped my tea and was about to switch on the television to watch the news when the landline rang. Lucy, Adrian or a friend calling for a chat? I wondered as I set down my mug and answered it.

A female voice I didn't recognize asked, 'Is that Cathy?'

'Yes, speaking.'

'I don't suppose you remember me. I used to foster in your area. Jenny McKay.'

I sat upright. This was more than a coincidence, surely?

'Yes, I remember you. You fostered Frazer.'

'You've got a good memory,' she said, then stopped. 'Or has someone been in touch?'

'If it's about Frazer, I've seen him recently,' I said.

'Yes, it is. Where was he?'

'Local,' I said, a little guardedly.

'How was he?'

'Not good but a bit better now. Sorry, but why are you asking? I don't mean to be rude but from what I've been told Frazer left you ten years ago and not in very good circumstances.'

Jenny went quiet for a moment, then said, 'You're right, although we have tried to put things right since and stay in touch with him.'

'You have?' I asked, surprised.

'After he left we tried to let him know we were there for him. But he was often angry and refused to take our calls. I'm phoning you now because we are very concerned for him. He went to see his birth mother, Mrs Labette, recently. She lives not far from you. They argued and Frazer left upset. He didn't tell me, his mother did,' Jenny continued. 'She was worried and phoned the social services, but because Frazer is an adult and no longer in care they couldn't help her. She then found some old paperwork with my number and called me. While we were talking your name came up. Apparently Frazer mentioned seeing you to his mother, although it was unclear if he'd spoken to you. She's worried about him but doesn't have his mobile number so I said I'd try to trace him if I could. It's the least we can do.'

'So you haven't seen or spoken to Frazer recently then?' I asked.

'No. Not for a long time.'

'He was sleeping rough when I first saw him,' I said. 'But he's in a hotel now because of Covid. I've only seen him a couple of times.'

'How is he – in himself?' she asked, concern in her voice. 'His mother said he wasn't good.'

'I don't know much. He obviously has some problems. He's been seeing a young lady who is staying with me. He talks to her more than he does me.'

'But he's safe and off the streets?'

'For now, yes.'

'I'll tell his mother,' Jenny said, winding up. 'And please tell him we still think of him and we're sorry for the way things ended. If he would like to get in touch we'd love to hear from him.' Which was slightly different to the impression Frazer had given me.

'I will,' I said. 'What's your number?'

She told me and I wrote it on the pad I kept by the phone.

'Thank you for your time. I won't keep you. I expect you are busy,' Jenny said apologetically, and was about to say goodbye.

'Jenny, before you go, perhaps you could fill me in on some gaps. If I'm honest I have concerns about the young lady I'm looking after. She hasn't known Frazer long and is becoming very attached to him. She has her own challenges and I'm not sure she's been told everything. She feels sorry for Frazer, as I do, but I wouldn't want to see her hurt.'

'I honestly don't know much about what happened after he left us,' Jenny admitted. 'Even when Frazer did answer our calls he didn't tell us much. And because we were no longer his foster carers the social services didn't keep us informed, although we asked them to. What I can say is that he was a good lad back then and it wasn't his fault it ended the way it did. My husband, Shawn, and I talked endlessly about it at the time. I don't know what you've been told but we were asked to foster two brothers, Micky and Davy. There was only a year between them and they were very close. Frazer appeared well settled by then, but right from the start it went wrong. The brothers were a handful and came with their own problems. Frazer resented the time I had to spend sorting them out. Shawn tried to make it up to Frazer by taking him out sometimes, but then Micky and Davy would play up.' She sighed.

'I was enjoying fostering until then,' Jenny continued, her voice catching. 'Frazer was more like a son to us. But it quickly went from bad to worse and then it all fell apart. With hindsight we made some mistakes, but no one really knew how badly Frazer was being affected. He was nearly a teenager and had hit puberty, so we thought that was affecting his behaviour. But he must have felt very rejected. Then it was too late, and he had to be moved.'

'The social services didn't suggest finding Davy and Micky a new home instead?' I asked. 'Frazer had been with you a long time.'

'Their social worker said the boys were settled, which they were. Frazer had gone by then and hated us, so there was little point in moving Micky and Davy. As it turned out they were only with us another year and then went to live with an aunt.'

'Did you continue fostering?' I asked, out of interest.

'Yes, we have a girl long term and she's still with us now.'

'That's good.' I paused. 'Jenny, I understand Frazer attacked Micky and Davy and was taken away by the police. It sounds dreadful.'

'It was. I've never seen him so angry. It was just me at home and I couldn't separate them from fighting. I thought one of them was going to get badly hurt so I called the police.'

'I understand,' I said. 'The young lady Frazer is seeing has a baby. Would you have any concerns about Frazer being around an infant? He seems very gentle and caring.'

'He was. I'm sure he still is, although we haven't seen him in years. Not sure if that helps or not.'

'Thank you. I'll tell Frazer you've been in touch and to call his mother. Do you want me to give him your number?'

'That would be good, although I doubt he'll want to phone us. And you and your family are well?' Jenny asked.

'Yes. I have a grandchild now.'

'Congratulations. I'm still waiting. Love to you all.'

We said a fond goodbye.

CHAPTER TWELVE

THERE'S SOMETHING I HAVEN'T TOLD YOU ...

Fostering is a small world and carers often keep mementoes and paperwork for years. I'd lived in the same house most of my adult life and had the same landline number, so it wasn't that unusual for someone from the past to contact me out of the blue, or even appear. It had happened with children I'd looked after who'd lost contact and then suddenly phoned or even arrived at my door. Like most foster carers, I am always pleased to see them again. I never forget a child I've looked after, regardless of how long ago it was.

I felt relieved that Jenny had confirmed what Frazer had told me regarding the circumstances in which he'd left them. I could understand why he'd played down that Jenny and Shawn had tried to stay in contact and let him know they still cared. He would have felt very rejected and probably still did to some degree, especially as his life had been difficult since. But time had moved on and his birth mother was trying to get in touch with him. He was using my old phone with a new SIM card and I didn't know the number, so I went upstairs to Lara, who was in her bedroom. I told her of Jenny's call and asked for Frazer's number so I could phone him and let him know his mother was trying to contact him.

'He doesn't want to see her,' she said bluntly.

'I understand, but I'd still like to talk to him.'

Reluctantly, Lara gave me Frazer's number and I entered it in my phone. I returned downstairs to the living room where I drank the last of my tea and then called Frazer.

'Yes?' he said, sounding bored.

'It's Cathy Glass. Are you free to talk?' I could hear a television in the background.

'Hang on,' he said, and silenced the television.

'Frazer, I've just had a call from Jenny McKay.'

'Why?' he asked suspiciously.

'I haven't spoken to her since you all moved away, but she phoned just now because your mother is trying to contact you. She called Jenny as she doesn't have your new mobile number.'

'I'll phone her,' he said, without much feeling.

'I think that would be good – just to let her know you're safe.'

I had little idea of the relationship Frazer had with his mother, if any, and he was an adult so it was his decision if he saw her or not.

'Also, I think it would be really nice if you could let Jenny and Shawn know how you're doing.'

'They kicked me out,' he replied.

'I know, and they deeply regret what happened. It's a pity the brothers went to live there, but it's a long time ago now. Jenny and Shawn still think about you. I believe they've phoned you over the years.'

'Sometimes,' he admitted begrudgingly.

'It's up to you, love, but I think it would mean a lot if you just texted Jenny.'

'I don't have her number.'

'I can give it to you when we've finished, then you can decide.'

'OK.'

'I'm looking after Arthur tomorrow so you and Lara can meet, but please be careful,' I added. 'I know you've tested negative, but it can change quickly. Until we have a vaccine we're all at risk.'

'I'll be careful,' he said. 'That guy died.'

I went cold. 'The one who tested positive where you are staying?'

'Yes. He wasn't much older than me. He had other health conditions, but we never thought he'd die. He went into hospital, but we've just been told he died.'

'I am so sorry.'

'I'm shocked,' Frazer admitted. 'He's the first person I know to die from Covid. I'll be careful when I see Lara tomorrow. I wouldn't want her or any of you catching it.'

'Stay out in the fresh air and don't get too close,' I said. 'Hopefully we'll have a vaccine before long.'

'It's scary,' he said.

'I know. Have you got everything you need there?'

'Yes.'

'OK, love. Let me know if you need anything. Take care.'

* * *

I'm sorry to say that the following day Arthur had another accident – his second since coming to live with me. Like the previous one, when Lara had chased him around the landing straight into his bedroom door, she was partly responsible. It was unintentional; she simply hadn't been careful enough.

It was after lunch and Lara was in her bedroom getting ready to go out to meet Frazer. I was downstairs looking after Arthur. Like many active infants his age he couldn't be left alone for a second; he was so quick, inquisitive and oblivious to danger. After a while I needed to use the bathroom, so I took him upstairs to Lara.

'Can you watch Arthur for a minute while I use the toilet?' I said. Coming out, I closed her bedroom door. Although the stairgate was in place at the top of the stairs, I knew if Arthur had access to the landing he would be in and out of the other rooms in seconds – doing damage and possibly hurting himself.

As I was washing my hands I heard him scream in pain. I rushed along the landing and into Lara's room.

'It was an accident, honest,' she said anxiously, holding Arthur to her. 'I didn't mean to.'

'What?' He was sobbing and clutching his hand, which was clearly hurting him.

'I shut his fingers in the wardrobe door,' Lara said.

I grimaced and went over to them. It was hurting him so much he wouldn't let Lara or me look at his injured hand.

'It was an accident,' she said again. 'I was trying to find something to wear, and I didn't realize his hand was in the door when I closed it.'

Paula, who'd been in her bedroom and had heard Arthur's cries, came to see what the matter was.

'I shut his fingers in the door,' Lara admitted, worried. 'It's not bad, is it?' she asked me.

As she held and comforted Arthur I managed to examine his hand. It wasn't bleeding, but there was a red indentation running across two fingers where the hinge of the door had closed. I was concerned a bone in his finger might be broken. Babies' bones are fragile. So as Lara calmed him down I got him to move his hand and wiggle his fingers. 'Like this,' I said, showing him.

He thought it was a game, stopped crying and copied me. Then he struggled to be put down – a sign the pain was easing and he was feeling better.

'I'll take him downstairs and keep an eye on him while you finish up here,' I told Lara.

'Thanks. Sorry,' she said.

Paula came with me and we played with Arthur in the living room. Every so often I checked his fingers. They weren't swelling and he was using them now, so I didn't think he'd broken a bone. By the time Lara appeared I was sure a trip to casualty wasn't necessary, but Lara needed to be more careful in future. Having looked after children for many years, like many parents and carers I could see danger everywhere. When it comes to young children you can't be too careful, and it was something Lara was still learning. She said goodbye and apologized to Arthur for hurting him.

'Say hi to Frazer,' I called after her.

I was expecting Lara to be gone for at least a couple of hours but forty-five minutes later she was back. I heard her key go in the front door and went into the hall, Arthur at my side. She was looking gloomy.

'What's the matter?'

'Frazer said we're not going to meet again until after lockdown is lifted,' she said, taking off her shoes. 'He's worried about passing on the virus as the infection rate is high.'

'That's sensible,' I said.

'I guess. I was thinking of seeing Shell on Saturday as I won't be seeing Frazer.'

'No, Lara,' I said firmly. 'Nothing is open, and you are not supposed to be socializing at all.'

'I was only asking,' she said irritably as she hung her coat on the stand.

'I know it's difficult for you, love. It is for us all. But you'll have to talk to your friends online for now.'

'So when can I go out?' she asked.

'I don't know. I don't make the rules. It depends on what happens when lockdown is lifted and we go into the tier system. Frazer seems to understand how serious it is.'

'He said to tell you he called his mother and also spoke to Jenny.'

'Oh, good.' I was pleased.

With less than four weeks to go to Christmas my online shopping continued in earnest, and boxes and packages arrived regularly. Often it was the same delivery driver, Adesh, a lovely guy who always had a smile. Following social-distancing guidelines, he placed the parcel in the porch, rang the bell and stood back as I answered the door and took in the parcel. Although he was clearly in a hurry to meet his targets, he always asked how I was and left telling me to have a good day – as I did him.

The majority of the packages that arrived were addressed to me as I had many to buy for at Christmas. As well as friends and family, there were children I'd fostered who'd kept in touch, and some had families of their own. Parcels also arrived for Paula or Lara. Aware that Lara was on a low income and living on benefits, I had told her not to buy Christmas presents for us, or, if she did, only something very small. I therefore assumed her purchases were for Arthur, which was confirmed when she showed me some of the gifts she'd bought. Of course she wanted to spoil him at Christmas as most mothers would, but I warned her not to get carried away. With hindsight perhaps I should have delved a bit deeper and found out how she was paying for these gifts, but she was an adult and I regularly talked to her about budgeting and managing her money. For example, when we went food shopping I passed on little tips like how the buy-one-get-one-half-price offer was only a money-saver if you were going to use the second product before it went out of date. I pointed out that the stores' own brands were often cheaper than brand names, and to buy fresh as much as possible. Not only was it the healthier option, it was also often cheaper.

But on Friday morning, ten minutes before we were due to log in to our weekly online meeting with her social worker, Lara came to me looking worried. I was in the kitchen finishing a quick coffee before we began. Arthur was with her.

'I'd better tell you before we speak to Claudette,' she said dubiously.

I set down my mug and looked at her. 'What?'

'You know Claudette always asks if I am managing my money?' she said, subdued.

'Yes. You've been doing all right.'

'Not really. There's something I haven't told either of you.' She threw me a tight smile.

I felt my anxiety level rise and waited for her to continue, moving the cat's bowl out of Arthur's reach.

'I've got a credit card and they are threatening legal action if I don't pay.'

'Oh no.'

'I know I've been silly but I took it out when Arthur was a baby so I could buy him nice clothes and stuff. Then when I lived with Diesel I bought him some things and it just keeps getting bigger and bigger and now I can't pay it back.'

'So you can't even meet the minimum repayment?' I asked.

'No.'

I decided to keep the lecture for later. 'How much do you owe?' I asked. 'Show me the letter and your most recent statement, please.'

'It's on my phone,' she replied. That explained why I hadn't seen a paper statement arrive from a credit card company, which might have set alarm bells ringing for me. Like many, Lara did all her banking on her phone.

'You'd better sit down,' she said, pulling a face.

With a feeling of impending doom, I led Arthur to the table and sat him on my lap as Lara found the statement on her phone and showed me.

'Good grief, Lara! Two thousand four hundred pounds!' I exclaimed.

'I know. I'm sorry. What shall I do?'

Good question, I thought. 'That's a lot of money. Have you told them you're struggling to pay?' I asked.

'No. I just ignored the letters.'

'That's the worst thing you can do. From what I know, if you have a problem repaying a loan you are supposed to inform the lender and work out a repayment plan.'

Lara wasn't the first person to get into a debt she couldn't repay using a credit card. It's far too easy to obtain credit, and of course the interest rate is so high that it quickly mounts up and before long you find you are only repaying interest and your debt is still building.

'I read online you can take out another card and transfer the balance. Shall I do that?' Lara naively asked.

'No. Absolutely not. You will just get into more debt. You need to stop using the card you've got. Let's see if Claudette has any ideas. We need to log in now.'

Worried for Lara, I left Arthur with her while I fetched my tablet, and when I returned to the living room we logged in to the meeting. Claudette wasn't there yet and didn't arrive for some minutes, which left Lara stewing as I tried to keep Arthur amused. When Claudette did log in she looked frazzled and apologized for being late. 'Sorry, I had an emergency to deal with.' She quickly recovered and asked brightly, 'So how are you all? Everyone well?'

'Yes,' I confirmed, then I let Lara say what she had to.

'I've got something to tell you,' Lara began. 'I've just told Cathy.'

'Oh yes?'

'I've run up a big debt using my credit card and now I can't pay it back.'

Claudette's expression gave nothing away. 'How big is the debt?' she asked.

'Two thousand four hundred pounds,' Lara replied. 'They are threatening to prosecute me, which is why I told Cathy.'

'What did you spend all that on?' Claudette asked evenly.

'Things for Arthur, and when I lived with Diesel stuff for him too. Cathy says I mustn't use my card again, but I don't know how I'm going to manage on benefits.'

'By spending less,' Claudette said, in a deadpan voice.

'Lara has shown me the letter and her recent statement online,' I said. 'I think we need to contact the company and try to work out a repayment plan she can afford, don't you?'

'Yes, I agree,' Claudette said. 'How does that sound to you, Lara?'

'OK, I guess, although I won't be able to buy much.'

'Cathy is helping you to budget, and in future you only buy what you can afford. How much of the debt was Diesel's?'

'A lot,' Lara admitted. 'He used to ask for my card.'

'He's not still using it, is he?' Claudette checked.

'No!' Lara replied indignantly. 'I'm not stupid.'

'I've seen the most recent statement and apart from mascara the rest of it was for Arthur,' I clarified.

'All right. So, learn from this, Lara,' Claudette said. 'Arthur won't know how much you paid for his clothes; the important thing is that he is adequately clothed and fed. Cut up the card and contact the lender.'

'I will,' Lara agreed.

We then turned to the other business of our meeting and I praised Lara for the progress she was making with Arthur – she needed it; she was looking pretty low. Claudette asked to see Arthur, so Lara lifted him onto her lap and got him to wave, then told her about the accident he'd had – 'He shut his fingers in the wardrobe door,' she said, as if he'd done it on purpose.

'It was an accident and he's fine now,' I added, as Claudette made a note. I felt guilty as they were both in my care.

Claudette then asked about Arthur's routine, and I reminded Lara to tell her of the new foods he'd been enjoying and that he was now trying to say the word 'cat' whenever he saw Sammy. Winding up, Claudette said she was on annual leave the following week so would see us again in two weeks' time, but if we needed help or advice we should contact the duty social worker.

Straight after we'd finished the meeting I gave Lara scissors and watched her cut up her credit card. I also asked her if she had any others. She said she didn't. I then helped her find the number we needed to call the credit company to talk about her account. We phoned a few numbers. Because so many of their staff were working from home due to Covid, we got passed from one advisor to another. They were courteous but weren't in a position to make a decision about a repayment plan and referred us to another number. By the afternoon we still hadn't got a definitive answer. We were both growing frustrated, and Arthur was becoming increasingly restless as we hadn't been out. Paula was looking after him. I then had an idea.

'How much can you afford to repay?' I asked Lara. She shrugged. 'Five pounds a week?' I suggested.

'I think so.'

'OK, let's reply to the letter you were sent and suggest that. I'll help you compose it.'

As Lara typed I dictated what I thought she should say: she was sorry she hadn't been repaying the loan but was a single parent living on benefits. That she was trying to contact an advisor to discuss a repayment plan, and while she was waiting to hear she would start paying back the loan at £20 a month, more in the future when she could afford it. I also suggested she make a lump-sum repayment of £100, which I thought would help show she was serious.

'But I haven't got a hundred pounds!' she exclaimed.

'I have. Look upon it as an early Christmas present,' I said.

'Thank you so much,' she said, and teared up. 'I've been so worried about this.'

'You should have told me sooner,' I said. 'I'm here to help.'

'I know, but I've spent my whole life taking care of myself. I'm not used to asking for help.'

We had a hug and then I paid off £100 using my debit card.

The following week Lara received a call from an advisor who said that because so many were suffering financial hardship as a result of job loss or reduced working hours during the pandemic they were relaxing their rules. Lara could repay the outstanding debt at £20 a month plus any lump sums she could manage. The advisor said they would put it in writing. We were both relieved and I hoped she had learnt her lesson, especially when I calculated that at £20 a month it would take her more than ten years to repay the debt, and interest was still being added!

CHAPTER THIRTEEN

FRAZER WILL HELP

'Have you thought any more about getting some quali-fications?' I asked Lara one evening the following week, as we sat in the living room and Arthur slept in his cot. I knew Lara hadn't done well at school and had scraped a few passes in her GCSE exams, but that was all. She'd dropped out of education at sixteen so hadn't gone on to college or attended vocational training. I felt she needed some direction in her life, something to aim for.

'I'm not going to get a job until Arthur is at school,' Lara said. 'I want him to feel wanted and loved. Anyway, I'm no good at studying.'

'If you found something you were interested in and made up your mind to do the work, I'm sure you could. You found the will power to stop smoking.'

'That's because I couldn't afford to smoke any more,' Lara replied.

'Even so, that took a lot of determination. Any thoughts on what you might be interested in?'

'Not really.' She shrugged. 'Frazer wants to go to college and do a building course.' She'd told me similar before; I found that when I tried to talk to Lara about something she might be interested in she replied with information about Frazer, as if he were more important than her.

'And what about you?' I asked, bringing her back on track.

'I worked in a supermarket for a while stacking shelves, but it was boring.'

'So what would you like to do?'

'Maybe become a beautician.'

'Have you researched what training and qualifications you would need?'

'No. Frazer said most of the college courses have been suspended because of Covid.'

'Yes, but if you found something you were interested in, you could register for when they open again.'

'Frazer says he wants to become a builder so he can get a steady job and provide for us. He's fed up with doing nothing. He says he's much more focused now he's met me and Arthur. It's given him a purpose in life.'

'That's good, but remember, you haven't been dating for long and are still getting to know each other,' I cautioned, as I had before. I was concerned by the speed at which their relationship was developing, and I didn't want to see either of them hurt.

That week we came out of lockdown and went into a tier system, where the restrictions on socializing reflected how fast Covid was spreading in the area. The county where I lived was placed in Tier 2, which meant we were allowed to meet up to six people outside, but not indoors. It was winter so this wasn't going to add much to our socializing. However, the rules were to be relaxed over Christmas, assuming the transmission rate didn't sharply rise, so my family Christmas could still go ahead as planned. The other good news was that the UK had approved the first vaccine to combat Covid-19 and vaccinations would begin the following week. Those in care homes and the most vulnerable would be vaccinated first. Mass vaccination was hailed as our passport out of this nightmare pandemic, and our spirits rose.

Now in the first week of December, we spent most of one day putting up our Christmas decorations. Lara was as excited as Arthur, if not more. She took lots of photographs, not only of Arthur 'helping', but selfies and photos of Paula and me too. It soon became clear she hadn't enjoyed a proper Christmas in a very long time, probably not since she'd been in care. As we worked – hanging garlands and dressing the tree with sparkling decorations – she asked if Frazer could come on Christmas Day, and since the rules over Christmas were to be relaxed, I agreed. None of us were deemed clinically vulnerable, the transmission rate in our area was stable, and we would follow government guidelines by keeping the house well ventilated and sticking to strict hygiene rules.

'I'll phone Frazer and tell him,' Lara said excitedly, and disappeared upstairs to her bedroom to make the call.

She returned fifteen minutes later happier than ever.

'Frazer says thanks, he'd love to come. This will be our best Christmas ever! We're going to meet in the park tomorrow as he hasn't seen Arthur in ages. Would you like to come?'

'Yes,' I said. Indeed, I'd have to go as I was still supposed to be supervising Lara with Arthur the whole time. It was something I would raise with Claudette when we next spoke. I felt Lara could be trusted to spend time alone with Arthur without my constant supervision, but I would need Claudette's approval first. I decided to email her, so she had time to think about it before our next meeting.

It was late afternoon by the time we finished putting up the Christmas decorations and as a result we hadn't been out of the house all day. I suggested that after dinner we went for a short walk. Paula and Lara agreed. We had cottage pie – a favourite of my family – with broccoli and lashings of gravy, which Lara and Arthur enjoyed too. Once we'd eaten we left the washing-up and, coats on, set off, Arthur tucked under a fleece in his stroller and his woollen hat pulled down over his ears.

It was a cold but clear evening and a moon shone in an inky-black sky. There was hardly anyone out, but we weren't the only ones who'd put up their Christmas decorations. As we passed other houses we paused to gaze at their festive lights. Arthur was fascinated and took it all in.

'Lights,' I said, pointing. 'Pretty lights.'

He made lots of noises and rocked with delight.

We continued into the High Street where festive lights shone from shop windows and were also strung between lampposts. The High Street was a different place decorated, and with few people and virtually no traffic. Magical.

'I like being out at night when there aren't others,' Lara said, gazing up at the night sky. 'It's soothing.'

'Yes,' I agreed. 'It is.'

Paula pushed the stroller for a while and Arthur, far from being tired, was enthralled. We took him out of his stroller so he could walk and peer in the shop windows. I told Lara that usually there was a Christmas Fayre in the High Street on the first weekend in December, but that it had been cancelled this year due to the pandemic.

On the way home we passed the church where we went on Christmas Eve for their wonderful family carol service. Numbers were being restricted this year due to indoor social distancing and I'd had to reserve our places in advance. But there would be no pantomime this year, not in our area at least, as our local theatre – like many others – wasn't big enough to put in place social distancing, so it had closed.

When we arrived home we had some pudding and a hot drink, and then I went upstairs with Lara while she put Arthur to bed. That evening I wrote up my log notes and then made a list of items I still needed to buy for Christmas. I always look forward to and enjoy Christmas, as do my family, but this year it seemed even more special. After the shocking year we'd had in the pandemic it shone like a beacon of light and hope for a brighter, better future.

The following afternoon I accompanied Lara and Arthur when they met Frazer. Paula stayed at home. Frazer was already in the park waiting for us, wearing jeans, a thick padded black jacket and a beanie hat. He smiled when he saw us and hurried over. He went to kiss Lara, but then, remembering the rules on physical contact, stopped and said hello instead.

We went into the children's play area where there was one other family. Lara took Arthur out of his stroller and began running after him, laughing excitedly as he darted from one piece of play equipment to another. Frazer joined in. It was safe for Arthur to run freely in here; designed for younger children, it was fenced off and had rubber flooring so if a child did take a tumble they shouldn't be badly hurt. I sat on the bench in the wintry sun and enjoyed watching them play. Every so often I saw Frazer glance in my direction. Then, as Lara lifted Arthur into a swing, she said something to him and he came over.

'He loves the swing,' I said as Frazer joined me on the bench.

He nodded, and then suddenly said, 'I wouldn't do anything to harm them. I know Diesel did, but I'm not like that.'

'Good. I'm sure you're not,' I said, wondering what had brought this on.

'I phoned my mum and texted Jenny like you said.'

'Yes, Lara told me.' I felt Frazer was psyching himself up to say something more.

'Jenny texted back and then phoned me. She said she was sorry for what happened and they still thought about me. Mum's still the same. She'll never change.'

'At least you contacted her,' I said.

'I want you to know I'm serious about Lara,' Frazer now said. 'I love her and she loves me. Once the pandemic is over I plan to get a proper job, maybe go to college, so we can all live together, and I can take care of Lara and Arthur. They will become my family. I want you to know my intentions are honourable.'

I was starting to feel a bit like a Victorian father being asked for his daughter's hand in marriage.

'I'm pleased to hear that,' I said. 'But you two haven't known each other for very long.'

'Does it matter?' Frazer asked. I saw Lara glance over and guessed she knew what Frazer was saying to me. 'My support worker had an arranged marriage and didn't meet his bride until the wedding. It worked for them,' Frazer added.

'It can do,' I said. 'But their parents would have very likely selected their partners based on their wisdom and what they knew of each other's families.'

'I've got a lot of stuff wrong in my life, but not this,' Frazer said. 'Shall I talk to their social worker about the two of us getting together?'

'If you wish. But Lara agreed to this mother-and-baby placement, which lasts a minimum of four months. If she were to suddenly leave, I think there is a good chance Arthur would be taken into care, without Lara.'

'But why?' Frazer asked indignantly. 'She didn't harm Arthur, Diesel did.'

'There are other reasons why Lara should stay with me,' I said gently. 'She's still learning parenting skills and how to put Arthur's needs first all the time. She's doing well and I wouldn't want to see all that thrown away.' I thought I should speak candidly as it seemed they planned to be together sooner rather than later.

'I can help Lara look after Arthur once we're together,' Frazer said.

'I'm sure you can be a big help. But I wouldn't suggest doing anything that could undermine Lara staying with me for the four months.' Frazer was looking sad and I felt sorry for him, but it needed to be said. 'The mother-and-baby placement is Lara's chance to prove herself,' I emphasized.

'I understand,' he said, with a deep sigh. 'I'll tell her. I just want us all to be together as a family.'

'I know, love,' I smiled.

'Thanks for having me on Christmas Day,' Frazer added. 'Jenny said I could go there but I wanted to spend it with Lara and Arthur. They're my life.'

The build-up to Christmas continued during the second week of December and we were all in the Christmas spirit. England's vaccination programme had begun with ninety-year-old Margaret Keenan becoming the first person to receive the vaccine and William Shakespeare, eighty-one, the second. Whether choosing someone with the Bard's name was planned or by chance I never found out. The number of Covid infections was falling apart from in a few 'hotspots' and all the talk of Brexit, which had dominated our news for so long, had almost been forgotten.

The not-so-good news was that Arthur nearly had another accident. It was avoidable and could have been very serious had I not been there to intervene. It was early morning, and we were all upstairs getting showered and dressed. Lara had got Arthur ready first and he was now running around the landing while she finished getting ready in her bedroom. Her bedroom door was open, the stairgate was in place, and I was keeping an eye on him too from the bathroom.

Once ready, Lara came out of her bedroom and opened the stairgate to go downstairs, then she realized she'd forgotten her phone. She returned to her bedroom to fetch it, without closing the stairgate. I saw Arthur heading for the stairs.

'Stop!' I cried at the top of my voice as I ran round the landing.

He was startled by my cry and stopped. I grabbed him and took him to safety. But my heart was in my mouth as I pictured what had so nearly happened: Arthur bouncing all the way down the stairs and crashing into the stairgate at the bottom.

Having heard my shout, Paula came out of her room. The colour must have drained from my face for she asked, 'Are you all right, Mum? You've gone very pale.'

I nodded and took a deep breath. Lara came out of her room, having found her phone, largely oblivious to Arthur's near-miss. 'What's he done now?' she asked lightly.

'Nearly fallen down the stairs,' I said pointedly, then I lectured her. 'Lara, you can't leave the stairgate open even for a few seconds. If I hadn't been here, he would have fallen for sure. Stairs can be lethal. He could have broken a bone or even died from a fall. You must be more careful.'

'I will,' she said, and tickled him under the chin, which made him laugh. It took me a lot longer to recover from the shock of what might have happened.

I didn't tell Claudette about the incident with the stairgate when we logged in to our weekly online meeting on Friday. Arthur hadn't been hurt and I'd entered it in my log notes, so I felt that was sufficient. Lara told Claudette about Arthur's routine, what he was eating, and that he only woke once at night now. Claudette asked about the credit card loan and Lara said the company had agreed to a reduced payment each month, and they were going to send her a letter confirming this. She also said she had cut up the card.

'Good. So how are you managing on your money?' Claudette asked.

'Cathy helps me out,' Lara replied honestly.

'You won't have her to help you out when you leave there,' Claudette pointed out.

'I know.' Lara sighed. 'I've given up smoking. I hardly go out. I don't know what else I can do.'

I appreciated it was difficult to manage on benefit money and many families struggle, which is why I was helping Lara.

'You'd have to use a food bank,' Claudette suggested.

'What, second-hand food?' Lara exclaimed, disgusted.

'It's not second hand,' Claudette said, with a smile. 'It's donated.'

'Frazer will help us,' Lara said confidently. 'He's going to get a job so he can look after Arthur and me.'

Claudette kept her expression neutral as she said, 'So I understand.'

'Did he phone you?' Lara asked impatiently.

'He did.'

'What did he say?'

'That he loves you and Arthur, and I have his permission to run a DBS check.' (This is the Disclosure and Barring Service to check if someone has a criminal record.)

'Have you done it?' Lara asked.

'Not yet, but we will if he has regular contact with Arthur.'

'We're going to live together,' Lara replied triumphantly.

'I understand that is your plan for the future,' Claudette said evenly. 'Now, can I see Arthur, please? Is he there?'

Lara picked him up and sat him on her lap. I felt, as I had at previous meetings, that Lara had spent too much time talking about herself and her plans rather than Arthur. As he grinned at Claudette and tried to grab her image on the screen, I emphasized how well they were both doing.

'Thank you for your email,' Claudette said to me. 'You're always so positive. Lara, Cathy feels you can manage with less supervision. What do you think?'

'Yes, I can. Does that mean I can take Arthur out alone?' Lara asked, child-like in her enthusiasm.

'I think Cathy meant less supervision in the home.'

I'd sent that email to Claudette before Arthur had nearly fallen down the stairs; now I was watching them like a hawk again.

'I look after him in the house myself already,' Lara said, not appreciating how often Paula and I took up the slack – keeping an eye on him when Lara wasn't in the same room, giving him a drink and a snack, or moving something out of his reach that could have been danger- ous to him. All the myriad little things you quickly learn to do when raising children.

Claudette must either have read my log or was just playing safe, for she said, 'I think we'll keep things as they are for now and then review again in the new year. Is that all right, Lara?'

'I guess,' she said, disappointed.

'In the meantime, I suggest you assume full responsi- bility for Arthur in the house. Pretend Cathy isn't there.'

* * *

Shortly after our online meeting with Claudette, Joy, my supervising social worker, telephoned. I hadn't heard from her since Lara and Arthur had been placed. Usually she was in regular contact. I soon learnt the reason why.

'Sorry I haven't called you sooner,' Joy said. 'My whole family has had Covid. We've all been very careful, so I don't know how we caught it.'

'Oh dear. Are you all right now?' I asked, concerned.

'I feel much better, thank you, just a bit tired, but my brother is still in hospital. He's only fifty-two and was fit before this. He had no underlying health conditions, but he's really bad. Our poor mother is in pieces. No one can visit him because of the risk of spreading the virus so we rely on daily phone calls from a nurse. The staff have been excellent, but to be honest it could go either way.'

'I'm so sorry,' I said, shocked and feeling for Joy. There was no visiting in any of our hospitals at present due to the risk of spreading coronavirus.

'Thank you. All we can do is hope. How have Lara and Arthur been? I've read some of your log notes and the minutes from the online meetings.'

'They're doing all right. We've just finished our weekly online meeting,' I said. I could tell from Joy's voice her heart wasn't really in it.

'Have you got everything you need?' she asked.

'Yes, thank you.'

'We're all still working from home as much as possible and I'm on reduced hours at present. If you can't get hold of me, call one of the team.'

'I will. I hope your brother gets better soon.'

'Thank you. So do I.' I heard her voice catch.

We said goodbye and I stayed where I was in the living

room, my heart going out to Joy and her brother, and what her family must be going through. It was a salutary reminder that this lethal virus was putting us all at risk, regardless of age or how fit or careful we were.

As I sat there in the living room the door burst open and Arthur rushed in. Lara was nowhere to be seen.

CHAPTER FOURTEEN

ASSUMING RESPONSIBILITY

'Lara!' I called. Taking Arthur by the hand, I led him out of the living room. 'Lara? Where are you?'

There was no reply. I looked in the front room and she wasn't there. The stairgates were closed so I assumed Arthur hadn't come down by himself.

'Is Lara up there?' I called to Paula, who was in her room.

'No.'

I went into the kitchen-diner and saw her through the kitchen window, talking on her phone and smoking a cigarette.

I knocked on the glass and signalled for her to come in. She could tell I wasn't pleased.

'It was only one,' she said, referring to the cigarette. 'I ran out of nicotine gum, and I find those meetings with Claudette so stressful.'

'We'll get you some more gum,' I said. 'But please don't start smoking again.'

'I won't. Sorry.'

'Lara, what also concerns me is that you left Arthur unattended while you went outside.'

'You were there,' she replied defensively. 'I heard you on the phone in the living room.'

'I know, but I won't always be on hand, and you didn't check with me first to see if I could look after Arthur. Claudette wants you to act as if I'm not here.'

'Oh, yes. I see. Is that what she meant? I won't do it again,' Lara said, worried.

'It's all right, love. I know it's difficult. But this is all supposed to be helping you work towards a time when you will be solely responsible for Arthur.'

'It'll be different then. I know I'll have to do it. And Frazer will be there to help.'

'I think you are placing too much emphasis on Frazer,' I said.

'He feels the same about me. We are going to get together and be a family as soon as we can.'

What else could I say? I'd said it all. I felt their impatience to create a family could in part be due to them not having families of their own. They'd idealized the notion of the family, seeing it as the answer to everything, which of course it isn't. All families have their ups and downs and the relationships within them sometimes become strained and have to be worked at. And on a practical level, Frazer had been sleeping on the streets until recently and had no permanent home of his own or a job. Lara's situation was tenuous too. She was only with me for a few months and was still having to prove her parenting skills. I wondered if Frazer would feel the same for Lara if she wasn't allowed to keep Arthur, or if their relationship would suffer as a result. But these were my thoughts and feelings and didn't form any part of my assessment. Overall, Lara was doing well, and I wanted to make sure it stayed that way.

I suggested to Lara she give Arthur a snack and a drink, and change his nappy, then we could walk to the High Street for what we needed, including her nicotine-replacement gum, which I would pay for. I thought she'd stopped using it as I hadn't seen her chewing it for a while, otherwise I would have bought her some more by now. If it helped her deal with stress then it was better than cigarettes.

Paula came with us to the High Street and on the way back we stopped off at the park for about fifteen minutes. As we were on our way home Lara asked, 'What's for lunch? I'm starving.'

I was about to reply with some suggestions but stopped myself. 'You tell me. Claudette wants you to behave as if I'm not in the house. What are you going to make for you and Arthur?'

While Lara thought about this I took the opportunity to explain to Paula what Claudette had said about Lara assuming full responsibility for Arthur in the house as if we weren't there. 'In preparation for hopefully taking Arthur out alone in the new year,' I added.

'That's good,' Paula said to Lara. 'Well done.'

Lara smiled, pleased. 'I can give Arthur one of those ready-meals for toddlers,' she said. 'I've still got some in the cupboard.'

'You could, or you could make something and save those for when you are in a rush or have run out of fresh food. If you're short of ideas, go online and see what suggestions come up for a fourteen-month-old.'

She used her phone to access the internet as we walked.

'How about cottage cheese sandwich with cucumber finger sticks?' she said.

'Sounds good to me,' I replied.

'But I don't like cottage cheese,' Lara added, pulling a face, and continued searching for suggestions. 'Scrambled egg with baked beans and cucumber sounds better.'

'OK, fine.'

'Supposing he doesn't like it?' Lara asked.

'If he really won't eat it you will have to give him something else. He can't go hungry.'

I'd already shown Lara how to scramble eggs, so once home I left her to prepare their lunch in the kitchen first before I made something for Paula and myself. As most parents and carers do, I like to feed my family, so it felt strange doing nothing, but that's what her social worker wanted – to prove Lara could do it. Once she'd finished in the kitchen she sat at the table with Arthur to eat as I made our lunch. Arthur enjoyed what Lara had made and she gave him yoghurt and fruit for dessert.

I'll admit I found it difficult giving Lara all the responsibility for Arthur and pretending I wasn't there. I'd spent years raising children, so I was in the mind-set of automatically recognizing and meeting their needs. It was second nature to me and also, to some extent, to Paula too, especially as she was at home all day. But it soon became clear just how much we had been doing. For example, Lara already settled Arthur in the evening or if he woke during the night; I'd insisted on it right from the start, although at present I was still getting up as well to supervise. But in the morning, if Arthur woke before Lara, I often saw to him while she got ready. That would have to change. Similarly, at present she was enjoying a leisurely shower each day without Arthur and using the toilet in peace. Add to that all the meals I made, the times I fed and changed him, and when Paula and I played with him, and we were probably doing as much for him if not more than Lara.

In some ways it was playing with Arthur that Lara really struggled with. Children learn through play and while Lara was very good at chasing him around the house and tickling him, she found it difficult to sit with him for any length of time and arrange activities. At fourteen months old he needed to be entertained with regular changes of activity and constructive play. Lara would sit with him for a few minutes, then quickly grow bored and expect him to watch television or a cartoon on my tablet. Arthur had arrived with toys and I had plenty in the cupboard. Lara knew where they were.

'Swap them regularly and join in,' I told her. 'Make it fun.'

'It's boring,' she said.

'Not for him.'

Then there was all the time Lara spent talking on the phone or texting when she expected Paula or me to look after Arthur. I stopped this and was now continually calling her to come and look after Arthur or taking him to her. 'Remember, I'm not here,' I said, and she sighed.

On Saturday afternoon I was in the living room, hoovering. Lara and Arthur were there, and she was texting Frazer about meeting up that evening. Lara looked upon Saturday as her night out, despite it being cold and nothing much being open. Absorbed in her phone, she didn't see Arthur suddenly grab her half-drunk mug of tea from where she'd left it on the coffee table until he'd tipped it all over himself. Neither did I or I would have intervened, but I wasn't supposed to be watching him. Thankfully it was only lukewarm.

'Look what you've done! I've got to clear up this mess!' Lara exclaimed, seeing that as the worst outcome of the accident.

'It's just as well it wasn't hot,' I said, 'or he would have been badly scalded. You can't leave anything within his reach.' Which I'd said countless times before.

Although I was babysitting Arthur that evening, I expected Lara to give him dinner and get him ready for bed before she left. At five o'clock she went into the kitchen to prepare his dinner without being reminded, which was good. What wasn't so good was that she was going to give him the rest of the can of baked beans she'd opened at lunchtime.

'He needs something different for his dinner, love,' I said.

'I know that really, just testing,' Lara said, with a laugh, and returned the beans to the fridge. 'But if you're pretending not to be here, you shouldn't have seen or said anything.'

'True,' I said, and smiled.

I liked Lara. There was no malice in her, although I was sure she would have given Arthur the rest of the baked beans for his dinner, had I not been there. And while it wasn't the end of the world, part of my role was to teach her to feed Arthur and herself a balanced, nutritious diet.

Lara now looked online again for some suggestions for Arthur's dinner. I had cookery books on a shelf in the kitchen, but, like Lara, I often turned to the internet for recipes and meal ideas.

'Mashed potatoes with peas and grated cheese,' she read out.

'Yes, that sounds fine. You know how to make mashed potatoes.'

'I do.'

Lara wasn't having any dinner herself as she and Frazer were going to get burgers and chips from the takeaway in the High Street. She was meeting him there as they were going to look at the Christmas decorations together. I said he should walk her home for safety, although he couldn't come in because of the Covid restrictions. Once Arthur had been fed and changed ready for bed, Paula and I looked after him while Lara got ready. She left at six-thirty, so we put him to bed. She was back two hours later, freezing cold, and clearly had something urgent to tell me. I was in the front room at my computer.

'Frazer is in my bubble so he should be allowed to come in here,' she said determinedly, even before she'd taken off her shoes and coat.

I saved the document I was working on and looked at her. Lara was referring to the support bubbles the government had introduced in the pandemic restrictions, which allowed two households to interact. As far as I knew these were for those who were living alone to try to reduce their isolation. It was only allowed in certain circumstances.

'I don't see how Frazer can be in a support bubble with you,' I said. 'But I'll check online.'

She took off her shoes and coat and stood beside me as I brought the government webpage onscreen and read the salient points.

'A support bubble links two households. Not everybody can form a support bubble. It is against the law to form a support bubble if you are not eligible. You can form a support bubble with another household of any size if you live by yourself – which neither of you do,' I added. 'Or if your household includes a child who is under the age of one, which Arthur is not.'

I read on, 'Or if your household includes a child with a disability who requires continuous care and is under the age of five. Or you are aged sixteen or seventeen and live with others of the same age, without any adults. Or you are a single adult living with one or more children who are under the age of eighteen. You and Frazer don't fit the criteria so you can't form a support bubble,' I concluded.

'What about a child-care bubble?' Lara asked. 'We found something online about that.'

I already knew the answer to this as all foster carers had received a letter explaining how child-care bubbles worked. 'You're not eligible, love,' I said. 'You look after Arthur and I'm here too. I'll find the letter explaining it.'

'Don't bother,' she said moodily, clearly disappointed. I guessed she and Frazer had set their hopes on forming a bubble. She moved away and then stopped and asked, 'So how is it that Frazer can come here on Christmas Day?'

'Because the government is going to relax the rules for Christmas. But we'll have to be very careful – lots of fresh air and hand sanitizing.'

Even so, like many others, I had concerns as to how safe it was going to be for us all to get together. Had my parents still been alive, I doubt I would have gone ahead with our Christmas plans. They had always come to us for Christmas, but coronavirus was far more dangerous to older people and was more likely to kill them. My other concern was that the transmission rate was rising in a number of areas, including ours.

Lara went into the kitchen to make herself a hot drink as I continued working at my computer. I could hear her talking to Frazer on her phone. She wasn't happy with me, but I didn't make the rules and I certainly wouldn't flout them – for all our sakes.

On Sunday morning I woke Lara at 6.30 as Arthur was awake, and she was now wholly responsible for him unless she had specifically asked me to babysit.

'It's too early,' she grumbled. Turning over, she pulled the pillow over her head.

I could hear Arthur in his cot jumping up and down with his cries of 'Mama!' growing louder.

'Come on, love, your son wants you. He's ready to start the day.'

'I'm not,' came Lara's muffled voice from under the pillow. 'Perhaps he'll go back to sleep.'

'He's not going to want any more sleep now. He's had eleven hours.'

She flung the pillow from her head and got up, not pleased. 'You should have put him to bed later,' she grumbled, as she went to see to Arthur.

I ignored her bad humour. Arthur had gone to bed at his normal time, so it was no good blaming me. But it was at times like this I had concerns about what Lara would have done if it was just her looking after Arthur. Would she have left him in his cot to become more and more upset? My heart clenched at the thought. Infants who are neglected learn that their needs won't be met and eventually give up, becoming silent and withdrawn. Thankfully Arthur wasn't like that, and it was important he stayed that way.

'If you are taking him into your bed, don't fall asleep,' I reminded Lara as she carried Arthur into her room.

'He can play on my phone,' she replied, and closed her bedroom door.

I listened out as I showered and dressed. Once ready, I left the bathroom and was about to go downstairs as Lara came out of her bedroom holding Arthur out in front of her.

'He's wet my bed!' she said, disgusted. 'His nappy must have overflowed.'

'Always best to change it first thing in the morning,' I replied.

'I think I might know that now,' she said bad-humouredly, and went into his bedroom to change him.

'Do you want me to strip your bed?' I called.

'Yes.'

By the time Lara came downstairs with Arthur she was fine with me again and eager to share the next drama.

'You'll never guess what!' she exclaimed, coming into the kitchen-diner where I was at the table drinking a coffee.

'No?'

'Shell is seeing Diesel again!'

'You're joking,' I said, and set down my mug.

'Shell texted me last night from his place. He's persuaded her I made it all up and he's a really nice guy. Courtney and I have tried to tell her what he's really like, but she doesn't want to know.'

'I have a nasty feeling she might learn the hard way in time,' I said.

'I can't believe Shell would do this to me. We're supposed to be friends.'

Lara then told me all about the messaging that had taken place during the night between her, Shell and Courtney, leaving her tired this morning.

Once we'd all had breakfast we met Lucy and family in a park. It was the first time they'd met Lara, and Emma loved chasing Arthur around. Lucy and Lara got on well and had a couple of long chats. Later, Paula and I video-called Adrian and Kirsty. Present coronavirus restrictions meant that only six people were allowed to meet up and that had to be outside, so I was taking it in turns to see my family. Not for the first time I thought how surreal and frightening normal life had become when something as simple as seeing my family needed to be rationed and planned.

CHAPTER FIFTEEN

NEW RESTRICTIONS

Since Lara had cut up her credit card, parcels addressed to her had stopped arriving. Even so, Arthur would have plenty of Christmas presents from her, plus the ones from me and my family. More than many children. We had begun wrapping presents secretly in our bedrooms, taking it in turns to share the wrapping paper, sticky tape, ribbon and bows I'd bought. Lara was so excited she started putting Arthur's presents under the tree as she wrapped them. Naturally Arthur began unwrapping them. She wrapped them again, using extra sticky tape, but that didn't stop him. Arthur didn't know they were to be saved for Christmas Day. I suggested to Lara that we put all our presents under the tree on Christmas Eve. I hadn't put any chocolate novelties or candy canes on the tree yet for the same reason. We'd taught Arthur not to pull over the tree, but it was a bit much to expect him not to eat sweets or unwrap enticingly wrapped presents. Lara agreed.

I was still teaching Arthur how to stroke our cat gently and not to pull his tail. Sammy was very patient but Arthur, like many children his age, could be heavy-handed. One afternoon I was sitting on the floor with

Arthur, showing him again how to lightly stroke Sammy. 'From his head, down his back to his tail,' I said. Lara was sitting on the sofa watching us.

'I was never allowed a pet,' she said. I assumed she was referring to her time in care.

'Not all families have pets,' I said. 'Some people have fur allergies and others simply don't like the idea of having animals in their home.'

'It wasn't that. Some of the foster families had pets but I wasn't allowed to have one of my own. I had to make do with theirs.'

'Like you do now,' I said. 'We all share Sammy.'

She shrugged.

I looked at her carefully. Whenever Lara talked of her time in care it was always in negative terms. I appreciated she'd had a bad deal with so many moves, but it hurt and saddened me that she appeared to have no happy memories from that time. It couldn't have been all bad.

'Surely some of the families you stayed with helped you and did nice things?' I said.

'I don't remember laughing much,' she replied. 'I always felt unhappy. I know I was angry and didn't understand why my mummy had left me.'

'Didn't someone explain?' I asked.

'They told me she'd died from a drug overdose, but that made it worse. Because she had a choice. If she'd been killed in a car accident or died from an illness, I think I could have accepted it better. But she took drugs, which killed her. She needn't have done that.'

'True,' I said. 'But I don't think for one moment your mother intended to die and leave you.'

'Who knows?' Lara said, with another shrug. 'One thing is for certain: Frazer and me will make sure it never happens to Arthur. I would never do drugs, and neither would Frazer.'

'Good. And make sure you stay off the cigarettes and alcohol too.'

I spent a fair amount of time that week reminding Lara to look after Arthur, and Paula not to. Lara huffed at me sometimes and grew irritated for 'always being on her case' as she put it. But I think – I hope – she appreciated why I was doing it. If she was going to be allowed to parent Arthur, her social worker would need to be sure she could keep him safe and meet his needs. She didn't have to be a 'super mum' as I'd told her many times, just 'good enough'.

By Friday's meeting with Claudette I felt we had made real progress. Lara was being more watchful of Arthur – recognizing situations and objects that could be danger-ous to him, rather than relying on me to point them out. She was starting to plan meals ahead and provide little healthy snacks and drinks in between without being told. She was also spending more time engaging with him in play, although not as much as I would have liked. But we had time to work on that.

Using my tablet, we logged in to the meeting and as usual Claudette asked how our week had gone. Lara spoke first, then I said what I had to, and so too did Arthur. He was sitting on the sofa between us, grinning, waving and running through his repertoire of words, some of which were recognizable – 'Mama', 'cat', 'ball' and 'azer', which Lara told us meant Frazer.

'So you've been seeing a lot of Frazer?' Claudette asked Lara.

'We video-call each other a lot,' she replied, which I knew.

Claudette nodded and made a note. Having been brought up to date, she praised Lara and then asked us what our Christmas plans were. This would be our last review before Christmas as there was only a week to go. I said that Lucy and her family and Frazer were coming to us on Christmas Day and my son, Adrian, and his wife were coming on Boxing Day.

'Let's hope nothing changes tomorrow to prevent that,' Claudette said.

'What do you mean?' Lara asked, immediately worried.

'The prime minister is addressing the nation again,' I said. Lara didn't follow the news as Paula and I did. The infection rate was rising and in tomorrow's televised address our prime minister was expected to announce further restrictions in some areas.

We finished by wishing each other a 'Merry Christmas' and a 'Happy New Year'. Next Friday was Christmas Day and the one following would be New Year's Day, so Claudette set our next meeting for Friday, 8 January, when Lara would be approximately halfway through her stay with me, unless it was extended. At that point, did I think she was going to be allowed to keep Arthur? Yes, unless anything went badly wrong.

The following afternoon, like many other households across England, we gathered in front of our television for the start of the coronavirus press conference. It was obvious straight away from the serious expressions on the faces of our prime minister and his advisors that what he was about to tell us wasn't good, even before he said, 'Good afternoon. I am sorry to report that the situation has deteriorated since I last spoke to you. Yesterday, I was briefed on the latest data showing the virus spreading … it is the new variant of the virus … which does appear to be passed on significantly more easily … This is early data. It is subject to review. It is the best we have at the moment, and we have to act on information as we have it because this is now spreading very fast. The UK has by far the best genomic sequencing ability in the world, which means we are better able to identify new strains like this. The Chief Medical Officer last night submitted our findings to the World Health Organization and we will continue to be totally transparent with our global partners. But we know enough already to be sure that we must act now. I met ministers on the Covid Operations Committee last night and again first thing this morning, and Cabinet met at lunchtime to agree the following actions. First, we will introduce new restrictions and look at Christmas again.'

I held my breath as he began to tell us about a new Tier 4, which was being imposed in some areas in England where the transmission rate was very high. 'Those living in Tier 4 areas should not mix with anyone outside their own household at Christmas, though support bubbles will remain in place for those at particular risk of loneliness or isolation. Across the rest of the country, the Christmas rules allowing up to three households to meet will now be limited to Christmas Day only, rather than the five days as previously set out …

'As before, there will be no relaxation on 31 December, so people must not break the rules at New Year. I know how much emotion people invest in this time of year, and how important it is for grandparents to see their grand-children, and for families to be together. So I know how disappointing this will be, but we have said throughout this pandemic that we must and we will be guided by the science ... When the virus changes its method of attack, we must change our method of defence. As your prime minister, I sincerely believe there is no alternative open to me. Without action, the evidence suggests infections would soar, hospitals would become overwhelmed and many thousands more would lose their lives ...

'Yes, Christmas this year will be very different, but we must be realistic. We are sacrificing our chance to see loved ones this Christmas so we have a better chance of protecting their lives so we can see them at future Christmases.'

It was rousing stuff, and very worrying. As the address finished we sat in stunned silence staring at the screen, where there was a shaded map of the UK showing the different tiers.

'We're not in Tier 4, are we?' Lara asked.

'No,' I replied, deep in thought.

'Great. Frazer can come to us on Christmas Day,' Lara said, not thinking of the wider implications.

'So that means Lucy can come on Christmas Day, but Adrian can't come on Boxing Day,' Paula said.

I nodded. 'Because the rules are only being relaxed for Christmas Day.'

Adrian and Kirsty had arranged to see her parents on Christmas Day and then to come to us on Boxing Day –

26 December. But as Paula had said, that wasn't allowed now as the rules on households mixing were only being relaxed for Christmas Day.

'But Frazer can still come on Christmas Day, can't he?' Lara persisted.

I didn't immediately reply as my thoughts were working overtime. It wasn't just the unfairness of only being able to see some of my family that was bothering me, but the safety aspect too. Had the area where we lived been put in Tier 4 none of us would have been able to meet indoors, just as in lockdown. But because we lived in another part of this (small) country, it was deemed safe.

'I'll tell Frazer he can still come,' Lara said, picking up her phone.

'Just a minute,' I said. 'I need to think about this.'

'What is there to think about?' she demanded.

'How fair it's going to be for all of us,' Paula replied.

'And if it's safe,' I added.

'They just said we could have Christmas Day,' Lara retaliated. 'It won't be fair if I can't see Frazer after you promised!'

I motioned to Paula not to say anything. I appreciated how much Lara had invested in Christmas, as we all had, but I honestly didn't know what to do for the best. As we were sitting there, with the television still on, a presenter now going over the regulations, the landline rang. Paula, nearest to the handset, picked it up.

'Hi,' she said. 'Yes … Sure … I'll put her on.'

'It's Lucy, she wants to talk to you,' Paula said, and passed the handset to me.

I muted the television. 'Hi, love, how are you?'

'OK. Did you watch the press conference?'

'Yes. Did you?'

'We did. We wondered if this would happen. This virus is everywhere. Mum, Darren and I have been talking and we both think it's better if we don't come to you on Christmas Day. We can swap presents outside in the fresh air. We'd never forgive ourselves if we were incubating the virus and passed it to you. We are going to say the same to Darren's parents as we were going there on Boxing Day. Is that all right?'

'Yes, love. I'm disappointed but I agree with you. I've been sitting here trying to work out what to do for the best. I think you and Darren are right. What will you do about your Christmas dinner?'

'We'll have something here. It will be weird not seeing you all, but it's not worth the risk.'

'I agree. I wonder if the church service on Christmas Eve will go ahead. They've put in place social-distancing measures – that's why we had to reserve tickets.'

'Don't go, Mum,' Lucy said. 'It's not worth it. I couldn't bear the thought of anything happening to you.' I heard her voice break, and my eyes filled.

'I won't go, love, you're right. Don't worry. I'll be careful.'

We talked for a few minutes longer, mainly about the virus. As nursery workers, Lucy and Darren were aware of how quickly it was spreading among families. Then she put Emma on.

'Hello, Nana,' she said cutely, which lifted my spirits. Aged two and a half, she knew a few hundred words, as most children her age do, and could make short sentences, including, 'Bye, Nana. Love you.'

The call ended and I looked at Paula and Lara, who'd got the gist of what Lucy and I had said.

'Lucy and Darren have decided not to come on Christmas Day,' I clarified. 'They don't feel it's safe. I need to call Adrian and see what he wants to do.' I pressed his number as Paula and Lara watched me in silence.

'Hi, love. Did you see the press conference?' I asked Adrian straight away.

'Yes, and Lucy's just texted to say she won't be going to yours for Christmas Day. Mum, Kirsty and I have made the same decision about coming to you on Boxing Day. It's not worth the risk. Kirsty is talking to her parents now and telling them we won't be with them for Christmas Day.'

'I think you're wise,' I said. 'Disappointing though it is. We'll arrange to meet outside to swap presents, and if you need any food for your Christmas dinner, let me know. I'll have plenty here. I've already bought lots of extras.'

'Sure, Mum.' We chatted for a while longer and then I passed the phone to Paula so she could say hi.

'But Frazer can still come here on Christmas Day, right?' Lara asked as Paula talked to her brother. 'Please?' she almost begged. 'We're allowed to.'

'I know, love, but that's not the point; it's about keeping us all safe,' I said. I was about to explain when Lara jumped up angrily from the sofa.

'If Frazer isn't allowed to come here then I'm going to his place!' she exclaimed, and stormed out of the room, leaving Paula and me to look after Arthur. I didn't call her back and remind her that Arthur was her responsibility. She was upset and I could understand why. Our

Christmas – so carefully planned and anticipated – was no more.

I gave Lara time to cool off in her bedroom, with the intention of then going up to talk to her. But ten minutes later she came down, surprisingly subdued and looking a bit shamefaced.

'Frazer's not coming,' she said quietly, and sat down. I was pleased she'd thought about it and was now acting maturely.

'You explained my concerns to him?' I asked.

'That's not the reason he can't come,' Lara said. 'The guy in the room next to his is ill with Covid so they all have to quarantine again.'

Which confirmed to me that we'd made the right decision. As Lucy had said, the virus was everywhere; anyone could be incubating it or have it without being symptomatic. It was impossible to know.

'We'll still have a nice Christmas,' I reassured Lara. 'It will just be smaller than planned.'

'I bought Frazer a present, but I won't be able to give it to him now,' Lara said, disappointed.

'Is it something that could be sent in the post?' I asked.

'Not sure. It's a photograph of me and Arthur. The frame has glass in it.'

'If we wrap it up well, it should be all right in the post. Can you show me?'

Lara fetched the framed photograph from her bedroom. It was already well packaged in a box with protective foam – a recent picture of her and Arthur mounted in a silver frame.

'Very nice,' I said. 'Where did you get it done?'

'I took a selfie and had it printed at that shop in the High Street. Frazer has got one of him for me.'

'Lovely.' I was also pleased that Lara hadn't bought something very expensive and beyond her means.

'Frazer and me agreed we wouldn't spend too much as we're saving up to get married.'

I nodded. 'I've bought Frazer a gift card he can spend online, so shall I send that in the parcel too?'

'Yes. His mother and Jenny are sending him gifts. Lucky him. He'll have far more than me,' Lara said, feeling a little sorry for herself.

'You'll have presents,' I said, and left it at that. As well as those from Paula and me, I knew Adrian and Kirsty, and Lucy and family, had also bought Lara and Arthur gifts as they did for all the children we fostered.

I fetched the gift wrap, sticky tape, bubble wrap and a large padded envelope. Paula and I looked after Arthur as Lara wrapped the present and put it into the envelope with mine. She didn't know Frazer's postcode, so I googled it and she carefully printed his name and full address on the envelope in black felt-tip. By the time she'd finished, her enthusiasm for Christmas had returned.

'Can we still play games and win prizes off the tree, like you said?' she asked me.

'Absolutely!'

The following day I received an email from our church saying that they'd made the difficult decision to cancel the Christmas Eve service this year due to coronavirus. They felt that even with the measures they'd put in place, the risk of spreading the virus was too great. It was the first time in living memory that the Christmas Eve service hadn't taken place and it seemed another harsh reminder of just how serious this pandemic was. I also started hearing from friends and extended family who were either scaling back their Christmas arrangements or not seeing anyone. Those who lived in the new Tier 4 areas, or had planned to spend Christmas with someone who did, had to scrap their plans completely as it was now illegal to travel in or out of a Tier 4 area or for households in that area to mix. It was a great disappointment and those I heard from either had too much festive food if they'd been expecting guests or not enough if they'd been planning on going to others for Christmas. It would have helped to have more notice of the restrictions, but most people appreciated these steps were necessary, given the rise in the number of new cases. And of course, as usual at Christmas, I was mindful that many people never enjoyed the Christmases we did, due to poverty, ill-health, isolation or suffering.

CHAPTER SIXTEEN

A DIFFERENT CHRISTMAS

I spent Monday morning packing up Christmas presents that could be sent in the post to those people we'd planned to see over the festive season but now wouldn't. I soon ran out of packaging so after lunch we went into the High Street to post what was already wrapped and to buy more packaging. We weren't the only ones. Outside the post office we joined a mask-wearing, socially distanced queue that moved forward very slowly so that social distancing was maintained inside. One in, one out. I guessed a lot of people were now posting presents they would normally have given in person. Arthur grew restless so Paula pushed him in the stroller to look in other shop windows as Lara and I continued to wait in the queue. She was posting her present to Frazer. Once inside, an assistant directed Lara to one cashier and me to another, then I bought more wrapping paper and bubble wrap. Pleased to be in the fresh air again, we took off our masks, and on the way home stopped off in the park so Arthur could have a run around.

That evening I wrapped the last of the presents that needed to be posted and the following day we went to the post office again. Because it was so close to Christmas now, delivery couldn't be guaranteed before Christmas, so I texted those affected and said their presents were on their way. Some of them had posted ours, while others said they'd wait until they could see us in person in the new year, thinking it wouldn't be too long.

On Wednesday, two days before Christmas, Paula, Lara and Arthur came with me in the car to help deliver presents to those who lived locally. It didn't really need all of us, but I hadn't got the OK from Claudette yet to leave Lara with Arthur unattended, and I still didn't feel completely comfortable giving Paula that responsibility. I'd texted each person in advance to say I was dropping off their present but wouldn't come in. Paula and Lara took it in turns to play postman, so as I pulled up outside the house one of them jumped out with the gift and placed it on the doorstep and rang the bell. Sometimes there was a gift waiting for us. If they came out we called 'Happy Christmas!' from the car and 'See you in the new year!' Then I drove to the next stop. Lara thought it was great fun.

'It's like being Santa Claus,' she told Arthur excitedly. Arthur was more interested in the snack she'd given him to keep him occupied.

We were out delivering presents around the area for over an hour. These were small gifts, nothing expensive, just a little something to people I'd known for years that said we were thinking of them at Christmas. The only presents left now were for my immediate family and we were planning to swap those outside on Christmas Day.

Thursday was Christmas Eve and that morning I checked on a couple of elderly neighbours to make sure they had everything they needed. One was still going to her son's for Christmas Day as planned. The other had made the decision not to take the risk and was staying at home, although her daughter was bringing her a cooked Christmas dinner.

'It's the first Christmas I've ever been alone,' she told me, and my heart went out to her.

'I would say you're welcome to come to us, but that would rather defeat the object,' I said.

'Yes. I'll be fine. I'll have a sherry and watch some television.' Which made my heart clench even more. Bless her.

'Call me if you need anything,' I said, and checked she had my telephone number. I and others who lived in the street had been keeping an eye on elderly neighbours since the start of the pandemic and especially during lockdown when we'd all been so isolated.

That afternoon I video-called Adrian and Kirsty, then Lucy and family. Emma was so excited. 'Father Christmas coming,' she said, over and over again.

'Yes, tomorrow. Are you going to hang up your Santa sack?'

'Father Christmas coming.'

'Yes, love. You'll have a great time.'

Her parents would take video clips to share with us.

Lara was very excited too, especially when I told her she could hang up a Santa sack. As well as her main presents, I'd bought some little things, as I had for Paula, to put in their sacks, which we traditionally hung on the front door before going to bed on Christmas Eve. Adrian and Lucy had continued this right up until they'd moved out, but don't tell their partners that!

Lara spent a lot of time on the phone to Frazer that day, even more than usual as he was fed up and bored with being alone in his room. Then, while Paula and I were in the kitchen putting the finishing touches to dinner, Lara took another call in the living room where she was with Arthur. We knew straight away from the rise in her voice that something had happened to someone.

'Oh no! ... Really? ... When?' she cried in indignation. 'I tried to tell her, but she wouldn't listen ... Really? He did! ... Where?'

And so it continued until dinner was ready. I told Lara and brought Arthur to the table.

'That was Courtney,' she said, eventually coming into the kitchen-diner where Paula, Arthur and I were already seated. 'Diesel attacked Shell and she's in hospital and no one can visit her because of the pandemic.'

'Dear me, how is she?' I asked, immediately concerned. 'Presumably her parents have spoken to a nurse?'

'There's only her mum, and the nurse told her Shell has got second-degree burns on her arm and she's been given very strong painkillers.'

'Burns? How did that happen?' I asked, horrified.

'Diesel threw boiling water over her because she wouldn't make him a cup of tea.'

Paula and I winced. We hadn't started eating yet but Arthur was hungry, so I popped a spoonful of dinner into his mouth.

Lara continued. 'Diesel and Shell were arguing. I don't know what about. It doesn't take much to set him off when he's in a mood. Then Shell filled the kettle to make herself a drink and Diesel told her to make him one too. She told him to make it himself and he grabbed the kettle and threw boiling water all over her. Shell must have really wound him up for Diesel to do that,' Lara finished.

I couldn't believe what I'd just heard. 'Lara, you're surely not suggesting it was Shell's fault? It doesn't matter how "wound up" Diesel was – he was to blame. He viciously attacked her. She could be scarred for life. And suppose a child had been in the room! Scalding water can kill an infant.'

Chastened, Lara sat down quietly.

Some years ago I did voluntary work in a refuge for those escaping domestic violence. I'd heard some victims there try to make excuses for their partner's appalling behaviour, including 'I seem to wind him up', 'I can't do anything right ...' and so forth. There is never any excuse for abuse, ever, and it is always the abuser's fault, not the victim's.

I gave Arthur another spoonful of dinner and then picked up my own knife and fork, although my appetite had largely gone. It was Christmas Eve and a young woman was in hospital after a vicious attack had left her with second-degree burns. Lara began to realize the wider implications.

'It could have been me,' she said, subdued.

'Or Arthur,' I added.

'I know.'

There was now little doubt in my mind that Diesel had been responsible for Arthur's injuries, but it would be impossible to prove.

'The police have arrested Diesel,' Lara said as she began feeding Arthur. 'Shell will have to make a statement when she is up to it. The nurse told her mum that she'll need to see a specialist from the burns unit.'

Of course, hearing all this dampened our festive spirits, but I did my best to rekindle them. After dinner Lara bathed Arthur, got him ready for bed, then took him downstairs to hang his Santa sack on the front door. The sack was bigger than him and Lara stood him inside it for some photos, which he found great fun. She took lots of pictures and I took some of the two of them hanging his sack on the front door, then putting out the Santa plate, which contained a sweet mince pie and milk for Santa, and carrots for his reindeer. By the time they'd finished we were in the Christmas mood again and Arthur was far from sleepy. It was after eight o'clock before Lara was able to leave him in his cot. But that's all part of the excitement of Christmas. Children all over the world lie awake on Christmas Eve.

Lara was happy that she could finally fill Arthur's sack with the presents she'd bought for him. Once full, she returned it to the front door for him to discover in the morning. She placed other presents for him under the Christmas tree and then said she was planning on having an early night. She looked at me expectantly and I knew why. She wanted to hang her Santa sack on the door. Smiling, I fetched hers and Paula's and then took photos of the two of them hanging up their sacks. Later, as I was arranging presents under the tree and generally getting ready for tomorrow, Lara came downstairs and said she'd received another text from Courtney. Shell was being allowed home that night but would have to go back to hospital in three days to have the dressing changed and the wound assessed. The whole of her arm was bandaged and she might need plastic surgery. I supposed the only consolation was that it could have been much worse.

Once I was sure Lara and Paula were asleep I filled their sacks and left them by the front door with Arthur's, then I took in the mince pie, carrot and milk, and went to bed. It was nearly midnight and I lay in bed gazing at the night sky through the parting in my bedroom curtains. It was a clear night where the ebony sky seemed deeper and darker than usual. Serene, as if nature was holding its breath ready to impart the glory and wonder of Christmas Day.

How long ago last Christmas seemed, I thought as I lay there, with all that had happened since. Back then the word 'pandemic' had been confined to movies, not part of real life. Now we were all familiar with this and other pandemic terms like 'contact tracing', 'lockdown', 'super-spreader', the 'R number', 'social distancing', 'isolating', 'quarantine', 'Zoom' and so on. The virus had created a strange and fearful dystopian existence, not just in my country but around the world, where intimacy was banned as we needed to treat others as potentially contagious and therefore a threat to our safety. I shuddered. Hopefully, now we had a vaccine, things would improve over the coming year. There was already talk of a 'new normal', whatever that meant.

Eventually I fell asleep thinking not of the coronavirus, but of my dear family, including my parents who, though no longer with us, were still held dear in our hearts and had made so many Christmases very special for us.

It seemed I had no sooner fallen asleep than I was awake. Not because of Arthur, but Lara. 'Father Christmas has been!' she cried excitedly as she thundered down the stairs.

I looked at my bedside clock. It was 6.50 a.m. Hauling myself out of bed, I threw on my dressing gown, went round the landing and downstairs. Lara was sitting on the bottom step completely absorbed in tearing the wrapping paper off the presents from her sack.

'Look what Father Christmas has brought me!' she cried joyously, and placed it with the others she'd already opened.

I joined her on the bottom stair.

Of course Lara knew it was me and not Father Christmas who'd filled her sack – at least, I hope she did! But she wasn't the first young person I'd fostered who'd embraced the fantasy and enchantment of Christmas, perhaps trying to make up for what they'd missed as children.

I sat with her as she finished unwrapping the presents, her face a picture of wonder, then she thanked me with a big hug and kissed my cheek.

'You're welcome, love. Merry Christmas,' I said, returning her hug.

'Shall we see if the mince pie and carrots have gone?' she asked eagerly.

We stood and Lara unlocked and opened the front door. 'The plate is empty!' she exclaimed, bringing it in to show me. 'Magic!'

We heard Arthur call 'Mama!' as he woke, and Lara didn't need to be told to go to him. She shot upstairs. 'Father Christmas has been!' she cried, going into his bedroom. I waited in the hall.

He looked a bit surprised at suddenly being plucked from his cot and whisked off downstairs with such enthusiasm. Lara often took a while to wake up properly, but not today.

'Father Christmas has been,' she told him again, and showed him the empty plate and then his Santa sack.

'Go into the living room to open his presents,' I suggested. 'It's more comfortable in there.'

Paula's bedroom door opened and, yawning, she came down in her dressing gown.

'Happy Christmas, love,' I said, and we hugged.

'And you, Mum.'

Paula took her sack from the front door while I went into the kitchen to let Sammy out for a run and make a drink for Arthur, which seemed to have been forgotten in all the excitement. I joined them in the living room where, to my surprise, was a Christmas stocking hanging from the mantelpiece for me.

'Thank you.'

With the Christmas decorations stirring in the warmth rising from the radiators, we sat together and unwrapped our Father Christmas presents. Lara videoed Arthur on her phone and I took some pictures on mine. She then collected her presents from where she'd left them in the hall and took Arthur upstairs to get ready while Paula and I cleared up all the wrapping paper. In the kitchen we made ourselves coffee and texted our family's WhatsApp group *Happy Christmas*. We'd have breakfast once we were dressed.

Upstairs I went into the bathroom to get ready, and before long I could hear Lara's excited whispers coming from the landing and Arthur running around. I wondered why she hadn't taken him downstairs to play with his toys if they were ready. When I came out I saw why. Arthur was dressed as a Christmas elf in a green, red and white suit with a matching bobble hat. And beside him, holding his hand, Lara was wearing a Mrs Claus outfit – a short, red velvety dress trimmed with white fur and matching hat.

'My! You both look wonderful,' I said, and Lara clapped her hands with delight.

I didn't know she'd bought them, and although they were extravagances she could ill afford, I certainly didn't say that.

Paula came out of her bedroom and admired Lara's and Arthur's costumes. She and I were wearing Christmas jumpers with glittering sequins, and leggings. Laughing, and in the Christmas mood, we went downstairs together where Lara took a selfie of us all by the tree. Traditionally in my house we open our Father Christmas – or rather Mummy Christmas – presents as soon as we wake, then those under the tree later when the rest of the family has arrived. As they weren't coming in this year, Paula suggested we open our tree presents after breakfast and Lara readily agreed. Frazer phoned and Lara disappeared off to take the call while I made breakfast and Paula looked after Arthur. We were at the table eating by the time Lara reappeared.

'Frazer said thank you for your present and card,' she said, joining us.

'I'm glad they arrived in time.'

'He hasn't sent me one,' she said, disappointed. 'I thought it had arrived and you'd put it away.'

'No, love. Frazer has been in quarantine so he couldn't go out to post it.'

'That's what he said, but I wondered if maybe he'd given it to someone else to post.'

'I think the whole house will be in quarantine,' I explained. I could see she was disheartened, and I hoped she hadn't given Frazer a hard time. 'Cheer up. It'll be something to look forward to after Christmas.'

'I guess.'

We kept our phones with us during breakfast and one or other of them was always bleeping with a *Happy Christmas* message from friends or family. Usually, phones were kept away from the table during mealtimes, but today was an exception. During lockdown our phones had become our lifelines and they now helped unite us on Christmas Day. A video of Emma opening her presents arrived on our WhatsApp group, and Lara heard from Frazer again. Shell and Courtney also messaged her. Shell sent a picture of her heavily bandaged arm as well as selfies of her in hospital, including one of her burnt arm before it was bandaged, which I declined to see.

After breakfast I put the turkey crown in the oven and Paula helped me prepare the vegetables for later. Usually, when all the family were expected for Christmas dinner, I did more preparation the night before, but as it was just us there wasn't that much to do. Nevertheless I intended to make a good Christmas for the four of us.

We opened our Christmas-tree presents, which included a box of chocolates from Lara to Paula and me, which was nice of her. We then played with some of Arthur's new toys – a magnetic fishing game, a musical puzzle and counting bricks. Before long he grew tired of sitting in one place and ran off. Lara chased after him and it quickly developed into Lara's favourite game of hide and seek, which Paula and I joined in with. Lara enjoyed it as much as, if not more than, Arthur. We played other games, won prizes off the tree, pulled crackers and ate our Christmas dinner with all the trimmings. Soon after, Arthur obligingly fell asleep on the sofa and Lara carried him upstairs and put him in his cot so we had the chance to get out a board game. Lara chose Monopoly.

As we played Lucy texted to say they'd just left Adrian's and were on their way to visit us. Arthur woke and Lara changed his nappy and brought him down. Five minutes later Lucy and family arrived; it was shortly after three o'clock. We put on our coats and went out the front into the cold fresh air, where we'd been told the risk of transmitting the virus was greatly reduced. Emma began chasing Arthur around the front garden. The gate was closed so it was safe. I fetched Lucy's, Darren's and Emma's Christmas presents and they gave us ours, which we would open later indoors in the comfort and warmth of our homes. I made us hot chocolate and warmed some homemade mince pies, which were Lucy's favourite, and we had them outside. I had included a box of mince pies for them to take home with their presents. They stayed for nearly an hour and then we stood on the pavement and waved them off. Another family further down the road was entertaining in their front garden too.

Adrian and Kirsty arrived half an hour later. Once again, we donned our coats and went into the front garden where I introduced them all. It was dark by then and Christmas lights from the houses shone out. The multi-coloured fairy lights I'd draped across our porch and the bay window of the front room looked magical, helping to create a really festive scene. A waxing moon rested lightly on a sea of slow-moving cloud in an otherwise clear, dark sky. The family further down the road was still partying in their front garden; indeed, their festivities had grown to include neighbours. We swapped presents with Adrian and Kirsty, then he produced a flask of mulled wine. I fetched glasses and warmed some more mince pies. We stood in the front garden and toasted each other with 'Merry Christmas and a Happy New Year', then later we waved them off.

Yes, it was a very different Christmas as our prime minister had warned us, but I felt we'd made the most of it.

CHAPTER SEVENTEEN

A BRIGHTER NEW YEAR?

Arthur didn't go to bed until nearly ten o'clock on Christmas Day, then Lara, Paula and I stayed up playing board games until 1 a.m. We all had a lie-in the following morning, Boxing Day, 26 December. It's traditionally when a lot of families go for a walk, having not been out the day before and being in need of some exercise after all the eating. Arthur certainly needed to use up some energy. As we were all getting washed and dressed I could hear him running around the landing.

'Lara, you need to watch him!' I called.

'Can you see to him?' she replied from her bedroom.

'I can, but Claudette wants you to,' I reminded her.

Yesterday had been different and we'd all entertained Arthur, but today we needed to get back on track. Giving Lara full responsibility for Arthur in the house was supposed to be paving the way for her taking him out alone.

Lara carried him into her bedroom and closed the door. A few minutes later I heard her telling him off for taking her mascara. I tried to think back to how I'd managed as a single parent with a young child. My husband had left us when my children had been very young.

I knocked on Lara's bedroom door and when she said, 'Yes?' I looked in. 'Has Arthur got some of his new toys in there to amuse him?' I asked.

'No. They're all downstairs.'

I popped downstairs and brought up some of his Christmas presents, including an activity centre, motorized ambulance, police car and books. 'He can play with these while you finish getting ready,' I suggested. 'Put them on the floor, not on the bed, so he can't fall off,' I reminded her.

She then had enough time to finish getting ready without any further mishaps.

I made breakfast for us all – Lara could make Arthur his lunch. As we ate, Lara received a text message from Frazer saying he wasn't feeling well and was staying in bed, waiting for the result of a Covid test.

'He was fine when I spoke to him yesterday,' Lara said, rather unsympathetically. She tried to phone him, but he didn't answer.

'He probably doesn't feel like talking if he's not well,' I said.

'He's not ill. He just had too much to drink last night,' she replied.

'Oh.'

'Well, there was nothing else for him to do.'

As it turned out Lara was right. Later we learnt that Frazer's Covid test was negative, and he was suffering from a hangover. Lara said he didn't usually drink much alcohol, so it had affected him. However, another resident in their hotel-cum-hostel had tested positive for

Covid. They were all tested regularly. I also heard from a friend that day who had contracted Covid just before Christmas and the whole family was ill. As in the first wave of the pandemic, it felt as if the virus was everywhere and closing in on us. I don't think I've ever felt so unsafe in my life.

Our walk that morning was just what we needed. It was another cold but bright day, and we went through the park and into open countryside. Arthur walked some of the way and was then happy to ride in his stroller. We were out for over two hours and once home we had lunch, mainly yesterday's leftovers – cold meat, nut roast, vegetables and pickles. Lara saw to Arthur's as I prepared ours.

In the afternoon Lara wanted to play more games as we had done on Christmas Day. However, there were no more prizes on the tree to be won so we used the chocolate novelties and candy canes instead. We had fun, but it was a pity the rest of my family weren't able to join us. Later, we sat down and watched a Christmas film together. Arthur was tired by now and nodded off for a while on the sofa beside his mother. Shell and Courtney texted Lara. Lara said ruefully that normally they'd be planning their New Year, but there'd be no clubbing or partying this year. Everything was closed due to the pandemic and the government was telling us to stay at home. Easing the restrictions in some areas had only been for Christmas Day, and an update on future measures was expected on 30 December.

Monday, 28 December, was the first day back at work for many and Claudette phoned Lara. She asked about her Christmas and told her that when we had our next online meeting, which was on Friday, 8 January, part of it would be observation, which set Lara into a spin. I explained to her that in normal circumstances Claudette would have been visiting us in person regularly and part of each meeting would have been her observing Lara and Arthur. It was necessary as, at present, Claudette just had mine and Lara's views on her progress, so she would need to see Lara's parenting skills for herself.

'Or lack of them,' Lara quipped.

'Have confidence in yourself,' I said. 'You're doing fine. Just remember to talk to Arthur when you play with him and don't leave him unattended.'

'I won't.'

Usually my supervising social worker, Joy, and other professionals connected with a case would have been visiting us, so Lara was getting off lightly. Even so, I could understand why she was anxious.

Claudette had also told Lara that at the next meeting they'd discuss her taking Arthur out alone for short periods, which was positive. Lara had a tendency to fixate on the negative rather than the positive.

Joy phoned me that afternoon and asked about our Christmas and how we all were. I asked after her brother. She said he was still in hospital but making progress. They'd spoken to him a few times on the phone, and he was expecting to be moved to another hospital soon, which offered intensive rehabilitation. She arranged an online meeting with us for Monday, 11 January. Lara groaned when I told her.

Frazer phoned Lara regularly during the day. Now over his hangover, he was bored and looking forward to when he could go out again and give Lara her Christmas present.

'What did Jenny send him?' I asked out of interest.

'A big box of presents including food, clothes and a shopping voucher. Do you want to see a picture?'

'Yes, please.'

Lara flicked through the photos on her phone to the ones Frazer had sent on Christmas Day. Jenny had clearly gone to a lot of trouble. There was a photo of a large festively wrapped box and then one with the lid off. It was packed full of individually wrapped gifts. The next picture showed the presents unwrapped and laid out on Frazer's bed: a Christmas cake, festive biscuits, two jumpers, two T-shirts, socks, pyjamas, dressing gown, a deodorant gift set and a £50 voucher for an online retailer.

'That's very generous of her,' I said.

'She can afford it,' Lara replied curtly.

This sort of comment didn't sit well with me.

'That's not the point, love,' I said. 'Jenny went to a lot of trouble when she didn't have to. It was nice of her.'

'Guilty conscience,' Lara said tartly. 'To make up for what happened.'

'Even so, it was nice of her.'

'If you say so.'

I let it go, but I felt it was a pity that Lara's resentment stopped her from seeing a good act when there was one. I appreciated that both she and Frazer had been let down and hadn't received the stable, loving childhood they deserved, but at some point she needed to let go of past injustices, otherwise it could blight her happiness in the future. I had the feeling that Frazer was more easy-going and ready to forgive than Lara.

* * *

The afternoon of 30 December saw us in the living room gathered around the television again for our prime minister's address to the nation. There'd been a lot of speculation about the changes he would make, but he began positively.

'I want to begin with the good news,' he said in his upbeat, affable way. 'The approval of the Oxford/AstraZeneca vaccine is a fantastic achievement and will allow us to vaccinate more people, more quickly ... On the downside, there is a new strain of the virus, which is spreading much faster and surging across the country ... [there has been a] 40-per-cent increase in cases in England in the last week alone, almost 15 per cent more patients in hospital – more than at the peak of the first wave. And yesterday, sadly, we recorded almost a thousand deaths across the UK, for the first time since April.' He paused and the tension built. Even little Arthur was quiet, seeming to sense the importance of what we were about to hear.

'At this critical moment, with the prospect of freedom within reach, we've got to redouble our efforts to contain the virus. More areas of England will be moving into Tier 4. No one regrets these measures more bitterly than I do. But we must take firm action now and that's why we have to think very hard about schools. In most of England, primary schools will still reassemble next week, as planned for the new term. But, in the areas we have just published today, I am afraid the start of the new term will be delayed until at least 18 January ...' There was then information about key workers' children and those considered vulnerable being exempt from this delayed start to the term, testing in secondary schools, and universities being asked to reduce the number of students returning to campus in January.

'All of these measures', our PM continued, 'are designed to save lives and to protect the NHS. For that very reason I must ask you to follow the rules and see in New Year safely at home. That means not meeting up with friends or family indoors, unless they are in the same household or support bubble, and avoiding large gatherings of any kind. We are still in the tunnel of this pandemic – the light is visible; the tunnel has been shortened and we are moving faster through it. So for now let's double our efforts, let's follow the rules, protect our NHS and together make 2021 the year we leave this tunnel behind us.' He stopped and a map of the country showing the new updated tier system came on screen as one of his advisors spoke.

'Where are we now?' Lara asked, sitting forward in her seat and breaking our silence.

'Tier 4,' I said. 'Like most of the country, which is pretty much the same as lockdown.'

'But I can still meet Frazer outside like I did before?'

'Yes, if you must, although no close contact. The virus has taken hold again and this is the second wave,' I said gloomily.

But Lara had only heard the part about being able to see Frazer and had shot from the room to phone him, leaving Paula and me to look after Arthur as we watched the rest of the broadcast. It was depressing. We had taken a big step back in our fight against coronavirus. I knew that Kirsty, a primary school teacher, would be teaching online again from home for at least a few weeks. Adrian, like many office workers, hadn't gone back to the office yet and would continue to work from home for the foreseeable future. The nursery where Lucy and Darren worked would be open for key workers and those who couldn't work from home, so they would be part-time.

Lara reappeared. 'You know tomorrow is New Year's Eve,' she said, phone in hand.

'Yes.'

'Can you babysit so I can see Frazer? He's out of isolation now and wants to give me his Christmas present.'

I would have preferred Lara to stay in, for there was no guarantee she was going to avoid close contact with Frazer, which ran the risk of her contracting the virus. But she was allowed to go out and meet another person, just as we all were.

'Yes, I'll babysit, but make it during the day, rather than the evening.'

'Why?'

'I think it's safer, and our prime minister has just told us to stay at home on New Year's Eve.' There was already talk on social media about large gatherings and partying taking place outside. Understandable, to some extent, as young people in particular were missing their freedom, but it was against the law. I didn't want Lara getting caught up in any trouble.

'How long can I stay out for?' she asked.

'Well, considering all cafés, bars and entertainment venues will be closed and it's the middle of winter, I suggest two hours.'

'Can we make it three?'

'All right, but during the day,' I emphasized.

She disappeared off again to phone Frazer. I gave her fifteen minutes and then called up to her bedroom that she needed to come down and look after Arthur.

'Yes, sure, sorry,' she said amicably, immediately appearing. 'Frazer said thanks for babysitting.'

'OK. Just be careful.'

The rest of the evening followed its usual pattern, with dinner, a bedtime story for Arthur, a bath and then Lara settling him in his cot.

The news that night was dominated by the spread of the virus and the increased threat of the new variant, not just in the UK but around the world. Although we'd been warned about the possibility of a second wave, most of us had thought if it did happen it wouldn't be as bad as the first. Now it seemed it was going to be worse and all we could do was to follow the rules to try to keep safe and wait for our turn to be vaccinated. Key workers, the elderly and the clinically vulnerable were being vaccinated first. At this time two doses were required for full immunity, but as there wasn't an infinite supply it had been decided to lengthen the gap between the first and second dose so that more people could receive one dose and thereby some protection. It made sense. It was likely that my age group would receive their first dose sometime in February. My children, that much younger, would be later in the year.

Paula and I watched a film that evening, while Lara spent most of the time in her bedroom, talking on her phone. When she appeared for a drink and a snack I took the opportunity to ask if her phone package was covering the cost of all her calls.

'Yes, I use the Wi-Fi in the house,' she said. Which meant it didn't come out of her call allowance.

'And you're still repaying your credit card at five pounds a week?' I checked.

'Yes.'

'Good. If you can repay a bit more then do so.'

'I can't.'

The following morning Lara, Paula and I took Arthur to the park for a while, then returned home for lunch. Lara had arranged to meet Frazer at three o'clock so Paula and I would give Arthur his evening meal and Lara would be home in time to put him to bed. Arthur was getting very attached to Paula and me, even sometimes calling us Mama, so the more Lara did for him the better.

She came back on time, freezing cold but happy at having seen Frazer and finally receiving his present – a framed photo of him, matching the one he had of her. As she showed us I smelt alcohol on her breath. I admired the photo and then asked lightly, 'How did you manage to buy a drink? I thought all non-essential shops were closed.'

'From the supermarket. They're still open,' she said easily. 'Don't worry, we didn't have much.'

'All right, love. I believe you.' She could have a drink on New Year's Eve if she wanted to. Most of us would.

She bathed Arthur and put him in bed. Once he was settled we got the Monopoly board out again, and like many other families that night we entertained ourselves at home as the new year approached. Just before midnight I fetched my tablet and logged in to my family's video call. To my surprise and delight Emma was still up to see in the new year. Lara's phone buzzed and it was Frazer video-calling her. So with us all online we counted down to midnight together. A few fireworks could be heard in the distance, but they were nothing compared to the normal celebrations. Having wished each other a Happy New Year we said goodnight, finished our game and went to bed, hoping for a brighter year to follow.

CHAPTER EIGHTEEN

AN OPPORTUNITY

January got off to a reasonable start. The news that morning showed that although some New Year parties had been broken up by the police, generally peopled had heeded the warning and stayed at home. Arthur was awake and raring to go at his usual time, so after breakfast Lara and I took him to the park, leaving Paula at home to have a lie-in.

I was standing by the roundabout as Lara turned it, making him chuckle, when I heard my name being called. I looked over and saw an old friend, Donna, coming along the path that ran beside the play area. I hadn't seen her since before the pandemic.

'Happy New Year! How are you?' she asked, warm and friendly, but keeping her distance as we were supposed to.

'All right, considering,' I said. 'Happy New Year.' I introduced her to Lara who had just enough time to say hi before Arthur wanted to be off the roundabout and play on something else.

'Still fostering then?' Donna asked me, with a smile.

'Yes. How are you all?'

She rolled her eyes. 'Busy. I've got my daughter, husband and their two children living with us until their house is finished. It's way behind schedule. They've been with us for six months already. Bruce is renovating their property in the evenings and weekends, and it should have been finished months ago.'

Bruce was her husband and ran a small building firm. Keeping an eye on Lara and Arthur as we talked, I now learnt that Donna's daughter and husband had bought an old house that needed a lot of work – the only one within their budget. Bruce was doing it up for them in his spare time, but it was taking a lot longer than anticipated due to the pandemic and also lack of skilled labour. He'd had two men working for him full-time, but one had left the country at short notice, in effect halving his work force. 'He's thinking of taking on an apprentice as he can't find anyone with experience,' Donna said. 'But of course they'll need training.' She sighed.

I sympathized. I knew how hard Bruce worked. I then asked how her son was and she asked after my family. We had a good chat as Lara played with Arthur. Eventually, Donna said, 'Oh well, I'd better be going. I need to buy some more milk so everyone can have coffee.' The path she'd taken offered a short cut from where she lived to the High Street.

'Once the restrictions are lifted we must get together,' I said.

'Yes, I'd like that. I'm sure I've still got your number – let me check.'

We both checked our phones and confirmed we had each other's current number. She said goodbye and was about to leave when I had an idea.

'Donna, what sort of person is your husband looking for as an apprentice?'

'Reliable, hardworking – he'll train them. Why? Do you know someone?'

I hesitated and glanced over at Lara who was on the far side of the play area. 'Lara has a boyfriend who is unemployed. I barely know him, although I fostered him for a short while years ago. A long story, but he's had a rough ride and is living in a homeless hostel. I really don't know how reliable or hardworking he is, just that he says he wants to work in building. He could do with a break.' Even as I said it I had doubts and felt asking was an imposition.

'I don't know,' Donna said, with a small shrug. 'Bruce may have already found someone, but I'll mention it to him.'

'Thank you.' We said goodbye and I returned to Lara, feeling embarrassed that I'd had the cheek to mention it and perhaps placed Donna in an awkward position. But then again, all she needed to do was text and say Bruce had found someone or just forget it and not text at all. It wouldn't affect our friendship.

Once Arthur had grown bored with the park, we returned home where the rest of the day disappeared pretty much as usual in keeping him amused, and feeding and changing him.

'When do they start using the toilet?' Lara asked, after changing another smelly nappy.

'Around the age of two, but children vary,' I replied.

'Gross.' She pulled a face and went off to put the nappy bag into the bin outside, which was progress in itself as she had been leaving them in the wastepaper basket in Arthur's bedroom until the smell had drifted downstairs.

* * *

Contrary to what I'd thought, Donna did text me that evening: *Hi Cathy, lovely to see you. Bruce says hi. I told him about your young lady's boyfriend and he said he can phone him for a chat. Not sure if you have Bruce's number so here it is – 07*** ******. Donna x*

My heart leapt with hope. Perhaps it wouldn't come to anything, but a chat with Bruce and any advice he could give Frazer would be invaluable. Bruce knew the building trade inside out.

I replied straight away: *Thank you so much. I'll tell him. He's called Frazer x*

Lara had finished putting Arthur to bed and was now in her bedroom relaxing. I already had Frazer's mobile number from when I'd spoken to him about contacting his mother, but I felt I should let Lara know what was going on. I went upstairs, lightly knocked on her bedroom door and, when she called, 'Come in,' opened it. She was sprawled on her bed listening to music on her phone. I could hear it leaking out from the earbuds. She removed one.

'I'm going to phone Frazer,' I said. She immediately removed the other and sat upright.

'Why?'

'You know that lady I was talking to in the park earlier – Donna?' She nodded. 'Her husband is a builder and he has offered to have a chat with Frazer about finding work. He has a vacancy so I'm going to call Frazer now.'

'I'll tell him,' Lara said, and replaced one earbud.

'I'll phone him as well. I just thought I'd let you know.'

'He probably won't answer.'

'Then I'll leave a message.'

Lara didn't seem to like me being in direct contact with Frazer. She shrugged and, returning the other earbud to her ear, continued listening to music. I hoped Frazer would show a bit more enthusiasm.

From habit, I checked on Arthur while I was upstairs. He was curled on his side, sound asleep. I came out of his room and continued downstairs where I sat in the living room and pressed for Frazer's number. He answered.

'It's Cathy, how are you?' I asked.

'OK.'

'Happy New Year. Are you free to talk?'

'Yes.'

'Frazer, this may come to nothing, but earlier today I was in the park with Lara and Arthur, and I met an old friend whose husband is a builder. He has a vacancy and is thinking about taking on a trainee. I mentioned you were looking for work and he said you could phone him for a chat.'

'What would I be doing?'

'I don't know, and the job's not yours, but it's worth speaking to him.'

'I guess.'

'You don't sound very enthusiastic.'

Frazer sighed. 'Nothing will come of it. I don't get breaks like this. It will be a waste of time.'

'It will if you have that attitude,' I said, perhaps a bit too sharply. 'Look, Bruce has offered to speak to you, which is positive. He needn't have done that. He's a very busy man. He might not offer you the job, but he is a nice guy with a lot of experience. He built his business up from scratch and knows the building trade well. I'm sure he can give you some advice, if nothing else.'

'I'll phone,' Frazer said, with no more keenness.

'But if you really aren't interested, I'll thank Bruce for his offer and leave it at that.'

'I've said I'll phone,' Frazer said. 'But don't expect me to be offered the job.'

'Just do your best. Good luck.'

As the call ended I felt deflated. I appreciated that life experience had taught young people like Lara and Frazer not to expect much, but that could blind them to opportunity. I cringed as I imagined Bruce receiving Frazer's call – if, in fact, he did phone – and hearing his despondent voice and apathy, compared to someone who was confident and could put themselves forward and showcase their talents. Someone whose upbringing had taught them self-worth and that good things could be theirs as much as anyone else's and they could achieve what they wanted. It was a sad indictment of Frazer's life that he was setting himself up for failure, but there was nothing more I could do other than hope that when he'd had a chance to think about it he'd share my enthusiasm.

The weekend passed much the same as most other days for those of us in Tier 4. We went out for a walk and kept in touch with family and friends by phone and online. On Sunday we took down the Christmas decorations, which made the house seem very bare.

On Monday Lara heard from Shell that the doctor had said her arm was healing, although she may need some reconstructive surgery later to help with the scarring. This seemed to emphasize just how bad the burn was. Shell had also told Lara that Diesel was being prosecuted for grievous bodily harm.

'Do you think I should tell Claudette?' Lara asked.

'Yes.'

Also on Monday our prime minister addressed the nation again and sombrely announced that due to a huge increase in Covid cases and the faster-spreading variant, we were going into another lockdown starting the following day. For those of us already in Tier 4 there wasn't much practical difference. Non-essential shops would close, and we should stay at home apart from the permitted exceptions. Other countries were in the same position and grappling with how best to protect their citizens. Borders were closed and all but essential travel had been banned. We rarely saw a plane in the sky now and were told the air was much cleaner, so I suppose every cloud has a silver lining, as the saying goes.

Despite Frazer promising to phone Bruce, he didn't. On Wednesday I received a text from Donna: *Is Frazer going to call Bruce? If so he needs to ASAP as there is someone else interested in the position.*

I was annoyed and felt I'd been wasting Donna's and Bruce's time. I texted back: *Sorry. I'll speak to him now.*

I didn't tell Lara I was contacting Frazer this time; I just shut myself in the front room and phoned him. It took a while for him to answer and when he did he sounded groggy, as though he had just woken, despite it being nearly midday.

'It's Cathy. Bruce's wife has texted me. I understand you haven't phoned Bruce.'

I heard him groan. 'I will,' he said, with no real commitment.

'It'll be too late soon. There is someone else interested in the position.'

Silence.

'Frazer, if you're interested, you need to call Bruce straight away.'

'OK,' he said lethargically.

'What's the matter? Have you gone off the idea of a career in building?'

'It's not that.'

'What is it then?'

More silence.

'Frazer, you've been telling Lara you love her and that you want a life together where you will support her and Arthur. You need a job to do that, and this is a good opportunity. The fact that Donna has bothered to contact me shows you're in with a chance.'

He didn't answer and I felt I'd said all I could. 'It's up to you, love, but either way, please phone or text Bruce and thank him for his trouble. It's polite.'

I don't know if what I said helped, but two hours later Lara told me Frazer had arranged to meet Bruce tomorrow on-site for a day's trial. I was ecstatic. Despite the restrictions, builders and other tradespeople could still work, following government guidelines.

'Wonderful!' I said. 'Tell him to make sure he arrives punctually – better to be early than late. And to show willing and ask if he's not sure about anything.'

'He knows that,' Lara said.

I texted Bruce: *Thank you so much for giving Frazer a chance. I am grateful.*

He replied: *You're welcome, Cathy. No promises. We'll see how it goes.*

I stopped myself from phoning Frazer and giving him all the advice I'd given my children when they'd gone for their first interview, for that's what this day's trial was. I thought Frazer would resent it. Instead, I just texted: *Good luck for tomorrow. Well done. I'm proud of you.* I knew how much courage it had taken for Frazer to call Bruce.

Arthur was fifteen months old now and into everything. Despite the experiences of his first year, he appeared a healthy, happy child who Paula and I had grown very close to. Of course we'd known right from the start that the aim of this placement was to give Lara the chance to develop the skills to successfully parent Arthur, so therefore at some point he would leave. But that didn't stop us from loving Arthur while helping Lara to keep him. It's one of the conundrums of fostering, and as a carer you have to get used to the revolving door of forming relationships and then having to say goodbye.

I had no doubt that Lara loved Arthur, although she was still finding some aspects of parenting him challenging – or 'boring', to use her term. Of course, there's a lot of routine in raising a child, especially a very young child. Most of the day is taken up with providing the basics of food, warmth, safety and so forth, and arranging stimulating play, which is good for their development but not necessarily for yours. However, it was as important as providing the basics, and giving the child stimulation was on my checklist of points to observe and comment on. Lara still had a habit of sitting Arthur in the middle of the living-room floor, surrounding him with toys, and then expecting him to amuse himself for hours while she got on with something else – namely checking her phone or watching daytime television. The average attention span of a child Arthur's age is two minutes and the time they can reasonably be expected to amuse themselves is ten to fifteen minutes maximum. I'd explained this to Lara.

'So you need to change his toys regularly and play with him,' I said. 'It will be more fun for him if you get involved.'

'But it's boring,' she said, as she had before.

Left to himself, Arthur soon got into trouble.

'Leave it!' Lara would cry, while trying to concentrate on her phone or the television. 'Come away now! Arthur! Now! Did you hear me?'

And so it would go on.

Paula and I still played with Arthur a lot, even though Lara was supposed to have full responsibility for him in the house now. I also felt Lara should be kissing and cuddling him more, showing him more warmth and affection. She did sometimes but not often, and at other times he appeared to be an irritation to her as she quickly grew frustrated with him. I appreciated she hadn't had a good, solid parenting role model herself, and this would be taken into account in Claudette's assessment. I discussed this with Lara as well as noting it in my daily log. She always said she would play with him more, which she did for about five minutes and then grew bored.

Lara spent most of Wednesday evening phoning Frazer until he told her he needed to have a shower and an early night as he had to be on-site with Bruce by 8 a.m. the following morning and it was two bus rides away.

'Rather him than me,' Lara said as she told me. 'It's freezing out there!'

'Builders work in all weathers,' I said. 'Frazer knows to wear plenty of layers and a waterproof jacket?' I checked.

'Of course,' Lara said, as if I was talking drivel.

But Frazer didn't, and the following day he had to be sent home.

CHAPTER NINETEEN

MISSING

When I saw Bruce's number flash up on my phone I guessed straight away something was wrong.

'Hello,' I said, my heart in my mouth.

'Cathy. I thought you should know, I've had to send Frazer home.'

'Oh no. Why?'

'It was either that or he developed frostbite,' Bruce said with a touch of humour in his voice. 'I'm afraid Frazer arrived dressed inadequately for the weather, and quickly turned blue with cold. I tried putting him in my van with the heater on, but his teeth wouldn't stop chattering.'

'Oh, I am sorry, Bruce,' I said. 'What on earth was he wearing?'

'Jeans and a jumper. He said he didn't want to get his coat dirty, so he left that at the hotel.'

'How silly. I am so sorry,' I said again, assuming Frazer had blown his chance of working for Bruce. But his tone as he spoke remained calm and stoical.

'Don't you worry. He didn't know. I've seen plenty of daft things in my time. Frazer's a nice enough lad. He was here early waiting for us and was cold by then. I've given him safety boots, but he'll need some more suitable clothing. I've told him what to get. I guessed he hasn't got much money, so I said if he buys what he needs over the weekend and brings me the receipt on Monday I'll reimburse him and give him another try.'

'Bruce, that's so kind of you,' I said, and my eyes filled. 'I don't know what to say. Thank you.'

'No need to thank me. The boy needs a break. If he does what I've told him and comes back on Monday, I'll make it a month's trial. He'll be paid, and if I like what I see I'll sign him up for an apprenticeship where he'll get time off for college.'

'Thank you,' I said again. A lump rose in my throat. 'I am grateful.'

'It's up to him now, Cathy.'

'Yes, indeed.'

Bruce's kindness moved me deeply. He'd gone that extra mile to give a young person a much-needed break when he hadn't needed to. Bless him, I thought. Acts of kindness like this restored my faith in human nature amid all the unhappiness I saw as a foster carer.

By the time Lara told me what had happened later that day, the story had been tweaked slightly. I'm not sure if it was by Frazer, wanting to save face, or Lara not wanting to admit I might have been right in checking Frazer knew what to wear.

'Frazer only had to work half a day and Bruce has given him the job,' Lara announced with aplomb.

'Yes, for a month's trial, I believe, which was nice of Bruce,' I said.

'How do you know?' she asked suspiciously.

'Bruce phoned me.'

'Oh.' She rolled her eyes and back-pedalled. 'But it's good Bruce wants him back, isn't it? I mean, he must have done well.'

'It's very good of Bruce to give Frazer another chance,' I said. 'He knows what to wear this time?'

She nodded. 'He just didn't want to ruin his jacket.'

'I know, love.'

I found Frazer's wish to protect his clothes at his own expense as sad as it was naive. But young adults can make silly mistakes, as they don't always have the same judgement skills an older adult with years of experience has. Thank goodness Bruce appreciated that.

The following morning Lara, Arthur and I sat in the living room ready for Claudette's virtual visit. I was using my tablet so I could move it around if necessary as some of the meeting would be Claudette observing Lara with Arthur. Claudette greeted us with a warm hello and then said she would do the observation first before Arthur grew restless. 'Just carry on as if I'm not here,' she told Lara.

I angled the tablet so Claudette could see Arthur. He'd just left the toys Lara had arranged in the centre of the room and gone to the patio window where he had his face pressed against the glass – a favourite pastime of his. I nodded to Lara to go to him. She was still sitting on the sofa beside me, but Claudette would expect to see her interacting with Arthur and meeting his needs.

Lara went over but then stood in awkward, self-conscious silence, apparently not knowing what to do or say.

'What do you think he can see through the window?' I prompted, expecting Lara to engage with Arthur and talk to him about what they could see, but she didn't.

'I've no idea,' she replied. 'There's nothing much out there.' Although there would be for Arthur as his world was full of new and exciting things.

'Can he see a bird?' I suggested, hoping Lara would run with it. 'Is the robin in the garden again?' I tried.

'No,' Lara replied,

Arthur began licking the glass, which made Lara laugh. Then, tired of that, he left the window and clambered onto the nearest armchair.

'Is he allowed to do that?' Lara asked Claudette.

'You tell me,' she replied.

Lara knew we discouraged Arthur from climbing on the furniture, both for his safety and the sake of the furniture. Perhaps she didn't like to take him away and risk a tantrum with Claudette watching, so she just stood there.

'He's not really allowed on there,' I said eventually.

'Get off!' Lara cried, with more firmness than necessary.

Arthur didn't get off and with a cheeky grin began jumping up and down on the chair, which was even more dangerous. If it had been my decision, I would have lifted him off by now.

'He never does what I say,' Lara told Claudette, as Arthur bounced precariously.

I knew this wasn't going well. Lara was nervous and Arthur seemed to be playing to the audience. He stopped jumping and then, giggling, tried to dive head-first over the chair back. Lara finally picked him up. He struggled and made a fuss. I nodded to the toy boxes. She carried him to the toys and then sat on the floor playing with him. I breathed a sigh of relief.

'Good boy,' I said, for Lara wasn't giving him any encouragement.

'Good boy,' Lara repeated.

But it wasn't long before Arthur returned to the window. 'Cat,' he said clearly, pointing.

'Well done,' I said, when Lara didn't.

'Well done,' Lara repeated. I hoped Claudette was making allowances for Lara's nervousness.

'Not Sammy, but another cat,' I prompted, and Lara nodded.

Arthur began sucking his fingers – a sign he was thirsty. He usually had a drink and a snack mid-morning.

'I think he may want a drink,' I said.

Lara headed for the living-room door.

'I'll follow with the tablet,' I said.

'Thank you,' Claudette said. I was used to these virtual visits now.

'Bring Arthur with us,' I quietly told Lara, for she'd been about to leave him unattended in the living room.

'Safety gate,' I whispered to her as Arthur followed Lara into the kitchen. She seemed to have forgotten everything.

Eventually Arthur was in his highchair at the table enjoying a drink and a healthy snack of fruit.

'Thank you,' Claudette said. 'That's fine. I've seen enough. Let's talk while Arthur is occupied. How is it going?'

'Frazer's got a job,' Lara said. I would rather she had begun by talking about Arthur's progress.

'So you're still managing to keep your relationship going despite all the restrictions?' Claudette asked.

'Yes. But we're not breaking the rules,' Lara replied.

Claudette nodded. I propped the tablet on the table so Claudette could see us and we her.

'And Diesel is going to be done for GBH because he threw that boiling water over Shell and she's scarred for life,' Lara continued, her voice rising. Now she was no longer being observed her usual flamboyance had returned.

'Shell?' Claudette queried.

'Yes, you know, my friend. I told you all about her when you phoned me after Christmas.'

'Yes, I remember. You're not seeing Diesel, are you?'

'No, of course not. I've got Frazer now.'

'And how have you been managing since taking full responsibility for Arthur in the house?' Claudette asked. So far this had all been about what was going on in Lara's life.

'Good,' Lara replied.

'No accidents or injuries?'

'No. So can I take Arthur out by myself like you said?' Lara asked.

'I believe I said we'd review it at this meeting. What does Cathy think? I've read your reports, thank you,' she said to me.

While I'd expressed some concerns, I knew that for Lara to stand any chance of Arthur returning to her we'd have to take this next step.

'I think for short periods first,' I said.

'Yes, I agree,' Claudette replied. 'Perhaps you could go out of the house and do some shopping or something to

begin with while Lara looks after Arthur,' she suggested
to me. 'Then build up to Lara taking him out by herself.
How does that sound, Lara?'

'OK, I guess.'

'I'll leave the exact timescale for the two of you
to arrange. Then we'll review at our meeting next
Friday.'

'Will I still be able to leave here at the end of February?'
Lara asked, making it sound like a prison sentence.

'The placement was for a minimum of four months,'
Claudette reminded her. 'And we may struggle to move
you then.'

'Why?' Lara asked, or rather demanded.

'Apart from completing your assessment, we need to
find you somewhere to live. Everything is taking longer
than usual at present.'

Lara didn't hide her disappointment and groaned.

'I'm not saying it won't happen, just that you need to
be prepared for staying longer,' Claudette said. 'Arthur
looks happy enough.'

'He is,' I said. 'He's doing very well. So is Lara.' I threw
her a smile.

'Good. Any questions?' Claudette asked.

'I don't think so,' I said.

Lara shook her head. But as soon as we'd said goodbye
and logged off, Lara had a question for me. 'When are
you going out like Claudette said?'

I needed a couple of items from the High Street, and
normally Lara and Arthur would come too and we'd stop
off at the park on the way back.

'Don't you need anything from the shops?' I asked.

'No. You can go and I'll stay here.'

Half an hour later I was on my way to the High Street, having left Lara at home with Arthur, and Paula in her bedroom. I'd told Paula what was happening, and I knew she'd listen out for them in case Lara needed help. It was the simple things that bothered me the most – things that could easily be overlooked, like closing the stairgates, putting Arthur in his cot if Lara needed to use the toilet, making sure he didn't put things in his mouth that were choking hazards and so forth. In theory, Lara had had full responsibility for Arthur in the house from before Christmas, but I'd always been there ready to remind her and help out if necessary so he was kept safe. On a personal level it felt strange being out alone – it was the first time since they'd arrived that I didn't have Arthur with me.

I hurried to the High Street, bought what I needed and, resisting the temptation to stop and talk to those I knew, went home. All was well, more or less. Lara was in the living room, sprawled on the sofa watching television. To keep Arthur quiet, she'd given him a bag of children's mini-biscuits. There were crumbs everywhere, and he had congealed biscuit around his face and squashed into both hands. Usually he had these snacks in his highchair at the table, unless we were out.

'I'll clear up when he's finished,' Lara said, brushing off some crumbs that had fallen on her.

'All right. You know where the hoover is.' I went into the kitchen to make myself a coffee.

I had to remind Lara twice to clear up the mess and eventually she did.

The following day I walked to the High Street again to give Lara some time alone with Arthur, although I didn't need to buy anything. When I returned she was again watching television as Arthur munched his way through another packet of mini-biscuits.

On Sunday Lara told me I could take Paula with me when I went out.

'Thank you, love,' I said, with just a hint of sarcasm. 'I'll ask her if she wants to come. I take it you don't?'

'No. I'm staying here with Arthur like Claudette said.'

Paula said she wanted to go for a walk so we did a circuit of the block, which took us about twenty minutes. When we arrived back Lara was in the kitchen searching the cupboards. Arthur was with her.

'He should be the other side of the safety gate,' I pointed out, and took him from the kitchen.

'We haven't got any of those biscuits he likes,' Lara said, as if it was my fault.

'Put them on your shopping list for tomorrow.'

Lara's eyes lit up. 'Yes, I can go shopping tomorrow, just Arthur with me. I'm allowed to now.'

'I know.'

I recognized that gradually I had to pass more and more responsibility to Lara in preparation for her being able to parent Arthur alone. Already, I wasn't always in the same room as them, and if Arthur woke during the night, which he still did sometimes, I now stayed in bed while Lara went to settle him. I never returned to sleep until he was settled, but I no longer shot out of bed to supervise Lara, nor did I feel the same anxiety for Arthur's wellbeing as I had in the early days. With some exceptions, I was satisfied that Lara was meeting Arthur's needs and keeping him safe, which is what I said in my reports.

* * *

On Monday Lara was very keen to go shopping in the High Street with Arthur. They were ready by ten o'clock. Before she left I checked she had a mask with her as well as her shopping list and enough money. I saw them off at the door, then cleared up her breakfast things. She could still be messy, but I didn't make an issue of it and concentrated on more important matters, like Arthur's care.

I was expecting Lara to be gone for an hour at the most. When an hour and a half passed I began to worry. All non-essential shops were closed so she wasn't trying on clothes, for example, or having her hair or nails done. So what was she doing? I called her mobile but she didn't answer, so I left a message on her voicemail, trying to keep the unease from my voice.

'It's Cathy, love. Are you on your way back now? Arthur will need his lunch soon.' It was after 11.30 and he usually ate at 12.00, having had a snack mid-morning.

Lara didn't return my call and I worried some more. Ten minutes later I tried her phone again, but it went through to voicemail. She must have seen that I'd called, and had very likely listened to my message; she was always checking her phone. I couldn't imagine why she hadn't returned my call or what she could be doing. When twelve o'clock came and went and Lara had been gone for two hours I knew something must be very wrong. Paula agreed.

'Nearly everything is closed,' she said. 'There is nothing to do. Perhaps Lara's had an accident.'

Which had been a worry of mine, too. 'Or Arthur has,' I said. 'But surely someone would have contacted us by now?'

All manner of frightening possibilities occurred to me, including that Lara had been so preoccupied on her phone that she hadn't checked the road before crossing and had pushed Arthur in the stroller into the path of an oncoming vehicle. I shuddered at the thought.

Or perhaps she'd met someone, I pondered. Not Frazer – he had started work today. Shell or Courtney? Or maybe someone I didn't know. Or had Lara run away with Arthur to make sure he couldn't be taken into care? But she hadn't taken a bag with her. I went upstairs and checked her bedroom and then Arthur's, but as far as I could tell their belongings were all there. I went into the kitchen where I found that Arthur's sippy cup was missing, but that only meant Lara had taken a drink for him. I suppose I should have been pleased she'd remembered, but now it added to my disquiet. Had Lara planned to be away longer than she'd told me? To go somewhere I didn't know?

By 12.15, when Lara had been gone for over two hours, I knew I had to phone Claudette and tell her. If she wasn't available, I'd speak to a colleague or the duty social worker. Before long I'd have to report Lara and Arthur missing to the police, but ideally the social services should be told first. I knew from experience that once I had reported them missing the police would quickly swing into action – a vulnerable infant in care effectively snatched by his mother.

'I wonder if I should just check the High Street first,' I said to Paula, thinking aloud. Then I immediately decided against it. 'There's no way they could have been there all this time.' Paula agreed.

I was about to call Claudette when my mobile rang. It wasn't Lara's number on the display, but Bruce's. 'Oh no, don't say Frazer hasn't turned up for work!' I said. For if he hadn't then the most likely outcome was that he and Lara had run away together.

'Hello, Bruce,' I said, my voice tight.

'Cathy, sorry to disturb you, but I think you need to come and collect Lara and the nipper. I'm afraid I can't leave the site.'

'Lara's there!' I gasped. 'Why?'

'The pair of them turned up about fifteen minutes ago, much to Frazer's surprise. They'd had to wait ages for the buses and the nipper was cold and miserable. They're sitting in my van with the heater on now. I've given the nipper one of my sandwiches as his mother said he was hungry.'

'Bruce, I am so sorry. I had no idea Lara was going there. She was supposed to be walking to the High Street. I was expecting her back ages ago and was about to report her missing. I've been worried sick.'

'She's safe. I think she knows she's done wrong.'

'Too right,' I said. 'I am sorry, Bruce, I'll come and collect them straight away.'

'Please. I need the van to fetch some supplies I ordered months ago from the builders' merchant. They've just come in. I'll text you the postcode of where we're working.'

'Thanks. I'm leaving now.'

I dropped my phone into my bag and hurriedly put on my shoes and coat.

'Lara's taken Arthur to where Frazer is working,' I told Paula.

'Why?' Paula asked, astounded.

'I've no idea. I can't believe she's done this on her first time out with Arthur!'

Grabbing my keys and bag, I shot out of the house and into my car.

CHAPTER TWENTY

UNWANTED

Bruce had been too polite to show his anger, but he had every right to be annoyed, I thought as I drove. I felt bad. He'd been kind enough to give Frazer a chance in life by offering him work and so far it had caused him nothing but trouble: Frazer had arrived on his trial day inadequately dressed for working outside and had to be sent home, and now Lara had turned up with Arthur!

Whatever had Lara been thinking? But that was the trouble with Lara: she didn't always think. Faced with her first day of being able to take Arthur out alone, she'd acted impulsively and done what she'd wanted to regardless of everyone else involved — Bruce, Frazer, me and most importantly little Arthur. This hadn't done her any good and I wondered what Claudette would say.

The roads were relatively clear as we were in lockdown, and although it had taken Lara two hours on the buses to get to where Bruce was working, I arrived in twenty minutes. I pulled up behind Bruce's van. The house they were working on was covered in scaffolding. I could see three men working on the platforms. Bruce spotted me and came down as I got out of my car. His van's engine was running, powering the heater that was keeping Lara and Arthur warm.

'Sorry for all the trouble, Bruce,' I said as he approached me.

'Thanks for coming quickly. I need to use my van and I couldn't really send them back on the bus.'

'I'll take them straight away,' I said.

He opened the passenger door of his van. 'Out you get,' he said. 'Time to go home.'

I waited on the pavement as Lara clambered out carrying Arthur, the crust of Bruce's sandwich still in his hand. Arthur grinned when he saw me, but Lara looked grumpy and couldn't meet my eyes.

'I think you'd better apologize to Bruce,' I said to Lara. For she'd been about to get into my car.

'Sorry,' she said sullenly, then looked up at the platform where the men were working. 'Can I say goodbye to Frazer?' she asked.

'He's busy,' I said.

But Bruce called over. 'Frazer, your young lady and the nipper are going now – do you want to say goodbye?'

'Bye,' Frazer returned, his voice flat. He didn't stop working or look at Lara, and I guessed he was annoyed and perhaps embarrassed too.

'Let's go,' I said to Lara, and I opened the rear door for her to put Arthur into his car seat.

'I'll be about an hour,' Bruce called up to the men.

'Thanks again,' I said to him.

He nodded, got into his van and immediately drove off. Lara's arrival had undoubtedly disrupted his day. She fastened Arthur's seatbelt and then, with a final glance up at the platform, got into the passenger seat. I started the car and pulled away, the atmosphere heavy. Lara texted someone and then said, 'Arthur's wet. I changed his nappy, but his clothes are sopping.'

'There's nothing we can do about it now,' I replied. 'We'll be home shortly.'

'It took me ages to get here on the buses,' she offered. 'There were lots of cancellations.'

'That's because we're in lockdown,' I said, trying to stem my annoyance and concentrate on the road. 'All public transport is on a reduced service as it's only to be used for essential travel. It's been on the news.'

'Frazer went on the bus,' Lara said, as if that made it all right.

'He's allowed to because he was going to work, it's essential travel.' I glanced at her.

'I knew you'd be annoyed,' she said, staring at the phone in her lap.

'With good reason, Lara. Apart from interrupting Bruce's work, you have exposed yourself and Arthur to the possibility of catching Covid. If you have picked up the virus on the bus, you are likely to pass it on to Paula and me. Why do you think we're all in lockdown and being told to stay at home?'

She shrugged.

I took a breath. 'Have you been using that hand sanitizer I bought you?' I asked.

'Yes.'

'Good. Once home, you and Arthur can go straight in the bath and I'll wash all your clothes.'

'Why?'

'To hopefully reduce the chances of us catching Covid. That's the advice schools are giving out. I looked after two children before you and after school each day I put them both in the bath and washed all their clothes.'

She shrugged again as if it didn't matter.

'Lara, do you realize how serious this is? As well as breaking lockdown rules and possibly exposing us all to the virus, you lied to me about where you were going. I was very worried something had happened to you and was close to reporting you both missing to the police.'

'I didn't tell you where I was going because I knew you wouldn't let me,' she replied, fiddling with her phone.

'It's not about letting you. You're an adult. You have to make responsible choices, and this wasn't one of them.'

'I can't stay cooped up forever!' she blurted, her voice catching with emotion. 'It's doing my head in.'

'I know, it's the same for most of us. Our lives have been put on hold and many are suffering, but we need to abide by the rules and try to stay safe. Some people who live alone haven't seen their families or friends for months. At least we have each other.'

I glanced at Lara again and she was looking very sad.

'Did you get the chance to speak to Frazer?' I asked.

'No. He didn't want to.'

'He was busy,' I said. 'Did he know you were going?'

She shook her head. 'It was supposed to be a surprise, but he wasn't pleased to see me.'

I felt sorry for Lara; she could be so naive.

'Because he was having to concentrate on his work,' I said gently. 'He wants to make a good impression.' Lara had very little experience of the world of work so perhaps didn't appreciate this. 'I'm sure if you phone Frazer this evening after work, he'll feel more like talking.'

Once home, I asked Lara to sanitize her hands before we went into the house, then she took Arthur upstairs and ran a bath for them both while I put all their clothes into the washer-dryer and made us all something to eat. Only then did I check my phone and saw a missed call from Joy. We'd had a virtual meeting booked for today and with all the worry and then having to collect Lara and Arthur, I'd completely forgotten about it. I quickly phoned her, apologized and explained what had happened. She understood, and rescheduled the meeting for the following morning.

In dry clothes and having had a cooked meal, Arthur was much happier. He'd been in his stroller for most of the day so had a lot of energy to burn off, which kept Paula and me on our toes. Lara was subdued and I assumed it was because she realized she'd acted wrongly.

'Just learn from it and move on,' I said that evening when she was still very quiet.

'It's not that,' she said. 'Frazer isn't answering my calls.'

'Give him a chance to unwind after work and get his dinner,' I said. 'Let him call you.'

Once Arthur was in his cot for the night, Lara went to her bedroom. Then just before 9 p.m., as I sat at my computer in the front room, she came to me, upset.

'Frazer says I'm not to contact him any more as he needs a break from me.'

I stopped what I was doing to comfort her. I wasn't wholly surprised. Lara had taken the initiative in their relationship and been all over Frazer right from the start. I'd wondered before if it was too much too soon. I guessed her going to his work might have been the final straw.

'I bet he's found someone else,' Lara said miserably, as I held her hand and offered words of support.

'Why should you think that?' I asked. 'There's a lot going on for him right now, starting a new job, and before long he'll have to find somewhere permanent to live.'

'I always pick the wrong blokes,' Lara lamented. 'I hate him.'

'No, you don't. From what I know of Frazer he's a good person, trying to make his way in life, just as you are. Give him the space he needs and see what happens.'

Fostering encompasses not only looking after a child's day-to-day needs, but offering advice and counselling where appropriate, helping to empower them so they can learn self-worth and make good decisions.

'I love Frazer and I thought he loved me,' Lara said, wiping her eyes.

'I know, love.'

'It's because of all these lockdowns,' Lara said. 'If we'd been together more this wouldn't have happened.' Which may or may not have been true.

I spent some time comforting Lara and then she said she was going to bed. I checked on her once she was in bed and saw that the photograph of Frazer was still on her bedside cabinet.

'Do you think he still has my photo?' she asked mournfully.

'I really don't know.'

'I'll throw it away if he doesn't get in touch.'

I said what I could to reassure her and then returned downstairs to my computer. As I worked my phone bleeped with a text message. It was from Frazer.

I hope Lara is OK. Don't think bad of me. I just needed some time to myself. Which confirmed what I thought: that Frazer was a decent person.

I texted back: *I understand. Don't worry. I've explained to Lara. Look after yourself x*

Although Joy's visit the following morning was virtual, it took the same format as if she'd been with us in person. We discussed Lara's progress, the routine she'd established for Arthur and how she was meeting his needs, as well as his general development. Joy spoke to Lara and saw Arthur. Then we talked about my training, which was all online at present. She knew of Lara's escapade to see Frazer at work as I'd told her when I'd phoned the day before, so there wasn't much more to say on that matter other than that their relationship was on hold at present.

'It will give her a chance to concentrate fully on Arthur,' Joy said, and I agreed.

I asked Joy how her brother was recovering from Covid, and she said he was in the rehabilitation hospital but his progress was slow. He was thought to have long Covid, which had only recently been recognized. I'd heard it mentioned on the news as it was affecting thousands. Instead of recovering from Covid, some people were experiencing persistent symptoms, including a high temperature, cough, headache, fatigue, chest and stomach pains, and a loss of appetite and concentration – or brain fog, as it was being called. I wished him well and we put a date for her next virtual visit in our diaries.

'Goodness knows when I'll see you in person,' Joy added.

'No, indeed.' For virtual had become the norm.

The week continued bitterly cold; indeed, January was set to become the coldest in England for ten years. The temperature plummeted but the infection rate continued to rise, despite lockdown. Our hopes lay with the vaccine, which was being rolled out in the UK at an unprecedented rate. The daily news bulletins now included the number of people vaccinated as well as new infections and, sadly, the number of fatalities from Covid. But people were getting fed up with all the restrictions and wanted to know when they were going to get their lives back. The government assured us that a 'roadmap' out of lockdown was being drawn up and in the meantime we were asked to stay safe and abide by the rules, which most of us were doing.

With Frazer no longer in the picture, Lara was less eager to go out with Arthur, although he still needed some fresh air and exercise each day. Sometimes Lara took him into the garden while Paula and I walked to the local shops for what we needed. Like me, Paula had to get out of the house each day to avoid 'cabin fever', as she put it. This resulted in Lara being left alone with Arthur, just as Claudette had said. Gradually I was becoming less anxious about leaving Arthur in her care. She seemed to be managing him better and there hadn't been any more accidents other than minor bumps and falls typical for a child his age.

On Friday, when Lara and I logged in for our weekly meeting with Claudette she began by asking Lara how the week had gone and apologized that she hadn't had a chance to read my notes. Lara spoke first.

'I've been doing well. But on Monday I took Arthur to see Frazer and was gone a long time. It won't happen again as we're not seeing each other any more.'

'All right,' Claudette said, looking slightly confused.

'It was Frazer's first day at work,' I explained. 'I didn't know where Lara was until I received a phone call from Frazer's boss asking me to collect Lara and Arthur. It's all in my notes.'

'I'll read them later. Apart from that incident, how is it going?'

'Still making good progress,' I said. I didn't go into my concern again that Lara was still too easily distracted and not always watching Arthur as she should, as that was also in my reports.

'How is Arthur?' Claudette asked Lara.

Lara picked him up and jiggled him up and down on her lap.

'Mama!' he cried, pointing at the screen.

'No, that's the social worker, you daft bugger,' Lara said. 'I'm your mama.'

'He's going through a phase of calling all women "Mama",' I explained. Many infants do.

Claudette nodded and asked Lara about Arthur's general health, if he'd had any accidents, and about his eating, sleeping and play – much as she did every meeting. She then told Lara to keep up the good work and that she'd see us online again next Friday.

Straight after we'd finished, Lara checked her phone. We kept our mobiles on silent during these online meetings.

'I've got a voicemail from a private number,' she said, puzzled, and put the phone to her ear.

I watched her as she listened to the message. Her face paled.

'The police want to speak to me,' she said.

My heart sank. 'Why?'

'It doesn't say. Just the name of someone and a number to call.'

'And you've no idea what it could be about?'

'No. Honest.'

'You'd better phone,' I said. 'I'll keep Arthur quiet. If there is something you're not certain about then ask me.'

We were in the living room and Lara went into the front room but returned almost immediately. 'It's gone through to voicemail.'

'Have you left a message?'

'No. Do you think I should?'

'Yes, just give your name and say someone phoned and you are returning their call.' Which seemed obvious to me as an adult, but wasn't necessarily to a young person.

Lara stayed in the room and left the message. We then had an anxious hour wondering why the police wanted to speak to her before anyone called back. We were having lunch when Lara's phone rang. 'It's a private number again,' she said, and answered it.

Paula and I watched Lara's expression as she listened to what the police officer had to say, then she said, 'Hang on, I need to ask my foster carer.' To me she said, 'The police want to know about Diesel.'

'Why are they calling you?'

'Because of what he did to Shell.'

'I see. They're gathering information?'

'Yes. Shall I tell them what I know?'

'Yes.'

Had Lara been a minor, under the age of eighteen, I would have asked her to put her phone on speaker so I could introduce myself to the police officer and explain that I would be there to support her, but Lara was an adult. As she kept the phone pressed to her ear and answered the officer's questions I learnt more about just how cruel and controlling Diesel had been to her. Paula took Arthur out of the room and kept him amused elsewhere. Lara was on the phone for about twenty minutes and when she'd finished I was shocked and saddened by what I'd heard. 'Why ever did you put up with all that?' I asked.

She shrugged. 'I guess I'm used to shit. That's what being an unwanted child does to you. You grow up expecting to be treated like that and you are usually right.'

I went to her and wrapped her in my arms. Of all the upsetting comments I'd heard from young people I'd fostered, this was one of the saddest. 'I'm sorry you've suffered in the past. I can't change that, but I promise I can help you to a better future.'

She didn't reply and I had the feeling she had heard similar platitudes before, but I meant it with all my heart.

CHAPTER TWENTY-ONE

CLOSE TO A DECISION

Time seemed to have slipped into a different dimension since the start of the pandemic with all the lockdowns. It was a year since we'd first heard of the deadly new virus that was spreading across the world, but it could easily have been last month or a lifetime ago. With our usual routines disrupted, isolated and unable to meet family and friends other than online, it was becoming increasingly difficult to remember how our lives used to be before the pandemic. The pace of life was slower now for many as we no longer rushed from one appointment to the next, but just switched on a computer. Having Arthur in the house helped keep us anchored and my heart went out to those who lived completely alone.

Lara didn't hear from Frazer again until the last weekend in January, by which time the framed photograph of him was no longer on her bedside cabinet, but in a drawer where she couldn't see it. It was Saturday morning and Lara came to me, phone in hand and smiling broadly.

'I've had a message from Frazer!' she said jubilantly, flashing the screen before my eyes just long enough for me to read: *How are you?*

'Shall I reply?' she asked excitedly.

'Do you want to?'

'Yes, of course.'

'Well, do so, then.'

'What shall I say? I don't want to mess up again.'

Since their break-up we'd had a few long chats about relationships. Lara had admitted she often rushed into them, declaring her feelings and disclosing all there was to know about her too quickly, and expecting the guy to do the same. Then she was disappointed when they didn't phone or text as often as she would like. She admitted she felt she needed a boyfriend to feel complete and I thought part of this might be due to feeling unwanted as a child. But I wasn't the best person to offer advice about dating, as I hadn't dated for some time.

'You could say you are well and ask how he is,' I suggested.

Beaming, she went off to text Frazer, then when her phone rang she vanished up to her room. I assumed the call was from him as she was talking for nearly an hour, leaving Paula and me to look after Arthur. When she returned she was aglow with pleasure and unable to contain her excitement.

'Can you babysit Arthur?' she asked. 'Frazer wants us to meet. We've got a lot of talking to do.'

'I can,' I said. 'When?'

'In about half an hour. He's catching the bus now. The lockdown rules allow us to meet another person from a different household outside.'

'I know, love. I'll babysit,' I confirmed.

'I won't touch him, so you needn't worry about catching the virus,' she continued in a highly excitable voice.

'You were right about him not liking it when I went to his work. I've said I'm sorry. He still loves me and I love him!'

I smiled. I could see how happy Frazer made Lara; she'd come alive again.

She quickly changed out of her jogging bottoms and into jeans, and, calling a general goodbye, she shot out the front door. She was gone for two hours and when she came back she said they were dating again. His photo was returned to her bedside cabinet. Lara saw Frazer again on Sunday and took Arthur with her, which was within the lockdown rules – you were permitted to take your child with you if you met someone from another household. I hoped that by being outside in the fresh air there was less chance of transferring the virus if Frazer was incubating it.

Lara didn't see Frazer again during the following week as he was at work, but they spoke on the phone each evening. Then on Thursday Bruce told Frazer he would like to keep him on and offered him an apprenticeship when the scheme began again after lockdown. I was delighted, as of course were Lara and Frazer. Although the month's trial wasn't quite over yet, Bruce had told Frazer he'd seen enough to know he was reliable and hardworking and would make a good employee. He also said that when restrictions were lifted he should go to his house for dinner, as his other employees did from time to time, and meet his wife. I texted a heartfelt thank-you to Bruce.

No need to thank me, he replied. *He's a good lad. I'll look into finding him some accommodation.*

When I asked Lara about this last comment she said that the hotel where Frazer was staying was going to revert back to paying guests soon so the homeless there had been asked to leave. Bruce knew someone who rented out rooms. Again, it seemed Bruce was going that extra mile for Frazer, and I felt that thanks to him there was a good chance Frazer would get his life on track. I also had a nice text message from Jenny saying how relieved she was that Frazer had found work, so I guessed that Frazer and she were still in touch and he had told her.

However, the week didn't end well. Just after 9 a.m. on Friday Lara left the breakfast table to take a phone call. I could hear her in the hall and her manner was quite terse.

'I said I'll bring him this afternoon!' she said. 'I just forgot.'

'Everything all right?' I asked as she returned to the table.

'I've got to take Arthur to the clinic later.'

'OK. Why?'

She shrugged. 'Don't know.'

'You must know, love.'

'For a check-up.'

'So what's the problem?'

'It was supposed to be on Monday but I forgot, and they are bound to tell Claudette.'

'Did the clinic send you a letter about the appointment?'

'No, a text.' Which I appreciated could be overlooked.

'Are you using the diary I bought you for Christmas?' I asked. I'd included a pretty personal diary in Lara's Santa sack.

'No, I wouldn't have looked at that either,' she said, clearly annoyed with herself for having forgotten the appointment.

'What about a wall calendar then?' I suggested.

'I can use the calendar on my phone.'

It was up to Lara how she remembered her appointments, as long as she did.

Lara still wasn't in the best humour when an hour later she joined me and we logged in for our weekly review meeting. When Claudette asked about Arthur, Lara included, 'He's got his check-up at the clinic this afternoon.' And left out that it had been rescheduled from Monday. If the clinic didn't say anything, neither would I.

Lara continued to talk about Arthur as Claudette nodded and took notes, then when he grew restless Paula looked after him in another room. Once Lara had finished I said my bit and then Claudette's expression grew serious.

'Something of concern has come up,' she said, looking directly at Lara. 'Diesel has made a statement to the police describing how you assaulted him and Arthur a number of times.'

'You're kidding me!' Lara exclaimed, and I was shocked.

'I'm not saying I believe him,' Claudette said. 'But you need to be aware of what he's claiming.'

'The scumbag!' Lara cried. 'He's lying! I didn't hurt Arthur or him. He's the one. He's much stronger than me. He was the one who hurt us. He's getting his own back because I told the police what he was like when they asked me about Shell.'

'That's possible,' Claudette said evenly. 'Did you ever push Arthur when you were angry or maybe slap him really hard? I need you to be honest, Lara.'

'No! Never! It was Diesel. He hurt him!'

'Did you ever witness Diesel harming Arthur?' Claudette asked.

'Not exactly,' Lara admitted. 'But when I used to get back after my Saturday night out Arthur was sometimes hurt and in his cot crying. Diesel always said he'd had an accident. I believed him because Arthur has accidents.'

Claudette was making notes.

'You do believe me, don't you?' Lara cried, desperation in her voice. For clearly this was serious and could affect her chances of keeping Arthur.

'Calm down,' Claudette said gently.

'I thought Diesel was being prosecuted for assaulting Shell,' I said.

'He is, but in his statement to the police he made these allegations against Lara. It seems he's saying Shell and Lara are very similar – both aggressive women who hate men and start arguments, and that he only acted in self-defence to protect himself.'

'That's ridiculous! He's a liar!' Lara cried, tears springing to her eyes. 'He doesn't want me to have Arthur and be happy. That's why he's making this up. When I was with him he said if I ever tried to leave, he would destroy me and make sure I couldn't keep Arthur.'

'I've never seen Lara very angry with Arthur or try to harm him,' I said.

Claudette nodded.

'Shall I talk to the police again and tell them?' Lara asked.

'Only if they want you to,' Claudette said. 'There's evidence against Diesel so the judge will decide.' She didn't tell us what that evidence was, though, so I guessed for legal reasons she couldn't.

'Try not to worry,' Claudette said, but I could appreciate why Lara was worried. I was too. 'Any plans for the weekend?' she asked, then added, 'I guess not as we're all in lockdown.'

'The usual,' I said. 'We'll go out for a walk each day.'

'OK. Anything else you want to discuss?'

Lara shook her head.

'So take care and see you both again next Friday. You know where I am if you need me.'

I said goodbye, although Lara couldn't.

'Diesel is such a shit!' she cried as soon as the meeting ended. 'I think I'll call him now and tell him what I think of him. The arsehole!' She reached for her phone.

'No. That's not a good idea,' I said. 'It could make things worse. I'm sure Claudette appreciates his motives. And the judge should see through him too.'

But of course mud can stick, as the saying goes. Although Lara didn't phone Diesel, she worried for the rest of the day what effect his allegations might have on her chances of keeping Arthur. She asked me to go with her to the clinic that afternoon, which I did, but when we arrived I wasn't allowed in. To reduce the risk of transmitting the virus they were limiting the numbers inside, so the appointments were for the child and one parent only. I had to wait outside, and it was cold. The receptionist saw me and after a while came out. 'The doctor shouldn't be long now,' she said kindly. 'We did tell everyone by text that only one person was allowed in.'

I smiled politely and thanked her. I didn't raise it with Lara when she finally came out. She either hadn't read the text properly or had forgotten. She was in a better mood as the paediatrician was satisfied with Arthur's development. So that was all that really mattered. Once home, I made us a hot drink and I gradually thawed out.

Lara saw Frazer on Saturday afternoon while Paula and I looked after Arthur. This was in place of me babysitting on Saturday evening, which, in normal circumstances, Lara looked upon as her night out. She saw Frazer again on Sunday, this time taking Arthur with her. Paula and I met Lucy, Darren and Emma briefly outside and then video-called Adrian and Kirsty.

On Monday I received a text message from my doctor inviting me to book an appointment for my first Covid vaccine, which I did straight away for the following morning. Having vaccinated the elderly, those clinically vulnerable and frontline health and social-care workers, they were now working down through the age groups, so Lara and my children wouldn't receive their first dose for some months yet. They were pleased I was receiving mine, though. I felt a bit unwell on Tuesday evening, as though I had mild flu, but after an early night I was fine again.

On Wednesday morning when I checked my email I saw one from Claudette. It said she wished to speak to me that afternoon and would book a telephone call for two o'clock if that suited me. I replied immediately, confirming that was all right and checking if it was just for the two of us. It was, so I wondered if it was in respect of the allegations Diesel had made about Lara.

At 2 p.m. I went to my bedroom so I had some privacy and waited for her call, having left Lara downstairs with

Arthur. Paula was at her laptop in the front room. Claudette began by asking how we all were and then said, 'We are nearing the end of the placement, so some decisions have to be made. I've got Lara's case conference tomorrow, and if she is going to parent Arthur I'll have to start looking for suitable accommodation for them soon. I need you to tell me candidly what you think, Cathy.'

This was going to take a while, so I sat on the edge of my bed.

'I don't believe what Diesel is claiming,' I began. 'I haven't seen anything to suggest that Lara has a bad temper or would intentionally harm anyone, certainly not Arthur. From what I know I think any non-accidental injuries Arthur sustained before he came into care were most likely inflicted by Diesel.'

'Yes, that's my feeling,' Claudette said.

'Having said that, Lara can put her own needs first at times, especially when it comes to her social life. Also, she still doesn't fully appreciate you have to watch a child of Arthur's age the whole time. You can't leave them alone to take a phone call or even go to the bathroom. Sometimes she simply forgets.' I'd included all these points in my reports and we'd talked about them during the weekly meetings, but I was now bringing it all together.

'Lara still finds it a struggle to manage her money,' I continued. 'But she has improved. She's repaying the credit card company and has given up smoking, so that's saving her money. There's no sign of her drinking heavily or taking drugs.'

'She hasn't really had the opportunity with all the lock-downs and living with you,' Claudette pointed out.

'True.' I couldn't argue with that.

'What about Arthur's general care – feeding and changing him?' Claudette asked.

'Yes, she has been doing most of that and can make him simple meals. She uses ready-meals sometimes, but then so do a lot of families. She usually remembers to give him drinks between meals and to change his nappy. She bathes him every night before she settles him in his cot. She goes to him within a reasonable time if he calls for her. They're in a much better routine than when they arrived. I would like to see her spending more time playing with Arthur, but she finds it boring after a short while.'

'So, on balance, you think she can provide a reasonable level of parenting?'

'Yes. I don't think Lara would intentionally harm Arthur, but she can leave him unattended when an accident could result,' I emphasized. 'If her phone rings, for example, she rushes off to talk and is sometimes gone for a long time. But then she knows Paula and I are here to look after Arthur. Whether it will be any different when she is alone with him I don't know. I've told Lara it's best to leave long calls to friends until the evening when he's asleep.'

'Who does she talk to on the phone?' Claudette asked.

'Frazer mainly, but also Shell and Courtney. Those are the only ones I know of.'

'How is it going with Frazer? They're seeing each other again.'

'Yes. Frazer is working now so they see each other at weekends but speak most evenings.'

'How is Frazer with Arthur?'

'From the little I've seen, good. Frazer has had a difficult past too and has spent most of his life in care.'

'Yes, I know.'

'I think Lara could parent Arthur with support,' I added.

'That's my thought too. We can't eliminate all risk, so we need to manage it. I've read your reports. Is there anything else you want to add?'

'Only that I'll keep in touch with Lara and help out when I can.'

'Thank you. I'll include that. See you both as usual on Friday.'

The call ended and I stayed where I was for a moment thinking about what I'd said. I felt I'd been honest, and fair to Lara. But what a difficult decision for Claudette or any social worker to have to make. It would be heart-breaking, although the safest option, to place Arthur with a long-term foster carer or for adoption, for if Lara was allowed to keep him and something happened, the social services would be held accountable. I thought Claudette's comment about managing the risk was spot on. Without doubt there was a risk in allowing Arthur to live with his mother, just as there was with many vulnerable families.

I stood, left my bedroom and began downstairs. As I did I heard Lara cry, 'Arthur! No! Stop!'

I ran down the rest of the stairs as Paula rushed out of the front room. We arrived in the kitchen together, to see Arthur standing in a puddle of flour. It was everywhere. It looked like a snowstorm.

'Sorry,' Lara said, pulling a face. 'He got into the cupboard before I could stop him.' She had been making herself a cup of tea.

'The flour can be cleaned up,' I said. 'But what concerns me is that Arthur's in the kitchen at all.'

'I forgot to close the safety gate,' Lara admitted.

'Try to remember in future,' I said. 'Next time it could be something dangerous he grabs, like the kettle.'

'I know.'

How to clear up flour? I wondered. It was everywhere. We tried the dustpan and brush first but that seemed to waft it even further. Then Paula fetched the vacuum cleaner and we hoovered up the rest, including from Arthur's trousers and slippers while they were on him, which he thought was great fun.

I didn't tell Lara of Claudette's phone call and that a decision on whether she would be allowed to keep Arthur was imminent. Claudette would tell her, I assumed at our weekly meeting on Friday. How much of a difference lockdown would make to the timescale of any move I didn't know. Lots of practices had changed in fostering since the start of the pandemic, as they had in many other areas of our lives. I wasn't in any hurry to see Lara and Arthur leave – they had become part of my life – but I recognized that whatever the decision, they would both have to leave at some point.

On the news that evening we were told that nearly 14 million people in the UK had received their first dose of the Covid vaccine and the infection rate was falling, which gave us hope we were past the worst of the pandemic.

CHAPTER TWENTY-TWO

ROADMAP OUT

Lara knew the placement didn't finish until the end of February at the earliest so wasn't anticipating a decision from Claudette on Friday. Also, her head was full of other things, namely Valentine's Day. It was on Sunday, and she was deciding how she and Frazer were going to celebrate with all pubs, clubs and restaurants closed.

'I'll buy a bottle of champagne and we'll have to drink it outside,' she said as we sat on the sofa in the living room ready for the meeting that morning.

'Do you know how much champagne costs?' I asked, agog.

'I'll get the pretend stuff then. As long as the cork flies off with a loud pop.'

'Yes, sparkling wine should do that,' I said.

Lara had already bought Frazer a very large Valentine's card – *To My Wonderful Boyfriend* – and was expecting one in return, with flowers and chocolates. I hoped she wasn't disappointed.

As I logged in to the meeting Lara picked Arthur up and sat him on her lap.

'Wave,' Lara told him as Claudette appeared on screen,

and flapped his arms. He chuckled and bounced up and down.

'You're in a good mood,' Claudette said.

'It's Valentine's Day on Sunday!' Lara cried.

'Is it?' Claudette said, the occasion apparently not having much significance for her, as it didn't for me. 'How are you all?'

'Fine,' Lara said. Arthur was already bored and scrambled down from Lara's lap. 'Have you finished with him?' Lara asked. 'He doesn't like sitting still.'

'He can go,' Claudette confirmed.

I took him to Paula and then returned to the sofa.

Claudette had begun telling Lara about the meeting she'd had yesterday. 'I've also spoken at length with Cathy,' she continued. 'We're all pleased with the progress you are making in this placement. With help, you have established a good working routine for Arthur. He now has regular meals and is sleeping much better. The paediatrician's report was satisfactory too. Are you pleased with your progress?'

'Yes,' Lara said tentatively. For there seemed to be a reservation in Claudette's manner. I felt it too.

'We do have some concerns, however,' Claudette continued, 'around how you will manage Arthur when there is just you. We feel further support would be useful. I'm recommending Arthur is returned to your care, but we [the social services] will apply for a supervision order. That will allow us to monitor and support you. We also think it would be very good for Arthur if he attended nursery part-time, five mornings or afternoons a week. It will help maintain the progress he has made and give you a break.' It would also add an extra

layer of supervision as the nursery staff would be monitoring Arthur too.

'Sounds good,' I said, when Lara didn't.

'Cathy has also offered to continue to support you after
you've left,' Claudette added.

'So can Frazer live with me?' Lara asked. 'He hasn't
got anywhere to go. They are all having to leave that
hotel. Bruce's friend might be able to find him something,
but it isn't definite. If he lives with me he won't need to
find his own accommodation.'

I explained who Bruce was but wished Lara hadn't
started talking about Frazer's needs and would instead
concentrate on Arthur's.

'Has Frazer asked to live with you?'

'No. Not yet.'

'I think Frazer can sort out his own accommodation,'
Claudette said. 'He seems to be managing, and your flat
is likely to be one bedroom or even a studio. We will look
into what is available.'

'But Frazer can visit me, can't he?' Lara persisted.
'And stay overnight?'

'If he does, we will need to do a DBS check, as I
mentioned before, and assess him,' Claudette said.

'He won't mind.'

Claudette looked at Lara thoughtfully. 'Do you feel
you can manage Arthur alone?'

'Yes,' Lara replied.

'Good. So you agree with our recommendations?'

Lara nodded.

'Any questions?'

'How long will that supervision order last?' Lara
asked, which was a fair question.

'A year, although it can be stopped earlier or extended for up to three years if appropriate.' A supervision order is granted by a judge and gives the local authority the legal power to monitor a child's needs and progress while they live at home.

'So you will keep visiting me during that time?' Lara asked.

'Either me or a colleague,' Claudette said. 'Do you have any more questions?'

'How long before you find me a flat?'

'I honestly don't know. You want to stay in this area, so it depends on what is available. I'm aiming for next month, but we'll have to see. I can't make any promises. Anything else you want to ask?'

Lara shook her head.

'All right, so tell me how your week has been.'

Once we'd both said our piece, Claudette wound up by saying she'd see us again next Friday and wished us a nice weekend.

I logged out, closed the tablet's case, and we both sat in silence for a while. There was a lot to take in.

'Well done,' I said to Lara, after a moment.

'Thanks.' But her voice was flat.

'What's the matter, love?' I could hear Paula playing with Arthur in the front room.

'I don't know.' Lara shrugged. 'I mean, I'm pleased I'll be able to keep Arthur, but it's going to be very strange, living alone, without you telling me what to do.'

I smiled and took her hand between mine. 'I'll be on the end of the phone so you can call any time. Also – and I'll need to check this – I think I can form a support bubble with you while lockdown lasts as you will be a single adult with a child. Claudette and the nursery staff will be on hand to support you too if necessary.'

Lara was still looking worried, and I appreciated how daunting this next step might appear.

'If you really don't feel you're ready to move out then we can ask Claudette to extend your time here with me,' I suggested.

'No. But I don't see why Frazer can't move in with me.'

'Claudette feels you and Arthur should be settled first, and so do I. Frazer has had a lot of uncertainty and change in his life, and so have you. This is your chance for some stability. You'll be able to see him, in line with current guidelines. And the lockdown won't last forever. This is your time, Lara. I am sure Frazer will understand.' Of course Lara was an adult so could live with Frazer if she chose, but the family would be carefully monitored by the social services to make sure her relationship wasn't negatively impacting on Arthur and he was safe and well cared for.

'Frazer isn't pressurizing you to let him move in, is he?' I asked.

'No. He wouldn't do that.' Which is what I'd thought. This was about Lara's insecurity, which was understandable.

We chatted for a while longer and I reassured her as best I could. Arthur burst into the living room, followed by Paula, and Lara told her what Claudette had said. Paula was pleased for her and said she'd keep in touch.

After lunch we walked to the High Street where Lara purchased a bottle of sparkling wine ready for Valentine's

Day on Sunday. I bought more mundane items like bread, milk and cheese. Paula didn't have any plans for Valentine's Day, and I knew Adrian and Kirsty, and Lucy and Darren, would be celebrating at home with a takeaway. Takeaway businesses had been doing very well during the lockdowns – probably the only ones that had.

That evening Frazer phoned Lara from the bus on his way home from work and said that tomorrow he was going to see a bedsitting room Bruce's friend rented out. He was going at 9.30 a.m. and the landlord needed a decision straight away as others wanted it.

'That's great,' I said.

'Frazer's pleased,' Lara replied gloomily. 'But if he likes it there, he might not ever want to live with me. Or he might meet someone else.'

'Lara, have more faith in yourself, love,' I said. 'If your relationship is strong, it will survive. Indeed, it could make it stronger, living apart.'

'Do you think so?'

'Yes. Just concentrate on yourself and Arthur, and see how it goes with Frazer.' Which I'd said in different ways many times before.

The following morning Frazer phoned Lara as soon as he'd seen the room and said he'd accepted it and was moving in straight away – that afternoon. There was no reason why he shouldn't. The room was available and many of the others in the hotel-cum-hostel had already left. In normal circumstances – if we weren't in the middle of a raging pandemic – I would have offered to move him in my car, but Lara said he had booked a cab and didn't have much stuff. I texted Bruce and thanked him, and also asked him to pass on my thanks to his friend, the landlord, for giving Frazer first option on the room.

Glad it worked out, Bruce replied.

That afternoon I received a step-by-step account from Lara of Frazer's moving through the text messages they swapped. Frazer was packing. He was leaving the hotel. He was in the cab. He had arrived at the flat. Then, around 4 p.m., after he'd unpacked, he sent Lara photographs of his accommodation, which she shared with us. It looked very comfortable. The bedsitting room was freshly painted, and furnished with a bed, wardrobe, shelves, table and a chest of drawers. It had its own en-suite, which was sparkling clean, as was the communal kitchen. The eight residents in the block shared the laundry room in the basement, and the monthly rent included heating, electricity, water and Wi-Fi. Because of Covid there were notices all around the building reminding residents to take extra care in the communal areas, and that visitors were not allowed because of the lockdown restrictions.

Lara was disappointed as she seemed to think she'd be able to visit Frazer.

'Lockdown won't last forever,' I said again, ever the optimist.

One thing I will say for Lara is that she never let the weather stop her from going out, not with Frazer at least. Playing with Arthur in the garden in winter was problematic, but when it came to meeting Frazer she would have battled her way through a hurricane if necessary.

The temperature overnight on Saturday had plummeted to below zero and on Sunday morning everywhere had a coating of frost. The temperature wasn't expected to rise above 2°C all day, but that didn't dent Lara's enthusiasm for going out. It was Valentine's Day and she had a boyfriend and they were going to celebrate.

The day couldn't pass quickly enough for Lara and at 6 p.m., with the next frost hanging in the air, I saw her off at the door. Coat zipped up and wearing the new boots, scarf and matching hat I'd bought her as part of her Christmas present, she had the huge Valentine's card for Frazer tucked under one arm and the bottle of sparkling wine in a bag. Paula and I played with Arthur for a while and then began his bedtime routine. Around 7.30 Lara texted a selfie. It was a lovely picture of her and Frazer sitting together on the bench in the churchyard and raising their glasses of sparkling wine as they smiled into the lens. The lamp in the churchyard shone down on them, giving the scene a rather magical, romantic feel.

Lovely, but don't get cold, I texted back.

We won't! came Lara's reply.

When I showed Paula the photo she said it was nice but then remarked, 'Aren't those your best wine glasses, Mum?'

I looked more closely and saw that indeed they were the cut-crystal glasses I'd inherited from my mother. I hoped they didn't get broken, but I was pleased they were being put to good use. Mum would have approved.

Lara returned just before 9 p.m. with a Valentine's card from Frazer – not as big as the one she'd given him, but containing very nice words. He'd also given her a box of chocolates. She said they'd agreed not to buy each other expensive gifts as they were saving up.

'Very sensible,' I said, and thought that some of my lectures about money had been listened to.

The wine glasses were quietly washed and returned to the cupboard.

On Monday Paula received an email from work saying she would be furloughed until July, which was half expected. Although we were both pleased she hadn't been made redundant, she would rather have been working, and the possibility of redundancy still loomed if the business failed to pick up, as it did for many others.

The rest of the week passed without major incident and was much the same as most others in lockdown. We went for a daily walk, where we now saw daffodil bulbs sprouting in the park, suggesting spring wasn't too far away.

Lara was anticipating that Claudette would have news about her moving by our next weekly meeting on Friday, and when that didn't happen she was disappointed. Lara wasn't due to go until the end of February at the earliest, but now the decision had been made she wanted it to happen 'now'.

'Why does everything take so long,' she moaned to Claudette. Patience wasn't Lara's strong point.

'I'll let you know as soon as I hear anything,' Claudette replied stoically. 'Now tell me about Arthur. How is he?'

'All right,' Lara said sullenly. 'Same as usual.'

She clearly wasn't in the mood to talk so I filled in the rest.

* * *

On Monday our prime minister addressed the country again in a live press conference – the much-awaited 'roadmap' out of lockdown. It would come in four stages, he said, but would be regularly reviewed as we went. The decisions were based on the latest scientific data, he emphasized. The first stage would start on 8 March when all primary and secondary schools would be allowed to reopen. Care-home visits could resume indoors and visitors could hold hands with their loved ones. Later in March rules on socializing in a public space would be relaxed so outdoor gatherings of up to six people or two households could take place. Outdoor sports facilities such as tennis and basketball courts and golf courses could reopen. The second phase in late April allowed for some hospitality to reopen but that may be restricted to serving outdoors only. Non-essential retail shops were expected to reopen then too, and universities and colleges could reopen their campuses. The third phase in the middle of May included pubs and restaurants being allowed to serve customers indoors, though there could still be a limit on the size of groups. Hairdressers and beauticians were likely to reopen then and people could travel for short breaks in the UK, with restrictions. But the date we all latched onto was 21 June – freedom day – when the last of the restrictions would hopefully be lifted and we'd no longer have to social distance, limit contact between households or wear a face covering. When life should return to near normal. But as Lara was quick to point out, that was months away.

* * *

On Wednesday morning Lara received the news she'd been waiting for. Claudette phoned her and said a housing officer would be in contact. She was over the moon and was expecting her move to happen instantly.

'I'd better start packing,' she said excitedly. 'Will you take me and Arthur and all our things in your car?'

'Yes, of course, love, although it might take a few trips.'

'I don't have a stroller or cot for Arthur,' Lara said, flying into a panic. She was using mine.

'You can take the ones from here or we'll buy what you need. You can probably apply for a grant. We'll have plenty of time. I don't think this is all going to happen straight away,' I cautioned.

'Why shouldn't it?' she asked.

'From what I know, you'll have a meeting with the housing officer first when they explain about the tenancy for social housing, then you view the property. If you want it there is another meeting where you sign the tenancy agreement. You will also need to apply for housing benefit as you're not working, or it might be universal credit. I'm not sure. Some of the procedures might have changed because of Covid, but that's generally what happens.'

I could tell from Lara's expression she thought I was being over-cautious. But as the rest of the day passed and then the next without Lara being contacted by the housing officer she began to believe me, and she wasn't happy. On Friday morning when we logged in for our weekly meeting with Claudette the first thing she said, rather accusingly, was, 'The housing officer didn't phone like you said they would.'

'I'll chase it up on Monday,' Claudette said evenly, and made a note.

'Monday? That's next week!' Lara exclaimed.

'That's right, Lara. I've got meetings for the rest of today and the offices close at the weekend.'

'I can phone them,' Lara said.

'You can if you wish, but no one will be there at the weekend, and I'll chase it on Monday.'

'What's their number?' Lara demanded.

If Claudette sighed with exasperation, she didn't show it. She found the number of the housing officer and read it out as Lara entered it into her mobile. The rest of the meeting continued as usual with us telling Claudette about Arthur. She saw him briefly and as soon as we'd finished, even before I'd closed my tablet, Lara was on the phone trying to contact the housing officer. She grew increasingly frustrated as the automated answering service asked her to press various numbers for different options. Finally, the automated voice told her that, due to the high number of calls, all the housing officers were busy with other clients, and she was invited to leave a message, which she did.

'Someone better call me back,' Lara said to me, annoyed. 'I'll keep phoning and make a nuisance of myself until they do.'

'Lara, many families are on the waiting list for social housing for years,' I said, trying to put it into some context. 'You're lucky; you have a home here and you're being made a priority because of your situation.'

'How long will it take?' she asked.

'I honestly don't know, love. But I'm sure Claudette will follow it up on Monday.'

Lara phoned the housing office twice more and left messages, then had to concede it was going to be next week before she heard. But that evening something happened that made Lara grateful to be living with me. Arthur was sick.

CHAPTER TWENTY-THREE

NEARING THE END

Shortly after Lara had put Arthur to bed on Friday night we heard him cry out in distress. Lara, Paula and I all arrived in his room together to find he'd vomited everywhere. It was down his front, in his hair and all over the bedding on the cot. He was very distraught, as many infants are when they're sick; he was standing up in his cot and crying.

Lara just stood there.

'Pick him up, love, and comfort him,' I told her.

'I can't. He's covered in sick,' Lara said, and stayed where she was.

Not pleased by her reaction, I quickly lifted Arthur from the cot and, comforting him, carried him into the bathroom, where he was sick again. Projectile vomiting is something to behold as it can travel quite some distance. Thankfully most of it went into the bath this time.

I talked to him gently, reassuring him as I ran his flannel under warm water and then lightly wiped his face, hands and hair. He could have a bath in the morning. I began undoing his sleep suit as Lara and Paula stayed by the bathroom door, both looking very concerned.

'Lara, come in here and comfort him,' I said as I took off his sleep suit.

She shook her head and stayed where she was.

'Come on, he's your responsibility.'

Reluctantly, she came in, but before I had a chance to hand Arthur to her he vomited again over the floor. Lara screamed.

'That's not going to help,' I said. 'You'll frighten him.'

Having raised three children of my own and fostered 150 more, I'd had to deal with a lot of sick and worse, but Lara was struggling and this was her child.

I held Arthur as he gradually calmed down and then began to recover. Infants can fall sick quickly and recover just as fast. It was impossible to know if he'd picked up a sickness bug or if it was something he'd eaten, although I couldn't think what that might be. He'd stopped crying and the colour was returning to his cheeks, so I placed him in Lara's arms.

'I'll get fresh clothes for him,' I said, and left Lara holding Arthur, with Paula by her side.

I fetched a clean sleep suit and vest for Arthur and gave them to Lara. Then I stripped the cot and carried the linen and Arthur's clothes downstairs, where I put them into the washing machine, together with my cardigan, which smelt of vomit. I took the thermometer from the first-aid kit, filled Arthur's beaker with water and a bucket with hot water and disinfectant, then returned to the bathroom. Lara had dressed Arthur in the sleep suit and he was looking much better.

'Has he ever been sick like that before?' I asked Lara as I took his temperature.

'Not really. He used to cough up mucus sometimes,

and when he was little he'd bring up some milk, but nothing like this.' It was the first time I'd seen Arthur sick.

His temperature was normal, and he was eager to be put down so clearly was feeling much better. Lara seemed to be taking longer than Arthur to recover, and I saw her hands trembling.

'Don't worry. Children can become sick very quickly and then recover just as quickly,' I said. 'You take him to his bedroom and give him some sips of water while I clear up.'

Paula remained by the bathroom door. 'Do you want some help, Mum?' she asked hesitantly.

'No, love, it's OK.'

Paula could be a bit squeamish about these things but was able to do what was needed if required. As Arthur's parent, Lara didn't have any option; she couldn't go to pieces if Arthur was ill and there was no one else around to help.

I cleaned the bathroom, then wiped Arthur's cot, and left Lara to put him back to bed. 'I'm sure he won't be sick again,' I reassured her.

I collected a new cardigan from my wardrobe and then waited on the landing as Lara resettled Arthur. Satisfied they were all right, I went downstairs. Paula was now in her bedroom.

Once Arthur was asleep, Lara came down.

'I know what you must be thinking,' she said, coming into the living room. 'I won't cope when it's just Arthur and me.'

'I am a bit worried, love,' I admitted. 'All children are sick sometimes.'

'I know, and I guess I'll have to force myself if it's just me. But I have a thing about sick.' She sat beside me on the sofa and fiddled with the sleeve of her jersey. 'You see, my mum was sick a lot, and she died by choking on her own vomit. It was me that found her. She was lying on her side in a pool of sick. If I see anyone being sick or even some on the pavement, I panic and it all comes back.'

'Oh, love,' I said, and took her hand.

I wasn't aware until then that Lara had been the one who'd found her mother dead. I knew she'd died from a drug overdose, but I hadn't ever been told the details. I assumed the social services had it on file somewhere.

'I am sorry,' I said. 'I'm glad you've told me. I now understand your reaction. Does Claudette know?'

She shrugged. 'No idea. I've had so many social workers.'

'I think you need to tell her.'

'I will. Thanks for being here for me. I don't know what I would have done without you.'

We talked for a while and I said I thought Lara's reaction may have been triggered as a result of post-traumatic stress, and that she might benefit from therapy to help her come to terms not only with finding her mother dead, but her past in general. I knew Lara had had some counselling many years before but hadn't found it helpful. Perhaps it hadn't been the right time. She agreed that something needed to be done as she had a lot of memories she just shut off, and said she'd talk to Claudette. I would also enter what had happened in my log notes, which Lara knew.

* * *

Arthur slept soundly for the rest of the night and woke on Saturday morning completely recovered, loud and active as he usually was. We still didn't know what had caused his sudden and violent sickness, and as long as it didn't keep happening I reassured Lara there was nothing to worry about. I also said that if Arthur had been repeatedly sick during the night or was running a high temperature, we would have sought medical advice. It was important she knew what to do.

That evening Lara met Frazer for a few hours outside while I babysat Arthur. When she returned, cold and wet from the rain, she said she was looking forward to when they could meet indoors, which, according to the latest update, wasn't until 17 May.

On Monday, fired up, and with any reluctance about leaving me having gone, Lara left answer-machine messages for Claudette and the housing officer – two for the latter, asking when she'd be offered a flat. Claudette returned her call later that day and said she'd spoken to the housing officer and someone would contact her, hopefully this week. This wasn't what Lara wanted to hear and Claudette patiently explained the housing office was very busy at present. There was always a shortage of social housing, now exacerbated by the 'hotels-for-the-homeless scheme' coming to an end. Lara was a priority, but others were before her on the list as she currently had somewhere to live.

'Perhaps I should make myself homeless,' she said as the call ended, and grumbled on and off for the rest of the day.

And the next day.

Thankfully, the housing officer phoned her on Wednesday with the news Lara had been waiting for, which put us all out of our misery. I really liked Lara, and she'd had to overcome a lot in her short life, but when she felt she had a grievance she let you know about it.

Lara was on the phone to the housing officer for over half an hour as he told her about a flat, the social housing tenancy agreement, regulations, requirements and procedure, some of which was different because of Covid. I wished I'd been able to hear what he was saying, for once they'd finished Lara told me piecemeal, suddenly remembering something and not understanding everything. The most important news was that she was being offered a one-bedroom flat and she had to meet the housing officer there at 11 a.m. on Friday. It was empty and had been deep-cleaned since the last tenant left. Lara was elated and her first priority was to text Claudette, not to thank her for all she'd done, but to tell her to cancel our weekly meeting as she was going to see a flat that morning. Claudette replied by text saying that was fine and we'd speak the following week.

Lara asked me to go with her to view the flat and of course I said I would. Then she remembered the housing officer, who may have been called Gary something, had said that due to Covid rules the viewing was for the tenant or tenants only and a carer if that was appropriate, which strictly speaking didn't include me. But Lara wanted me there so we decided I would go and if I wasn't allowed into the property I'd wait outside with Arthur. I could have asked Paula to look after Arthur, but she'd done a lot already and I felt she needed some time to herself. Later, Lara remembered she had to take ID with her and that Gary had told her about a website that would help her access the benefits she was entitled to.

While Lara was researching this online she also put the address of the flat into a search engine. She found various road-side photographs of the outside of the block of flats, a three-storey brick building fronted by a grass verge. I knew roughly where the estate was – a 1980s development about a twenty-minute drive away.

Lara naturally told Frazer about the flat offer, then Shell and Courtney. Courtney said she'd go with Lara on Friday 'to save me the bother'. When Lara told me I reminded her what the housing officer had said – that the viewing was for the tenant only.

'We can say I'm your foster carer, but you can't really take a friend,' I said. Then I had a nasty thought. 'Have you told Shell and Courtney the address of the flat?'

'I guess so, why?'

'I hope they don't tell Diesel.'

'No, they won't,' she said adamantly. 'They're not in contact with him, not after what he did to Shell.' Then she thought some more about it. 'I'll make sure they know not to tell him.'

'Yes. It sounds as though he can be very persuasive, and it's so easy to find people on the internet. You don't want him turning up at your flat.'

I didn't want to alarm Lara, but years of fostering had taught me to be cautious and to consider all possibilities.

Lara phoned Shell and Courtney and they both confirmed they weren't in contact with Diesel or his mates and wouldn't divulge Lara's address. I hoped it stayed that way. This was a new beginning for Lara.

* * *

At 10.30 a.m. on Friday the three of us set off in my car, the address of Lara's flat in my satnav. Arthur was in his car seat in the rear and Lara was sitting in the passenger seat beside me, the 'baby bag' containing everything Arthur needed for the morning at her feet. Lara packed this now herself and it included a change of nappy, spare clothes, a drink, snack and small toys to keep him amused. Lara was both excited and apprehensive at seeing the flat for the first time, which I could understand. It was a big step. This could become her home for the foreseeable future.

The roads were quiet with the schools still out, many workers furloughed and others told to work from home. We arrived ten minutes early and I parked outside the block of flats. Half a dozen lads in their early teens sat astride bikes on the grass verge at the front, presumably having had enough of home learning.

'We're going to see our new flat,' Lara told Arthur, and lifted him from his car seat.

She set him down on the pavement and holding his hand we walked up the short path to the entrance, face masks at the ready.

'It's number seven,' she said

The main door to the building was wedged open and that led into a central corridor. We put on our masks and went in, then checked the numbers on the doors. Flat one was on our left and two was on our right at the front of the block. Three and four were at the back.

'It must be upstairs,' Lara said.

She picked up Arthur and carried him up the flight of stairs. I followed, our footsteps echoing on the wooden steps. There were another four flats leading off this landing; one had a child's scooter parked outside. A flat at the rear had its door propped open. A tall young man in his late twenties came out. He was wearing a grey face mask the exact shade of his jacket. 'Lara Lewisham?' he asked, maintaining social distance.

'Yes,' Lara replied.

'I'm Gary Sabala, your appointed housing officer. Thank you for being so punctual.'

'I'm the foster carer for Lara and Arthur,' I said. 'They are living with me at present.'

This seemed to satisfy Gary and he nodded.

'I have to ask you both, are either of you running a high temperature or showing signs of Covid, or having to self-isolate, or living with someone who has tested positive or is having to self-isolate?' It had become a standard question at the start of many appointments.

'No,' we both confirmed.

'Thank you. In line with current practice, I have opened all the windows in the property and would ask you not to touch anything unnecessarily. You don't have a problem using hand gel?'

'No.'

Gary produced a bottle of antibacterial gel from his briefcase and squirted it into our open hands. Lara had put Arthur down to do this and he immediately ran into the flat. I quickly followed, not knowing how safe it was for him or what damage he might do. I found him in the living room. It was cold. The flat was unoccupied so the heating was off and the windows were all open to let in the fresh air. Lara and Gary came in too.

'I'll show you around,' Gary said. 'So, this is the one main room with the kitchenette over there.'

Lara didn't say anything, and I thought she seemed a bit disappointed. She wasn't as enthusiastic as I would have expected.

'The bedroom is through there,' Gary said, pointing to one of the other open doors leading off the small hall. 'And the bathroom is next to it.'

Gary stayed in the living room by the open window as Lara, Arthur and I went into the bedroom. It was compact like the rest of the flat and would just about hold a bed, cot and a small chest of drawers. We went into the bathroom, which was dated but clean.

Lara still hadn't shown any enthusiasm and I followed her back into the living room.

'The flat has been empty for a month,' Gary said. 'The elderly gentleman who was living here died and his relatives had to clear it out.'

'He didn't die here?' Lara asked, horrified.

'No, in hospital, I think,' Gary said. 'But we've given the place a deep clean.'

I could see that. The flat was clean but it was well worn. It was completely unfurnished. There were no curtains or blinds and the whole flat needed decorating.

'It's nice being at the back of the building,' I said encouragingly to Lara, glancing out of the window. 'There's a lawn and you're not overlooked.'

Lara was still subdued and looking apprehensive, and she was now struggling with Arthur who wanted to run off, which it wasn't safe to do as the door to the flat was wedged wide open.

'A coat of paint will make all the difference,' I said to her. 'I'll help you. You can choose your own colour scheme.' Then I checked with Gary: 'She can repaint the flat?'

'Yes, but tenants aren't allowed to make structural changes. It's all in the tenancy agreement.'

Lara didn't reply. I think Gary saw her apprehension as he said, 'You don't have to make up your mind now about having the flat. You can go away and think about it and call me tomorrow. But there are others interested.'

Arthur broke free of Lara's hand and ran into the bedroom. Lara and I followed.

'What's the matter, love?' I asked her. 'I thought you would be pleased to have your own flat. Once it's painted and furnished it will be really nice.'

'I know, but I had a flashback as we walked in. It reminded me so much of where I lived with my mother. Our last place was just like this and it all came rushing back.'

'The flat where you found your mother on the floor?'

'Yes, and all the struggles we had. She couldn't cope with being a mother and it makes me think that I won't cope either.'

'Lara, you don't take drugs. There is no reason why you shouldn't cope. History won't repeat itself. My daughter Lucy had similar doubts about being able to parent when she was expecting Emma, but look at her now. She's a great mother, and you will be too.'

Lara managed a weak smile from behind her mask. 'I hope you're right, but it's such a big step, living by myself and looking after Arthur.'

'I know, but you can do it, love. I wouldn't have told Claudette you could if I didn't believe it. I'll do what I can to help.'

'Thank you.' I saw her eyes fill. 'I wish I'd had you in my life earlier. I promise I won't let you down.'

I swallowed hard. 'You won't.'

Lara straightened, took a deep breath and, picking up Arthur, strode purposefully into the living room.

'I'll take it,' she said to Gary. 'I'll have the flat.'

'Sure?'

'Yes.'

'If you've finished in here then we'll go outside, and I'll explain what happens next and check your ID. I have some forms for you to read and sign, and the rest is online.'

We filed out of the flat, down the stairs and into the fresh air. As Gary talked to Lara I walked Arthur up and down the grass verge. He'd had enough of standing still and adults talking. As we walked and I felt his little hand in mine, and I saw his wonder and inquisitiveness at everything we passed, I reminded myself that his time with me was limited. Very soon he would be living with his mother, and although it was the right decision, I would still miss him and Lara. So would Paula, for they had been as big a part of her life as they had mine.

CHAPTER TWENTY-FOUR

LEAVING BUT NOT GOODBYE

A week later Lara was given the keys to her flat and then the work began. I had helped her apply for the benefits she needed online, not just to cover the rent and day-to-day living expenses, but for one-off charitable grants towards essential purchases. To get started I bought the paint that Lara chose, and while Paula looked after Arthur at home we began decorating. Lara thought we could start painting straight away, so I showed her how to wash and prepare the woodwork and walls first to get a better finish. I'd always done most of the decorating at home, although my family helped once they were old enough.

We made good progress and at the weekend Frazer helped Lara, arriving at 9 a.m. and leaving after 9 p.m. on both Saturday and Sunday. I sent sandwiches with Lara for both of them and on Sunday they also ordered a take-away and 'had a picnic on the living-room floor'. Paula and I looked after Arthur for the whole weekend.

Lara chose roller blinds online for the windows and had them delivered to the flat. Frazer fitted them. Some money came through towards a cot and I suggested she bought one that converted into a bed that could be used for a number of years to come. We also ordered flat-pack furniture, which Frazer helped Lara assemble the following weekend. We found a reasonably priced cooker and arranged to have it installed. Each time a delivery was due at her flat I took Lara and Arthur in the car, which gave them a chance to get used to their new home. The once tired-looking flat was quickly becoming a bright new home.

I gave Lara some of my spare cutlery, china and glasses. She ordered bedding online. We were using my credit card to make these purchases as the grants took a while to come through and didn't cover the full cost – nowhere near. I'd asked Lara to keep a note of what we were spending, not because I would ask her to repay it, but because it was important she knew and budgeted. When I first suggested she buy a second-hand sofa and table she rejected the idea and wanted to buy new.

'If only I had a credit card,' she sighed.

'Absolutely not!' I said firmly. 'Please don't be tempted to apply for another one. I use my credit card but I clear it every month so I don't pay any interest.' However, there was nothing to stop Lara from applying for another card even though she still had a large outstanding debt on the other one. Personally, I think credit card lending needs to be better regulated so people aren't encouraged to get into debt.

There was a large charity shop I knew of just out of town that sold really good-quality second-hand furniture but it was closed due to lockdown, otherwise I would have taken Lara there. Instead, I persuaded her to look at second-hand furniture on a website where local people advertised items for sale. Reluctant at first, she became more enthusiastic when she saw the quality and prices of some of the items. Often people just wanted to get rid of something, so it was really cheap. She found a sofa and a small dining table with four chairs at a give-away price and contacted the seller, who assured her they were in 'nearly new' condition and the reason for the sale was that they were moving from a house to a flat and needed the space. The only drawback was that the items would need to be collected. Lara told the seller she'd have the furniture even if she had to bring it on the bus!

While I researched the price of hiring a van or using a firm to collect the furniture, unbeknown to me Lara asked Frazer if Bruce could collect the items in his van. He said he would after work one evening. When I found out I was embarrassed he'd been put in that position but grateful for his offer, as the cost of hiring a van was more than the furniture itself. I texted Bruce an apology and thanked him.

No problem, he replied. *Happy to help them out.* He was such a lovely man.

Bruce and Frazer collected the furniture on Wednesday evening and Frazer paid the seller in cash. Once the sofa, table and chairs were in, Frazer texted Lara a photo. She was pleased. So by the end of March Lara's flat was ready for her and Arthur to live in. All we had to do was move her personal possessions so they could start living there. As far as I was concerned there was no rush, but Claudette and Joy needed to set a date for her to leave, when the placement would officially end.

Lara started to prevaricate, making excuses for not going, and then suggested that she should live in the flat for a while 'to get used to it'.

'And leave Arthur with me?' I asked.

She gave a small nod.

'Don't you think Arthur would find that very confusing? All this time you've been telling him the flat is going to be your new home and then you disappear without him. I don't think Claudette will agree to that either.'

'But supposing he's sick or has an accident when there's just me?' Lara asked, a crisis in confidence looming.

'He's not likely to be sick again,' I said. 'It's happened once in all the time you've been with me, and if he is sick you comfort him and clear up the mess. If he's really ill you call for medical help, and if necessary an ambulance.'

'What if he falls and hurts himself?' Lara asked. 'They [the social services] are sure to blame me.'

'No, they won't. He's bound to have some minor accidents. All children do. Just watch him like we have been doing here. And maybe keep that diary or log I mentioned. It can help if you are ever asked about a particular incident or concern.'

Lara was clearly struggling again, so I suggested we talked to Claudette, and she set up an online meeting for the next day. Lara freely admitted her concerns, and Claudette spent time reassuring her. Claudette was an experienced and empathetic social worker, and said if all her mother-and-baby placements were like Lara she would be very pleased indeed, which helped boost Lara's confidence. It was what she needed to hear. Claudette reminded her that the supervision order would allow her to visit and support Lara, and she said she'd make her first visit – in person – the week Lara moved in. 'Cathy will be offering support and I expect Frazer will too,' Claudette added. 'We've applied for his DBS.'

'He said you had,' Lara replied. 'OK, I'll move in this Saturday.'

'Excellent,' Claudette said, and made a note of the day. 'I'll phone you on Monday and visit later in the week.'

I now helped Lara start to pack her and Arthur's personal possessions. It was surprising how much they had accumulated in five months. On Thursday we went to her flat and took some of their belongings, including toys for Arthur, and stayed for a couple of hours. We plugged in the fridge-freezer, threw out the empty fizzy-drink bottles and takeaway containers from when she and Frazer had eaten there, and fixed childproof clips to the cupboards Arthur could reach. We returned on Friday with milk and other food items and Lara made me a cup of tea – the first in her new home. We sat on her nearly new sofa, which was immaculate, as Arthur played nearby, then went off to explore. A great advantage of the flat being compact and having just one main room was that it was much easier to watch him and there were no stairgates to remember to close. Apart from the risk of him climbing on the furniture and falling, there were few hazards that I could see.

'Make sure you hold his hand before you open your front door,' I said to Lara. The communal staircase was only a few steps away and I shuddered at the thought of Arthur running out and going down head-first.

Paula hadn't seen Lara's flat yet so she decided to come with us on Saturday and say goodbye there. We had breakfast together and it was subdued. Even Arthur was quieter than usual, perhaps sensing the atmosphere and aware that many of his belongings had disappeared.

'My last meal here,' Lara said gloomily, as she finished the eggs on toast I'd cooked.

'It needn't be,' I said. 'Once all the restrictions are lifted you can come here as often as you like.'

Although restrictions were gradually easing – we were now allowed to meet up to six people or two different households – it had to be outside, as evidence continued to suggest the virus didn't thrive so well in the fresh air. Once Lara had left she would be forming another household, and in order to visit I would be in her 'support bubble'.

After breakfast Lara changed Arthur's nappy, washed his face and hands, then packed the last of their belongings, while I cleared up the breakfast dishes and checked for any of their stray items. We then placed their bags in the hall ready for the off. Sammy, sensing something was going on, came to investigate, then took up his favourite place on a stair just the other side of the safety gate. Paula now gave Lara a leaving card, which had a voucher inside. I gave Lara my leaving card but there was nothing inside it. She looked a little disappointed, although she tried not to show it.

'Come with me,' I said. 'There's something I need to do before you leave.' She came with me into the front room where I logged in to my computer. 'How much do you owe on your credit card?'

'I don't know exactly. A lot. It makes me depressed when I look at the statement, so I don't. But I haven't used it again, honestly. You remember, we cut it up.'

'Yes, I know, love – don't look so worried. Use my computer to log in to your account and check how much is still outstanding, please.'

I moved over so she could use the keyboard. She logged in and showed me the most recent statement. I could see £20 coming off each month but interest was still being added so the original debt was no smaller. At this rate it was still going to take more than ten years to repay it.

'My leaving present is to help you with this,' I said.

'Oh. Thank you – like you did just before Christmas.'

'Yes.'

Last year, when I'd found out about her credit card debt, I'd given her £100 to help towards reducing it, calling it part of her Christmas present. However, I now used my debit card to clear the whole of the outstanding debt.

'A clean start,' I said.

Lara stared at the screen and then looked at me in disbelief. 'You've done that for me?' she asked incredulously. I nodded. Resting her head on my shoulder, she cried openly. 'Thank you, thank you so much.'

'You're welcome, love. You don't have to worry about that any more, but no more credit cards,' I reminded her.

'I won't. I've learnt my lesson. Thank you.' She wiped her eyes.

I was in the happy position of being able to help Lara financially; not all foster carers are. I would have done the same for my children, so it seemed right to do it for Lara. Obviously, I couldn't stop her from applying for more credit, but I hoped she had learnt her lesson and that during her time with me she'd also learnt about budgeting as well as parenting. She knew it was going to be very tight managing on benefits, and as Claudette had said, she may have to use a food bank.

I reminded Lara to hold Arthur's hand and I opened the front door to an overcast sky. It was early April and although the air was mild, rain was forecast later. Lara put Arthur into his car seat as Paula and I loaded the car. Seeing the front door wide open, Sammy leapt over the stairgate and came out. He sauntered down the front garden path, then sat just outside the gate, as if he'd come to see us off.

I checked we'd taken all the bags from the hall and closed the front door. Lara was in the front passenger seat, so Paula got into the back next to Arthur.

'Sammy has come to say goodbye,' I told Arthur as I sat in the driving seat.

'Sammy,' he said clearly, pointing through the glass of his side window.

'Yes. Good boy.'

Lara put her earbuds in so she could listen to music on her phone, as she'd got into the habit of doing on these trips. As I drove, Paula and I talked to Arthur. She was holding his hand and pointing out some objects we passed. 'House', 'Bicycle', 'Shop' and so forth. Arthur was repeating some of the words. 'Lorry!' he cried very clearly.

'Well done!' I said, and smiled at him in the interior mirror. He looked back with a gorgeous grin and my heart melted.

'We're going to miss you,' I said to him in the mirror.

'Very much,' Paula agreed.

Over the years we'd had to get used to children leaving to return to live with their parents, a relative or a new forever family, but it's not something you become immune to. You learn to manage your feelings, wish them well for the future, and hope they keep in touch.

Fifteen minutes later I drove onto the estate where Lara's flat was, then pulled into her road. I was surprised to see Frazer waiting outside the flats, but Lara wasn't.

'Oh good, he's early,' she said, taking out her earbuds.

'You were expecting him?' I asked.

'Yes, but he said he might not be here until later.'

Lara jumped out of the car as soon as I parked and ran to Frazer. They hugged.

'So that's Frazer,' Paula said. She'd heard a lot about him but hadn't met him since we'd fostered him all those years ago.

I got out and opened the rear door on the pavement side. 'Your new home,' I told Arthur, and helped him out.

Paula joined me on the pavement as Frazer and Lara came over holding hands.

'Paula, Frazer,' I said, introducing them.

'I remember you,' Frazer said a little self-consciously. 'I hope I wasn't too much of a pain.'

'Not at all,' Paula said. 'I remember you too.'

'Would you have recognized me?' Frazer asked convivially.

'I think so. How are you doing?'

'Good. How are you? You've been furloughed?'

'Yes, until July.'

'Bruce is keeping me on, which is great,' Frazer said.

'Yes, I heard. Well done.'

I think Frazer and Paula would have continued talking but Lara, never appreciating Frazer's attention being diverted from her, tugged his hand. 'Come on, we need to get my stuff out of the car so Cathy can go.'

'There's no rush,' I said. 'But let's unload and then have a chat inside.'

It only needed two trips up and down the stairs with all of us helping; even Arthur carried his favourite cuddly toy in one hand and held mine with the other. We stacked everything in their living room and then Lara showed Paula the rest of the flat.

'It's really nice,' Paula said as they returned to the living room. Frazer and I were there chatting.

There was an awkward silence as we all stood looking at each other and it soon became clear Lara wanted to be alone with Frazer. I didn't blame her; this was her home and she only saw him at weekends. I'd visit her again in a few days.

'So, you have everything you need?' I checked.

'Yes,' Lara said. 'Thanks. I'll phone you.'

'Frazer, nice to see you again,' I said.

'And you. Hopefully we can get together again before long,' he said to Paula and me.

Arthur was now in the bedroom. I could hear him bouncing on the bed.

'We'll say goodbye to Arthur and leave you to it,' I said.

Paula and I went into the bedroom, leaving Lara and Frazer in the living room. Arthur stopped bouncing when he saw me and grinned cheekily, for he knew he wasn't supposed to bounce on the beds in my house.

I lifted him off, and hugged and kissed him. Then I passed him to Paula who did the same. 'Bye, Arthur,' she said. 'Hopefully see you again soon.'

I wasn't going to leave him unattended in the bedroom, so Paula carried him into the living room. I closed the bedroom door behind us. Frazer and Lara were having a quick kiss and cuddle but pulled away when they saw us.

'Have a good weekend,' I said. 'Phone me if you need anything.'

'We will,' Frazer replied, holding Lara's hand.

Paula gave Arthur one final hug and set him down. We headed for the front door. Arthur ran after us, and it was Frazer who picked him up while I opened the door.

'Bye,' I said. 'Look after him.'

'We will,' Frazer replied.

He closed their front door and Paula and I made our way down the echoing stairs. I was deep in thought. Parenting didn't have to be perfect but 'good enough', and I hoped Lara's was. I thought so, but it seemed I'd had more responsibility than usual in the making of the decision. Claudette had been monitoring and assessing Lara through our weekly meetings, but because of the pandemic they had all been online. She'd only visited us once in person and that was when she'd first placed Lara and Arthur six months before. She'd relied heavily on my observations, and I'd tried to be accurate and objective. Yes, there were still some concerns, but as Claudette had said it's about managing the risk, not removing it, and she'd be able to do that with the supervision order.

As we left the building Paula voiced my thoughts. 'I think Frazer is going to be a big help to Lara.'

'Yes, so do I, love.'

CHAPTER TWENTY-FIVE

MARG

Sammy was sitting by the front door when Paula and I arrived home from moving Lara and Arthur to their new home. I let us in. The house was quiet – uncannily so without Arthur. I'd found it best in the past to keep busy when a child left, so Paula and I set about giving Lara's and Arthur's bedrooms a good clean. This also served the purpose of having them ready in case they were needed again quickly. I was hoping for a short break, but that couldn't be guaranteed, especially at present. The number of children coming into care was rising, and some foster carers were still being advised to shield so weren't taking new foster children.

I opened the windows in the bedrooms to let in the fresh air. We stripped the bed and cot and I put the linen into the washing machine. Paula then made us lunch while I went to my computer in the front room and completed my log notes, including the move, as I was expected to. I said it had gone well and that Frazer had been at their flat when we'd arrived. I would also add a few lines each time I visited Lara.

Paula and I sat at the table to have our lunch with Lara's place and Arthur's highchair glaringly empty. I'd offered the highchair to Lara, but she'd bought an inexpensive booster seat, which Arthur would be able to use for some years to come. I'd also offered her the stroller, but she hadn't wanted it, saying it was 'old and tatty – no offence'. None taken. True, it had been well used, but it worked fine. Lara was planning on buying a new stroller when her benefit money came through.

After lunch Paula and I put the highchair, stairgates and stroller out of sight in what had been Arthur's bedroom and closed the door. We'd stow them in the loft at some point. Downstairs, we returned the boxes of early-years toys to the cupboards, and then we walked into the High Street for the groceries we needed before the rain set in. It was strange being out without Arthur when we were so used to one of us pushing him in the stroller or holding his hand if he wanted to walk. It was as if we had a limb missing. It was also strange buying food for the two of us without having to consider Arthur's or Lara's preferences. I thought back to when they'd first arrived with little or no routine and Arthur just having bottles of formula, and how far they'd come. I wondered what Lara was giving him to eat today.

'I hope Lara remembered to give Arthur lunch,' I said out loud. Then I caught myself and smiled.

'I'm sure she or Frazer will have given him lunch,' Paula said.

'I know.' I needed to stop worrying and start to let go. But it was difficult.

I resisted the temptation to contact Lara until the evening, when I texted her: *How's it going?*

She replied with a thumb's-up emoji.

The heavy rain that had been forecast didn't arrive and

the following day was set to be fine, so I sent a message to my children on our WhatsApp group: *Are you free to meet up tomorrow?*

They replied saying they were, and we made arrangements to meet in a park with a picnic. I also told them that Lara and Arthur were now settled in their flat. In normal circumstances they would have seen more of them, but Covid had stopped that.

Although I was going to support Lara as necessary, it was difficult to know how often to contact her. It was a casual arrangement, and I didn't want to appear overbearing, as if I was continually checking up on her, so I left it until Sunday evening before phoning. She sounded all right, but said she was busy with Arthur, then added, 'Frazer says hi.' So I assumed he'd been there the whole weekend. I said I was thinking of visiting her tomorrow, but she said she was meeting Shell and Courtney. I said I'd go on Tuesday but to call if she needed anything.

On Monday I received a text message from my doctor inviting me to book my second Covid jab, which was a relief. Lara texted to say Claudette had phoned her and Arthur had a place at nursery, starting the following week. She had to take him for a visit on Friday and then he would go 9 a.m.–12.30 p.m. each weekday, and it would include his lunch. The message ended with an emoji showing relief.

Do you need anything bringing when I come to see you tomorrow? I asked.

Bacon, it's expensive. And some ready-meals, please.

Lara liked bacon, and I guessed she'd been using

ready-meals over the weekend, for there'd been plenty when I'd moved her.

OK. Looking forward to seeing you both tomorrow morning x

Don't come before 11 a.m., she replied. *We won't be ready.*

I confirmed I'd be there shortly after 11 a.m., although I thought she'd have to be ready a lot earlier than that the following week when Arthur started nursery at 9 a.m.

Paula decided not to come with me on Tuesday as I wasn't sure how long I was going to be at Lara's. I stopped off at a supermarket en route to buy the bacon and ready-meals Lara had asked for. I also included some fancy chocolate desserts I knew she liked, and some fruit. As I drove I felt optimistic. Nothing had gone wrong at the last minute and as long as Lara kept Arthur safe all should be well. I had some concerns in respect of how Lara would manage long-term when it was just her looking after Arthur day after day, week after week, but he would be at nursery soon for part of every day, which should take the pressure off. I thought it was good that Lara had been able to see her friends the day before, as well as having Frazer there at the weekend. It was company for her. Being a single parent can be very isolating. As I parked the car and then made my way up the stairs I assumed Lara would be in a good mood.

I was wrong.

I rang the bell and heard Arthur's footsteps run along the hall, then his little fists pounding on the front door, as he used to do at my house. It was a few moments before Lara answered and I knew straight away something was wrong. She had her phone pressed to her ear, her cheeks were flushed and her eyes glistened with tears.

'I've got to go, Cathy's here,' she said to the person on the phone.

'What's the matter?' I asked, going in. Arthur was smiling, pleased to see me.

'The old bat downstairs is going to report me!' Lara cried, with a mixture of upset and anger.

'Report you? For what? What do you mean?'

'For not looking after Arthur properly and making too much noise. She said she's phoning the council and the social services. I need this like a hole in the head. They'll take Arthur away for sure.' Lara dissolved into tears.

'No, they won't. Come and sit down and tell me exactly what's happened,' I said.

Taking Lara by the arm, I drew her into the living room and to the sofa. I put the bag of shopping in the kitchenette, then gathered together some of Arthur's toys, which were strewn all over the floor, and sat him by them so he could play.

'He won't stay there,' Lara said miserably. 'He never does.'

'You're doing fine. Calm down,' I said, and sat beside her. Clearly everything had got on top of her, I assumed because of the woman's comments and threat of reporting her.

I passed Lara a tissue from the packet I kept in my bag, then waited while she dried her eyes.

'I should have stayed with you,' she said. 'We were safe there.'

'That wasn't an option, love, was it? Now, tell me what's happened and we'll think of a way to put it right.'

'I don't think you can,' she said hopelessly, and took a deep breath. 'On Saturday afternoon, we'd only been here about three hours, the woman who lives in the flat below came up and complained we were making too much noise. Frazer was here and we apologized, although we didn't think we were making a lot of noise. Arthur was playing and we were unpacking. Then on Sunday we went out for a walk and as we passed her door she came out and said she hadn't slept all night because of the noise we were making. She was really rude and said the flat was only meant for one person. I didn't see what business it was of hers, and the only noise we made during the night was when Arthur woke and I had to see to him. He's become a bit unsettled.'

'He's bound to for a while,' I said. 'Living here is new for him. It will probably take him the best part of a week to settle.'

Lara gave a small nod. 'But that's not all,' she continued. 'Frazer left for work early yesterday morning and then I met up with Shell and Courtney – outside like we're supposed to. We had a nice time and got chips and ate them in the park. I felt good. But later, when I was getting Arthur's dinner, that woman came up again and knocked hard on the door. I wasn't going to answer but she kept knocking so I had to in the end. She was horrible and said she was trying to watch television and couldn't because of the noise Arthur was making and she'd report me to the council. He wasn't making a lot of noise, just playing like he does.' I nodded. 'Then this morning, about an hour ago, she came up again and had a right go at me. She said she'd had enough and was going to report me to the social services for not being a responsible parent.'

Lara's eyes filled again and her voice broke. 'I'm doing my best, Cathy, honest. I don't know what else to do. I can't stop him running around and playing.'

'No, of course you can't. She's being unreasonable. Dry your eyes.' I passed her another tissue. 'I seem to remember the housing officer saying there was an elderly man living here before you, so I guess she's not used to hearing a child. Also, this laminate flooring doesn't help; it won't absorb noise like carpet does. You do take off your shoes when you come in?' I asked.

'Yes, like we did at your house.'

'Good. Now, what should we do for the best?' I said, thinking out loud. Arthur had left the toys and come to us carrying a picture book. I lifted him onto the sofa between us and opened the book. 'Have you told Claudette?' I asked Lara.

'No, just Shell. That's who I was on the phone to when you arrived.'

'Horse,' I said to Arthur, pointing to the picture in his book. Then to Lara, 'I think we need to tell Claudette in case that woman phones the social services. It's better if it comes from us. Also, I think I'll go down and talk to her. It might help.'

'Really? You're brave. She scares me,' Lara admitted.

'You stay here with Arthur and if I don't reappear in ten minutes, send a search party,' I joked. 'Come on, cheer up. You didn't need this, but we'll deal with it.'

'Thank you so much.'

I left Lara and Arthur on the sofa looking at the picture book and let myself out of their flat. The woman's hostile attitude and comments to Lara had really knocked her confidence and I could understand why. As I went down the flight of stairs I tried to think what to say for the best. My protective instinct was to give the woman a piece of my mind for upsetting Lara, but I knew that wouldn't help and was likely to make matters worse. I needed to try to defuse the situation.

The flat where the woman lived was directly below Lara's and looked out over the lawn at the rear, as Lara's did. Beside the doormat was a pot of sad-looking plastic flowers. I steeled myself, pressed the doorbell and took a step back. The door was opened immediately by a stern-looking woman with grey cropped hair, who I guessed to be around seventy. She also kept her distance.

'I'm sorry to trouble you,' I began. 'I'm a friend of Lara's and …'

'I know,' she said testily. 'I've seen you here before.'

'That's right. I've been helping Lara to decorate and move in. I've come to have a chat as Lara is rather upset …'

'She's upset!' she interrupted. 'I haven't slept a wink since her and that child moved in.'

'I'm sorry to hear that,' I said, keeping my voice even and conciliatory. 'Lara is doing all she can to settle her son and stop him from making excessive noise. But I'm guessing that having a young, active child living above you is very different from an elderly gentleman.'

'There's three of them there,' she said accusingly, in the same hostile manner.

'Lara and her son are living there, and I understand her partner visited at the weekend.'

'The flat's not big enough.'

'I agree, but it's all that was offered so they are having to make the most of it.'

She tutted disapprovingly. 'It really isn't good enough.'

'No, but they are nice young people, and you could do a lot worse with new neighbours. I appreciate it's a big change for you. I understand the gentleman lived there for many years.'

'Over twenty. Bert moved in around the same time I did. We were good friends.'

'You must miss him. I'm sorry for your loss,' I said, and finally I saw her manner soften a little.

'I do. I helped him a lot with his shopping and cooking when he was poorly, and sometimes I just sat with him when he needed company. We were good friends for a long time, and after he passed his family cleared out his flat without even saying goodbye to me.'

'Oh dear, that was thoughtless. I won't keep you further, I just wanted to see you to explain. You must have wondered what was going on with all the comings and goings.' She gave a small, stiff nod. 'If you have the time, perhaps you would like to meet Lara and Arthur properly?'

'Not now. I'm busy.'

'All right, maybe another time. I'm sure Lara would appreciate your company. It can be very lonely bringing up a child by yourself.'

'I know. I did it for years,' she said sympathetically, then spoilt it by adding, 'But I didn't upset my neighbours. I made sure my kids were kept quiet and under control.'

'As Lara is trying to do. Arthur will be starting nursery next week so that will help. And I'll give the social services a ring and explain what's happened. I'm a foster carer so I know them quite well. I'll let you get on with your day, but if you would like to pop upstairs any time and say hi to Lara, I'm sure she'd be pleased. I'm Cathy, by the way.'

'Marg.'

'Nice to meet you, Marg. Hopefully see you again before too long.'

I smiled as I came away, but my heart was racing. Formidable and judgemental best described Marg on first meeting. I could see why Lara had felt intimidated. But in my experience people like Marg tend to have had challenging lives themselves, often resulting in them feeling frustrated and unhappy. Instead of reaching out to people and making friends, they push them away. Anyway, I felt I'd done my best.

Lara was waiting anxiously by her front door when I arrived. We went in before I told her what had been said.

'Do you think she really will come up and say hi?' she asked incredulously.

'I doubt it. But hopefully I've defused the situation a little and she'll think twice before complaining again. I think she's set in her ways and misses Bert – the man who used to live here. Maybe she's lonely, but she's also hurt by the way Bert's family treated her. Sometimes we can struggle to show we're hurt, and express it through anger instead.'

'I think I used to do that,' Lara said reflectively.

'I think we all do at times. Anyway, I'll email Claudette when I get home and tell her what's happened.'

'Thank you. I hope she doesn't hold it against me.'

'I'm sure she won't.'

I helped Lara tidy up the living room and wash the dishes stacked in the sink, then I took her and Arthur out for lunch. We stopped in the park on the estate on the way back and it was nearly 4 p.m. when we arrived at her flat. There was no sign of Marg. I went up to Lara's flat and checked she had everything she needed, then, telling her to call me if there were any problems, I kissed them both goodbye and left.

As soon as I arrived home I emailed Claudette and explained what had happened and the reason I thought Marg had reacted as she had. Joy phoned to check Lara and Arthur's move had gone well. In normal circumstances she would have visited us to say goodbye before they left. Claudette would still be Lara and Arthur's social worker, but Joy's involvement with them had ended with the placement. I asked Joy how her brother was, and she said he was still making steady but slow progress. She reminded me to fill in the end-of-placement form online, which was really a self-appraisal – what had gone well and what I could have done better. It seemed there was a form for everything in fostering now.

'So, you are free to take a new child from tomorrow?' Joy asked.

'Let's make it next week unless it's an emergency,' I replied. 'I've got a few things I need to do first.' One of which was to visit my parents' graves. The cemetery gardens had been closed during lockdown and had recently reopened.

'From Monday then. Speak soon.'

Claudette replied, thanking me for my email and saying she would visit Lara later in the week and would ask her about the situation with the neighbour then. That evening I texted Lara to make sure she was all right; she replied that she was and Arthur was asleep so she was watching television.

The following afternoon I had my second Covid jab. As I was walking back from the doctor's surgery my mobile rang. When I saw it was Lara's number I immediately thought something else had gone wrong.

'Hello, love,' I said tentatively.

'You'll never guess what!' Lara began.

'No?'

'Marg, that woman who lives below me ...'

'Yes?' I braced myself for what I was about to hear, although Lara didn't sound upset, more animated.

'She's just left!'

'Your flat?'

'Yes. Don't worry, she's fully vaccinated and I had the windows open. She's been here for over two hours! She baked me a cake and apologized for being rude. She's OK when you get to know her. We've had a good chat, just like I used to with you.'

'Wonderful,' I said, relief flooding through me. 'That is good. Well done.' As I continued walking home Lara told me all about Marg's visit.

'She speaks her mind, like I do, but we got on really well. I couldn't believe it when I opened the door and saw her standing there with a cake on a plate. She said it was a peace offering and she was sorry for being rude. I asked her in and made us tea. She was really nice to Arthur and said how lovely I'd made the flat. I told her you'd helped. She didn't know you were my foster carer.'

'No, I told her I was a friend.'

'She said her parents had died when she was a child and she was brought up by an aunt who wasn't very nice to her. I said some of my carers weren't nice either, but you were.'

'Thank you, love.'

'Praise where it's due,' Lara said. I hadn't heard her use that expression before. 'That's what Marg says,' Lara added. '"Praise where it's due."' I thought Marg had made quite an impression on Lara.

'I told her about Diesel,' Lara continued as I walked. 'She said her marriage hadn't been good and she never wanted to marry again after her husband left her. I said that was a pity as I had found Frazer, so there were some good guys out there but you had to find them. I think she and Bert were just friends. She has two adult children and a grandchild, but they live in Australia and she hasn't seen them for three years. She looked sad when she told me that and I felt sorry for her. The cake was nice, and she said she'd give me the recipe. I said better still if she could bake it for me as I was the queen of ready-meals. She laughed at that and said she liked my frankness, and how nice it must be to be young in this day and age. I set her straight on that and said it was a very worrying time for many of us, especially if, like me, you had a young child and no job. I told her I was thinking or becoming a beautician and she said she'd be my first customer. She could do with a makeover, but I didn't tell her that.' I laughed. 'As she left she said if I wanted to go out with my young man when we were allowed to and everything was open again she was happy to babysit – saves you the trouble.'

'I see. That was nice of her,' I said. 'Sounds like you two really hit it off.' I put my key into my front door and let myself in.

'We did, but I still want you to visit me.'
'Yes, of course, love.'
'At least until Frazer moves in.'

CHAPTER TWENTY-SIX

A WANTED CHILD

The following week I visited Lara on Monday and Wednesday afternoon. Arthur had started nursery that week and I wanted to know how he was getting on as well as make sure Lara was managing. The flat was messy as usual but not too awful. Lara was in a positive mood and seemed to be coping. However, what she didn't tell me was that she'd been arriving very late for nursery every morning.

I didn't find out until Thursday when Lara telephoned me just before 11 a.m. She was on her way home from nursery and sounded upset and anxious. She said that when she'd arrived that morning the manager of the nursery had taken her aside and told her she was very concerned about Lara's timekeeping. She said it was disruptive for the staff and other children to have Arthur keep arriving so late. She explained it was a waste of resources and if he wasn't going to attend then his place could be offered to another child on the waiting list. She pointed out that Arthur had been prioritized because of their situation, and that her social worker would be wanting feedback soon. The manager had asked Lara why she kept being so late and Lara had been honest and said she wasn't good at getting up in the morning, which I knew, although she had improved during her time with me.

'How late have you been taking Arthur?' I asked.

'About an hour,' she admitted. That was a lot, and the nursery was only a fifteen-minute walk from her flat.

'So what's been going wrong?'

'I haven't got you to wake me.'

'But you're setting your alarm?'

'Yes, but I switch it off and go back off to sleep and then suddenly it's nearly nine o'clock.'

'And where's Arthur when you've fallen asleep again?' I asked, concerned.

'In his cot so he can't do any damage. He's often awake before my alarm. When he's had enough he shouts, "Mama, Mama!" at the top of his voice, then I have to get up.' Lara seemed to find this acceptable, but I didn't.

'That's not fair on him,' I said. 'He's been in his cot all night. You need to get into a better routine, Lara, like you were here.'

'I know,' she said despondently.

'What time are you going to bed?'

'Late. One o'clock, sometimes after. I watch a film and then talk to Courtney and Shell. They're always up.'

'So, not Frazer then?'

'No, he goes to bed at ten as he has to be up early for work.'

'And so do you, Lara. It's all right for Shell and Courtney, they don't have a small child.' As far as I knew they didn't have jobs either. 'You need to start going to bed earlier and getting up when Arthur wakes like you did here.'

'I know.'

'I'd better start phoning you each morning until you are in a better routine. You can't keep arriving late.'

'I know, and I've got Claudette coming tomorrow.' She sighed. 'I'd better tell her, and that it won't happen again.'

'Yes.'

So I began calling Lara at 7 a.m. each morning and I waited until she answered, often groggily: 'Yes, I'm getting out of bed.'

I then telephoned her every half an hour until they'd left the flat and were on their way to nursery – usually by then she sounded much brighter. Sometimes I spoke to Arthur too; he was saying ''ello, Caffy' now.

Lara wasn't late at all the following week and the manager took her aside again and said how pleased she was with the changes she'd made. I also visited Lara and Arthur twice that week. I was looking after another child, so I went while he was at school. Once Lara was in a better routine I just texted her to make sure she was up.

The weather turned really warm as spring gave way to summer, and with restaurants and pubs reopening (albeit still with restrictions on numbers and social distancing), Lara took up Marg's offer of babysitting. They had become unlikely friends and saw each other regularly. Marg babysitting Arthur on a Saturday night became a regular occurrence, so Lara finally got her much-looked-forward-to night out again. Usually she went out with Frazer, but sometimes Shell and Courtney.

Lara told me that Diesel's court date had been set. He was still pleading not guilty, although he'd changed his statement to say that the boiling water spilt over Shell had been an accident and wasn't in self-defence as he'd originally claimed. Lara had been asked to make a statement about Diesel's abuse of her. The police were as confident as they could be that Diesel would be convicted. Shell's arm was healing, but she will be scarred.

When Lara had been living with me and we'd been talking about photographs from her past, she said she only had one and that was of her mother. She'd admitted she'd destroyed her Life Story Book, which had contained other pictures, when she'd been angry. I'd told her that most foster carers kept photographs of the children they'd looked after and suggested her social worker could help her with this. Lara hadn't seemed very keen at the time, but then she'd mentioned it to Claudette, who was looking into it.

Frazer began his apprenticeship when the colleges reopened in September, working with Bruce four days a week and attending college one day. Bruce and Donna are lovely people and took Frazer under their wing. As soon as restrictions were lifted they invited him and Lara to their house for a barbecue, and at least once a week Frazer has his dinner with them after work, then Bruce takes him home. Frazer has seen his mother again and she has met Lara and Arthur. Frazer's foster carer Jenny is still in touch.

I am in regular contact with Lara, Frazer and of course little Arthur. I think I always will be, as they were such a big part of my life. Arthur calls Frazer 'Daddy' and it was no surprise that towards the end of the year Frazer gave notice on his accommodation and moved in with

Lara and Arthur. Frazer's DBS check had come back and as far as I knew it was clear. Claudette continues to visit under the supervision order, and I trust it is as obvious to her as it is to me how much Lara and Frazer adore each other and Arthur. They are giving him the childhood they didn't have.

Lara's and Frazer's lives began very similarly. Their parents were addicts and couldn't look after their children. Frazer's mother developed mental health problems largely as a result of her addiction, and Lara's mother died from a substance overdose. Both Lara and Frazer grew up feeling unwanted and unloved. But then by chance on a cold winter evening during the pandemic they found each other and everything changed. Arthur couldn't be more loved and wanted. Well done, Lara and Frazer.

For the latest on Lara, Frazer and Arthur, and others in my fostering memoirs, please visit https://cathyglass. co.uk/updates

SUGGESTED TOPICS FOR
READING-GROUP DISCUSSION

Cathy is keen to establish a routine for Arthur. Why are routines important for a child?

Lara clearly loves Arthur, but how does she put him at risk?

How did Covid impact on fostering?

We are told that parenting doesn't have to be perfect but 'good enough'. Discuss what that phrase might mean.

Lara and Frazer have quite different personalities. How might their experiences have shaped them? Do their personalities complement each other?

How much of Frazer's and Lara's urgency to be together is a result of them not having families of their own?

Lara suffered at the hands of Diesel. Why did she stay with him for so long?

The care system didn't provide the stability it should have for Lara and Frazer. What do you think went wrong? How might it have been put right?

Towards the end of the book, when Claudette is considering whether Arthur should live with his mother, she talks about 'managing the risk'. What do you think she means by this?

Readers of Cathy's books often comment that they feel they are there with her, in the same room, as part of the family. How does the author achieve this? Perhaps give a few examples from the text.

CHRONOLOGY

If you would like to read, or re-read, my books in chronological order, here is the list to date:

Cut	*Damaged*
The Silent Cry	*Hidden*
Daddy's Little Princess	*Mummy Told Me Not to Tell*
Nobody's Son	*Another Forgotten Child*
Cruel to be Kind	*The Child Bride*
The Night the Angels Came	*Can I Let You Go?*
A Long Way from Home	*Finding Stevie*
A Baby's Cry	*Innocent*
The Saddest Girl in the World	*Too Scared to Tell*
Please Don't Take My Baby	*A Terrible Secret*
Will You Love Me?	*A Life Lost*
I Miss Mummy	*An Innocent Baby*
Saving Danny	*Neglected*
Girl Alone	*A Family Torn Apart*
Where Has Mummy Gone?	*Unwanted*

The titles below can be slotted in anywhere, as can my Lisa Stone thrillers: http://lisastonebooks.co.uk/:

The Girl in the Mirror	*Happy Adults*
My Dad's a Policeman	*Happy Mealtimes for Kids*
Run, Mummy, Run	*About Writing and How*
Happy Kids	*to Publish*

This list is also on the books page of my website: https://cathyglass.co.uk/true-stories-cathy-glass/

Cathy Glass

_____

One remarkable woman, more
than **150** foster children cared for.

Cathy Glass has been a foster carer
for 30 years, during which time she has
looked after more than 150 children, as well
as raising three children of her own. She was
awarded a degree in education and psychology
as a mature student, and writes under a
pseudonym. To find out more about Cathy
and her story visit **www.cathyglass.co.uk**.

A Family Torn Apart

Angie and Polly are loved and looked-after by their parents, so why are they brought into foster care?

But as they settle with Cathy, and start to talk of life at home, it becomes clear something is badly wrong.

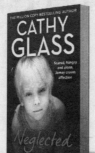

Neglected

The police remove Jamey from home as an emergency and take him to foster carer Cathy

But as Jamey starts to settle in and make progress a new threat emerges, which changes everything.

An Innocent Baby

Abandoned at birth, Darcy-May is brought to Cathy with a police escort

Her teenage mother wants nothing to do with her, but why? She is an adorable baby.

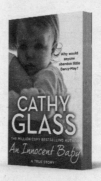

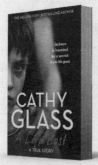

A Life Lost

Jackson is aggressive, confrontational and often volatile

Then, in a dramatic turn of events, the true reason for Jackson's behaviour comes to light . . .

A Terrible Secret

Tilly is so frightened of her stepfather, Dave, that she asks to go into foster care

The more Cathy learns about Dave's behaviour, the more worried she becomes …

Too Scared to Tell

Oskar has been arriving at school hungry, unkempt and bruised. His mother has gone abroad and left him in the care of 'friends'

As the weeks pass, Cathy's concerns deepen. Oskar is clearly frightened of someone – but who? And why?

Innocent

Siblings Molly and Kit arrive at Cathy's frightened, injured and ill

The parents say they are not to blame. Could the social services have got it wrong?

Finding Stevie

Fourteen-year-old Stevie is exploring his gender identity

Like many young people, he spends time online, but Cathy is shocked when she learns his terrible secret.

Where Has Mummy Gone?

When Melody is taken into care, she fears her mother won't cope alone

It is only when Melody's mother vanishes that what has really been going on at home comes to light.

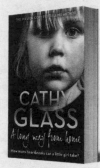

A Long Way from Home

Abandoned in an orphanage, Anna's future looks bleak until she is adopted

Anna's new parents love her, so why does she end up in foster care?

Cruel to be Kind

Max is shockingly overweight and struggles to make friends

Cathy faces a challenge to help this unhappy boy.

Nobody's Son

Born in prison and brought up in care, Alex has only ever known rejection

He is longing for a family of his own, but again the system fails him.

Can I Let You Go?

Faye is 24, pregnant and has learning difficulties as a result of her mother's alcoholism

Can Cathy help Faye learn enough to parent her child?

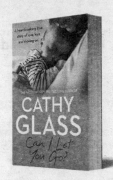

The Silent Cry

A mother battling depression. A family in denial

Cathy is desperate to help before something terrible happens.

Girl Alone

An angry, traumatized young girl on a path to self-destruction

Can Cathy discover the truth behind Joss's dangerous behaviour before it's too late?

Saving Danny

Danny's parents can no longer cope with his challenging behaviour

Calling on all her expertise, Cathy discovers a frightened little boy who just wants to be loved.

The Child Bride

A girl blamed and abused for dishonouring her community

Cathy discovers the devastating truth.

Daddy's Little Princess

A sweet-natured girl with a complicated past

Cathy picks up the pieces after events take a dramatic turn.

Will You Love Me?

A broken child desperate for a loving home

The true story of Cathy's adopted daughter Lucy.

Please Don't Take My Baby

Seventeen-year-old Jade is pregnant, homeless and alone

Cathy has room in her heart for two.

Another Forgotten Child

Eight-year-old Aimee was on the child-protection register at birth

Cathy is determined to give her the happy home she deserves.

A Baby's Cry

A newborn, only hours old, taken into care

Cathy protects tiny Harrison from the potentially fatal secrets that surround his existence.

The Night the Angels Came

A little boy on the brink of bereavement

Cathy and her family make sure Michael is never alone.

Mummy Told Me Not to Tell

A troubled boy sworn to secrecy

After his dark past has been revealed, Cathy helps Reece to rebuild his life.

I Miss Mummy

Four-year-old Alice doesn't understand why she's in care

Cathy fights for her to have the happy home she deserves.

The Saddest Girl in the World

A haunted child who refuses to speak

Do Donna's scars run too deep for Cathy to help?

Cut

Dawn is desperate to be loved

Abused and abandoned, this vulnerable child pushes Cathy and her family to their limits.

Hidden

The boy with no past

Can Cathy help Tayo to feel like he belongs again?

Damaged

A forgotten child

Cathy is Jodie's last hope. For the first time, this abused young girl has found someone she can trust.

Run, Mummy, Run

The gripping story of a woman caught in a horrific cycle of abuse, and the desperate measures she must take to escape.

My Dad's a Policeman

The dramatic short story about a young boy's desperate bid to keep his family together.

The Girl in the Mirror

Trying to piece together her past, Mandy uncovers a dreadful family secret that has been blanked from her memory for years.

About Writing
and How to Publish

A clear, concise practical guide on writing and the best ways to get published.

Happy Mealtimes
for Kids

A guide to healthy eating with simple recipes that children love.

Happy Adults

A practical guide to achieving lasting happiness, contentment and success. The essential manual for getting the best out of life.

Happy Kids

A clear and concise guide to raising confident, well-behaved and happy children.

CATHY GLASS WRITING AS
LISA STONE

The new crime thrillers that will chill you to the bone . . .

THE COTTAGE

Is someone out there?

TAKEN

Have you seen Leila?

THE DOCTOR

How much do you know about
the couple next door?

STALKER

Security cameras are there to keep us safe. Aren't they?

THE DARKNESS WITHIN

You know your son better than anyone. Don't you?

Be amazed
Be moved
Be inspired

Follow Cathy:

 /cathy.glass.180

 @CathyGlassUK

www.cathyglass.co.uk

Cathy loves to hear from readers and reads
and replies to posts, but she asks that no plot
spoilers are posted, please. We're sure
you appreciate why.

MOVING
Memoirs

Stories of hope, courage and
the power of love . . .

Sign up to the Moving Memoirs email and you'll
be the first to hear about new books, discounts,
and get sneak previews from your
favourite authors!

Sign up at

www.moving-memoirs.com